Soldier Talk

Soldier Talk
The Vietnam War in Oral Narrative

Edited by Paul Budra and Michael Zeitlin

Indiana University Press
BLOOMINGTON AND INDIANAPOLIS

This book is a publication of

Indiana University Press
601 North Morton Street
Bloomington, IN 47404-3797 USA

http://iupress.indiana.edu

Telephone orders   800-842-6796
Fax orders   812-855-7931
Orders by e-mail   iuporder@indiana.edu

The paper used in this publication meets the minimum requirements of
American National Standard for Information Sciences—Permanence
of Paper for Printed Library Materials, ANSI Z39.48-1984.

Manufactured in the United States of America

Library of Congress Cataloging-in-Publication Data

Soldier talk : the Vietnam War in oral narrative /
edited by Paul Budra and Michael Zeitlin.
     p.   cm.
Includes bibliographical references and index.
   ISBN 0-253-34433-6 (cloth : alk. paper) — ISBN 0-253-21697-4
(pbk. : alk. paper)
   1. Vietnamese Conflict, 1961–1975. I. Budra, Paul Vincent, date
II. Zeitlin, Michael, date
   DS557.7.S648 2004
   959.704'3'0922—dc22
                    2003026469

1 2 3 4 5   09 08 07 06 05 04

For my father, Victor Budra
P.B.

For Isaiah, Daniel, and Jonathan
M.Z.

CONTENTS

ACKNOWLEDGMENTS

We wish to thank Mike Briggs, Robert Sloan, Maria Ticinovic, Geoffrey Winthrop-Young, David Boulding, Marilyn Young, Marlene Briggs, and Denyse Wilson for their suggestions and support during this project. We would also like to thank the readers and editors at Indiana University Press for their insightful criticism of the original manuscript. The idea for this book emerged from a seminar held at the annual meeting of the Canadian Association for American Studies; our thanks to the members of that organization for their input. Finally, we are sincerely grateful to the contributors who made this volume possible. All editors should have the like privilege of working with scholars who are so professional and patient.

Soldier Talk

1. Introduction
Talk the Talk

MICHAEL ZEITLIN AND PAUL BUDRA

He had come to love what editorial writers were fond of calling the democratic principle with its faith in the common man. He found that principle and that man in the Army, but what none of the editorial writers ever mentioned was that that noble common man was obscene as an old goat, and his obscenity was what saved him. The sanity of said common democratic man was in his humor, his humor was in his obscenity.

—Norman Mailer, *The Armies of the Night*

Walk like a man
Talk like a man
Walk like a man my son.

—Frankie Valli

In Gustav Hasford's novel *The Short-Timers*, a squad of American Marines is killing time out in the boonies, the enemy jungle of Vietnam. Sitting beside a trail, idly playing a few hands of poker, they curse the "lifers," the commanding officers who have made a career out of the military. The "grunts" are ashamed of their collective impotence, and their sense of betrayal and resentment has no outlet in meaningful action. " 'That's an amen,' says Alice, up the trail. He swats a mosquito away from his face. 'We talk the talk, but we don't walk the walk' " (65).[1] Talk, for the Vietnam combatant, is cheap, a way of releasing tension, of articulating fantasies of freedom from a military hierarchy that is opaque and capricious. In Stanley Kubrick's film *Full Metal Jacket*, an adaptation of *The Short-Timers*, the same line is recontextualized. A psychotic infantryman named Animal Mother — a soldier so combat-crazed that his platoon-mates believe he will need to spend the rest of his life having grenades thrown at him just so that he will feel normal — confronts a combat correspondent named Joker. In an exchange of escalating taunts, Joker gains the upper hand. Animal Mother then brings the dialogue to a point of menacing tension: "You talk the talk. Do you walk the walk?" Animal Mother draws the line between verbal posturing and physical action, between machismo threat and actual violence, knowing he would win a real fight even if, against Joker, he could never win a battle of words. But it is Joker who is the intelligence of the movie as a whole. It is his observations that form the voice-over narration, and it is his subjectivity that gives perspective to the carnage, absurdity, and calamitous mischances of an ugly war. And so it is in virtually every major American film about Vietnam: a central character tells the story, a reflective human voice speaks the war, someone talks the talk.[2]

The Vietnam War is being told and remembered in oral language, the language of the combat veteran. It is his voice, his point of view, his representation of his own experience, his way of "talking the talk" that is the primary focus of this book.[3] Never before in the history of American military conflicts has such a vast archive of recorded voices — transcribed and published — become available, giving us an unprecedented opportunity to confront the brutal secrets of a devastating war through the testimonies of its historical protagonists. This book is about how to read, and how to hear, the historical, psychological, and narrative truths inherent in the soldiers' talk.[4]

After a period of silence and avoidance that extended well beyond the war's end in 1975, Vietnam War oral history came into its own as a fundamental form of American witnessing and remembrance in the 1980s.[5] The rush of oral history publication reached flood proportions in the 1990s and shows no sign of waning.[6] In the broadest sense, the Vietnam War oral history project proceeds from the deeply felt recognition that there is something unfinished and incomplete, perhaps even something false, about the official accounts of the war. As Mark Baker put it in his introduction to *Nam*, "Something is missing . . . something personal and palpable. . . . No one has bothered to talk to the men and women who went to Vietnam and fought the war" (xii). As a combat correspondent during the early years of America's involvement in Vietnam, and through the Tet offensive in January 1968 and beyond, Michael Herr had already felt that the war was not being told by the ones who were fighting it on the ground:

> There was a Marine in Hue who had come after me as I walked toward the truck that would take me to the airstrip, he'd been locked in that horror for nearly two weeks while I'd shuttled in and out for two or three days at a time.

> We knew each other by now, and when he caught up with me he grabbed my
> sleeve so violently that I thought he was going to accuse me or, worse, try to
> stop me from going. His face was all but blank with exhaustion, but he had
> enough feeling left to say, "Okay, man, you go on, you go on out of here you
> cocksucker, but I mean it, you tell it! You tell it, man. If you don't tell it . . . "
> (Herr 207)

Herr's encounter poses a question at once political and narratological:
How is the war to be told, and by whom? The first fact from which this book
proceeds is that the soldiers themselves have been "telling it" for a long while
now, in a colloquial and often obscene language. But if their voices enrich our
quest after historical knowledge, insofar as they represent what Michel Foucault has called "the living openness of history" (13), they also complicate
it, deferring our attempts to resolve and conclude. The testimony of living
voices (or voices caught live on tape) serves to forestall the desired closures
imposed by an objective historiography. "Indeed," Marita Sturken observes,
"history operates more efficiently when its agents are dead" (5).

The voices of the soldiers help keep alive the dynamically fractured and
contentious domain of cultural memory, a turbulent and ongoing process of
collective remembrance that inevitably is

> bound up in complex political stakes and meanings. [Cultural memory] both
> defines a culture and is the means by which its divisions and conflicting agen-
> das are revealed. To define a memory as cultural is, in effect, to enter into a
> debate about what that memory means. . . . Cultural memory is a field of
> cultural negotiation through which different stories vie for a place in history.
> (Sturken 1)

The "field" of cultural memory is also to be understood as an imaginary
and symbolic American ground upon which the terrain of Vietnam, along
with America's history of involvement there, has become overlaid, despite
some efforts to bury it out of sight once and for all.[7] Citing the concluding
mantra of Michael Herr's *Dispatches* — "Vietnam Vietnam Vietnam, we've
all been there" — Fred Turner develops the metaphor productively:

> like Herr, I believe that there *is* a sense in which we have all been to Vietnam
> and even a sense in which we linger there today. This Vietnam is not the his-
> torical landscape on which the fighting and dying took place, but the land-
> scape of public memory. Its battlegrounds are monuments, movie screens, and
> public libraries, presidential campaign trails and the Oval Office. At each of
> these sites, we struggle with one another and ourselves to recall the war and to
> put our recollections to use in the present. (x)

The struggle Turner defines has taken form since the early 1960s as a
collective process of dialogue and contestation across a vast and proliferating
range of genres, including speeches, manifestoes, policy papers, secret Pen-

tagon reports, novels, poems, plays, memoirs, newspaper articles, magazine essays, scholarly histories, films, and, finally, Web pages and Internet discussion lists. Amid this prodigious and expanding mass of narrative material — visual, oral, and written — the published oral testimonies of the war's active participants have assumed a central value and importance that this book sets out to analyze and appreciate from a variety of perspectives.

"WHAT DOES THAT ASSHOLE KNOW ABOUT TUNNELS?"

One factor that distinguishes the Vietnam War oral narratives from those previously gathered after World War II (when the portable tape recorder had already become an established tool of the oral historian) is its overwhelming emphasis on the verbal testimony of the infantryman, "the grunt."[8] In this sense, as both dialogic practice and narrative genre, oral history post-World War II participates in that general movement toward the writing of a relatively unmediated social history of "the common man." Looking back in the year 1994 upon the Great War and World War II, historian Sir Martin Gilbert reflects that history should be "an attempt to tell, within the framework of commanders, strategies and vast numbers, the story of individuals" (xxi).[9] As the individual subjects of history — soldiers, civilians, victims, and, with varying degrees of willingness or coercion, perpetrators (see especially Browning) — tell their own stories, the literary domain of personal narrative, autobiography, memoir, and oral history expands. Thus the response to the polemical question, "what is history and what is not, who is in it and who is not?" (Portelli 8) has become increasingly clear. History — and the genre of oral history so often inherent in it — is "more intrinsically itself," observes Alessandro Portelli, "when it listens to speakers who are not already recognized protagonists in the public sphere" (6).[10] Gathering the individual voices of history thus marks a "politically engaged social practice" (Portelli xvi) aimed at recovering, or reconstituting, "the history, memory, and subjectivity of working-class people" (xvii).[11] As Christopher Browning summarizes the matter in *Ordinary Men: Reserve Battalion 101 and the Final Solution in Poland*, "In recent decades the historical profession in general has been increasingly concerned with writing history 'from the bottom up,' with reconstructing the experiences of the bulk of the population ignored in the history of high politics and high culture hitherto so dominant" (xix).[12]

In his indispensable discussion entitled "The Warrior's Knowledge: Social Stratification and the Book Corpus of Vietnam" (the appendix to his book, *The Perfect War: Technowar in Vietnam*), James William Gibson defines the manner in which the division of narrative genres organizing the representation of the Vietnam War — including history, oral history, fiction, and nonfiction — reflects an American politics of social stratification:

> The warrior's knowledge as expressed in memoirs, novels, poems and plays by the soldiers, together with reports by oral historians and essay journalists, posits a literature about the war that contradicts the war-managers at virtually every level. Yet these narratives have failed to influence the conventional assessments by both the "error in judgment" and the "self-imposed restraint" schools. How can a major war like Vietnam be absorbed into the historical record without listening to those who fought the war, especially when over 200 books have been written by soldiers and their close observers? What are the tacit rules governing "legitimate" knowledge about the war, and how have they marginalized and discredited the warrior's knowledge? (461)

The infantryman's social position translates into his literal position on the battlefield itself, a place of "limited" perspective as compared to the "bigpicture" tableaux claimed to be visible by those occupying more elevated and more distant vantages. The typical oral testimony of the American grunt can indeed exhibit powerlessness, isolation, fragmentation, and narrowed focus. The testimony of Lieutenant Robert Jeanette, 1st Air Cavalry Division, survivor of the terrible battles of the Ia Drang valley in 1965, is representative: "I really had absolutely no idea what happened other than what happened in our own little area. Everything was so individualized. Everything was so vicious. Everything was happening around you, and you had no time to worry or interest in what was happening elsewhere" (Steinman 68). Yet it is precisely this ground-level perspective that is so valuable to the historian interested in the actual experience of warfare itself. Writing of the First Indochina War culminating in the French defeat in Vietnam, made especially visible to an Anglo-American audience by Graham Greene's *The Quiet American*, Frances Fitzgerald, in introducing a volume of Vietnamese voices, has observed,

> As the landscape of Vietnam, like the landscape of France, changes perceptibly every ten miles, so the war in Vietnam has been uneven, inconsistent, and thus almost impenetrable to those who think only in generalities. Even after the arrival of the American forces, the war consisted not of fronts and flanking movements but of a series of isolated incidents — a mortar attack here, a bombing strike there — that resisted all the American attempts at rationalization. Thus, these stories in a sense tell more about the war and its consequences than any compendium of reports and statistics. The writers have a narrow, focused perspective; they are interested not in ideologies or global strategies but in the detail of a life, an emotion. They have borne witness to the fate of the individual in a country that has been devastated by abstractions. (xv)

Vietnam War oral history cherishes the irreducible truth of this individual, ground-level perspective while postulating an uncountable multiplicity of such perspectives, each representing the place where, in Portelli's words, "history and story, two directly related words, overlap and coalesce. War as event and oral history as discourse, therefore, share the fact of being the grounds of encounters between personal experience and history, the spaces where the individual narrative of biography meets the collective narrative of history" (161).[13] It is the particularity of the soldier's vision that gives it its value as a window on what might be termed the hidden microhistory of the war.

Indeed, a major theme in the testimonies of the Vietnam soldiers is the distance they perceive between "the lived reality of actual warfare" (Gibson 468) and the narrative representations of the war in contemporaneous newspaper and magazine accounts. The American infantryman experienced a war so distinct from these accounts as to seem a different reality altogether. The soldiers' oral narratives therefore clash with the dominant discourses of a media apparatus that collaborated, sometimes willingly, sometimes unwittingly, with the war managers' attempt to monopolize the representation of historical truth and fact:

> The professional rules of what constitutes news virtually dictated that the news media would report on what the war-managers said about the war. News as a form of knowledge is professionally defined by journalists as what the highest levels of bureaucracies say about the world, not what people in subordinate levels have to say. (Gibson 469)

Again and again, a central command's singular point of view replaces the multiple and diverse narratives of ground-level participants and observers. As Michael Herr notes, the news institution, which, during the earlier years of the war, placed itself largely in the service of the military command, ensured that the subjective, pointed, or idiosyncratic dispatches from the field would be "worked over into that uni-prose which all news magazines and papers maintained" (212) — thus "allowing the living, fragile, pulsating 'history' to slip through their fingers" (Foucault 11). In some cases, moreover, actual accounts from the front lines were deemed to be superfluous altogether. Stanley Karnow describes a particularly glaring instance of this phenomenon in recounting how the American media machine reported — in living color — what was eventually revealed to be the purely fictitious "second" Tonkin Gulf incident of August, 1964:

> Though no correspondents had been present, the American press published vivid eyewitness accounts of the incident, dramatized by news editors with inspiration from Pentagon officials. As "the night glowed eerily," wrote *Time*,

the Communist "intruders boldly sped" toward the destroyers, firing with "automatic weapons," while *Life* had the American ships "under continuous torpedo attack" as they "weaved through the night sea, evading more torpedoes." Not to be outdone, *Newsweek* described "U.S. jets diving, strafing, flattening out . . . and diving again" at the enemy boats, one of which "burst into flames and sank." Now, having won the battle, *Newsweek* concluded, "it was time for American might to strike back." (386–87)

Here official discourse, masquerading as objective truth, reveals itself as nothing but pure fiction. And yet, such official accounts were deemed to be more reliable and veracious than the eyewitness testimonies of the soldiers themselves.[14] If truth, then, is a matter of correspondence between a narrative account and a verifiable reality, it is also a matter of power and politics, of who is in control of its definition, production, and distribution. For Karl Marx, the revolutionary subject of history "must *prove* the truth, i.e., the reality and power, the 'this-sidedness' of [human] thinking in practice" (67, emphasis added), against the class that controls not only the material means of production but also the means of mental production — the dominant ideas and illusions which the ruling class perpetuates about itself and the world.

If language, in wartime especially, is inherently opaque and metaphorical, capable of absorbing heavy loads of patriotic sentiment or ideological abstraction, and if, moreover, the media in war is more or less controlled or intimidated by a central command structure pursuing its own interests, then language itself is one of the primary battle sites of war.[15] For Hemingway, in a famous passage from *A Farewell to Arms,* one experiences the mendacity of official language as a kind of embarrassment and nausea:

> "What has been done this summer cannot have been done in vain."
>
> I did not say anything. I was always embarrassed by the words sacred, glorious, and sacrifice and the expression in vain. We had heard them, sometimes standing in the rain almost out of earshot, so that only the shouted words came through, and had read them, on proclamations that were slapped up by billposters over other proclamations, now for a long time, and I had seen nothing sacred, and the things that were glorious had no glory and the sacrifices were like the stockyards at Chicago if nothing was done with the meat except to bury it. There were many words that you could not stand to hear and finally only the names of places had dignity. Certain numbers were the same way and certain dates and these with the names of the places were all you could say and have them mean anything. Abstract words such as glory, honor, courage, or hallow were obscene beside the concrete names of villages, the numbers of roads, the names of rivers, the numbers of regiments and the dates. (185)

For Hemingway, a central figure in the American tradition of war narrative, everything is at stake in keeping the "word mirror" clean so that it might give as undistorted a reflection of reality as possible. To operate in this way, language must be grounded in the sensory experiences, material conditions, and life processes of real, active men reporting from the field. If, then, "abstract words such as glory, honor, courage, or hallow were obscene," that is because they obscured the real obscenity of war behind a cloud of abstraction or sentiment. In "How to Tell a True War Story," Tim O'Brien explains:

> A true war story is never moral. It does not instruct, nor encourage virtue, nor suggest models of proper human behavior, nor restrain men from doing the things men have always done. If a story seems moral, do not believe it. If at the end of a war story you feel uplifted, or if you feel that some small bit of rectitude has been salvaged from the larger waste, then you have been made the victim of a very old and terrible lie. There is no rectitude whatsoever. There is no virtue. As a first rule of thumb, therefore, you can tell a true war story by its absolute and uncompromising allegiance to obscenity and evil. . . . If you don't care for obscenity, you don't care for the truth; if you don't care for the truth, watch how you vote. Send guys to war, they come home talking dirty. (69)[16]

Obscene talk, then, is to be understood as a kind of insurrection against an official, sanitized account that shies away from the real obscenity of war:

> One way to understand the difference [between "official" and "unofficial" discourse] is to note that the warrior's knowledge is most often written in *colloquial* language as opposed to educated prose; it is often *obscene* language as well. Some obscenities are the normal expletives, but words like "gook" and "crispy critters" tell the reader about a world different from the one described in official accounts of a war against communism, battles against Vietcong and NVA troops, and the categories of casualty reports. If all intellectual discourse must be written in "civil" terms, then the warrior's knowledge is automatically moved to the margins. (Gibson 467)

What is obscene, finally, is a usage of language unacquainted with the reality of wartime conditions on the ground or, indeed, beneath it:

> By the time that Westmoreland came home that fall [1967, i.e., just before the Tet offensive of January 1968] to cheerlead and request-beg another quarter of a million men, with his light-at-the-end-of-the tunnel collateral, there were people leaning so far out to hear good news that a lot of them slipped over the edge and said that they could see it too. (Outside of Tay Ninh City a man whose work kept him "up to fucking here" in tunnels, lobbing grenades into them, shooting his gun into them, popping CS smoke into them, crawling down into them himself to bring the bad guys out dead or alive, he almost smiled when he heard that one and said, "What does that asshole know about tunnels?") (Herr 47)

"MEMORIES, GUESSES, SECOND GUESSES, EXPERIENCES (NEW, OLD, REAL, IMAGINED, STOLEN); HISTORIES, ATTITUDES" (Herr 42)

In his introduction to *Strange Ground: Americans in Vietnam, 1945–1975: An Oral History,* Harry Maurer isolates a key question for us — the question of veracity — yet arrives at a dubious editorial procedure:

> For reasons that will be obvious, four speakers in this book remain anonymous. All the others agreed to be identified, which I wanted to do partly as a way of screening out tall tales. William Broyles, in an *Esquire* article called "Why Men Love War," remarks that "I have never once heard a grunt tell a reporter a war story that wasn't a lie, just as some of the stories that I tell about the war are lies." He goes on to say: "Not that even the lies aren't true, on a certain level. They have a moral, even a mythic, truth, rather than a literal one." I am not much convinced by that argument, so I have done my best, as many vets advised, to "keep my bullshit detectors out." Stories, even whole interviews, do not appear here because they did not ring true. But I have not tried to check these accounts. Some, undoubtedly, stretch the facts. I hoped that by asking people, in effect, to sign their names to what they said, I would minimize the "mythic truth" and stay close to what happened. (4–5)

Indeed there is a long history of distrusting the stories of soldiers. In Western drama, the "miles gloriosus," or "braggart soldier," has long been a comic caricature. Soldiers are known to exaggerate. A war front creates its own myths as surely as it requires its own jargon. And young men, caught in daily tests of courage, slip easily into a rhetoric of machismo that masks fear and lauds excess. For this reason, the language of the grunt has found virtually no place in the official records of war. The traditional historian interviews generals and reads reports, but instinctively mistrusts the testosterone-addled accounts of the combatants in the field. Yet in "screening out tall tales" and stories that "did not ring true" Maurer loses, we feel, an invaluable source of knowledge about *the soldiers themselves,* and about what it was like to be a soldier in the Vietnam War.

Additionally, if "staying close to what happened" includes a propensity to exclude what are deemed to be the "mythic truths" recounted by the soldiers, then the power of determining "what happened" is yielded to those who would confine themselves within the categorical boundary of "non-fictional" discourse claimed as the preserve of the conventional historian. As Gibson observes,

> "Nonfictional" texts are thought to monopolize the representations of all real experiences. "Nonfictional" texts are thought to represent "what really happened," as opposed to "fictional" texts, which deal in matters that "never

really happened"; experiences that are not real experiences, but only imaginary ones. (471)

A major effect of the fictional/non-fictional binary is that it sanctions the
discrediting (by those who were "never there") of a certain way of "soldier
talking" as a source of truthful or historical claims.

We suggest that, as it pertains to the document of oral history, the fictional/
non-fictional binary is a false one to be resolved dialectically in the direction
of a new synthesis: oral *narrative*. Perhaps it should not be surprising that we
have arrived at this position: most of the contributors to this volume are not
historians, nor are we experts on oral history as defined by the academic
discipline that goes by that name, although much research into this field has
been undertaken by all of us here. This book, rather, is about oral history as a
literary genre; it is, moreover, an exploration of what happens when literary
critics and serious readers from other disciplines are confronted with a narrative genre that has become associated with a specific historical event. Literary
critics emphasize things that historians generally do not: symbolism and
imagery; narrative point of view; issues of voice, memory, and subjectivity;
and what historian Hayden White has called the "tropics of discourse."[17]

As someone who was exposed to warfare and was lucky to survive it,
Michael Herr captures the essence of the encounter we are interested in
exploring, the site at which "what happened" converges with memory and
language:

> Sometimes I didn't know if an action took a second or an hour or if I dreamed
> it or what. In war more than in other life you don't really know what you're
> doing most of the time, you're just behaving, and afterward you can make up
> any kind of bullshit you want about it, say you felt good or bad, loved it or
> hated it, did this or that, the right thing or the wrong thing; still, what hap-
> pened happened. (20–21)

"*Still, what happened happened.*" Indeed, finding out "what happened"
should be the goal of any historical project. Who killed whom, for example
at My Lai, is crucial to know. Yet determining "what happened" after the fact
is inseparable from the *narrative act*. It is a natural question, in turn, to ask
whether the testimonies of living witnesses, or, as Foucault maintains, the
representations inherent in historical documents, are

> telling the truth, and by what right they could claim to be doing so, whether
> they were sincere or deliberately misleading, well informed or ignorant, au-
> thentic or tampered with. But each of these questions, and all this critical
> concern, pointed to one and the same end: the reconstitution, on the basis of
> what the documents say, and sometimes merely hint at, of the past from which
> they emanate and which has now disappeared far behind them. (Foucault 6)

Insofar as human narratives assume their forms in response to real historical pressures, we are interested not only in what the soldier says but also in the narrative shape of what he says. "What happened," then, is never completely separable from what Maurer pejoratively calls mythic truth and personal "distortion": it is the reaction of the subject to what happened, the forms of compensation and elaboration forced upon him by the pressure of dreadful events, that is the real subject of oral history. In sum, the question we pose to the combat veteran, and attempt to learn to listen for in his discourse, is not so much "What happened" as "Who are you?" and "What was it like to have been you, in Vietnam?" Finally, we do think our book shows that many important *historical* aspects of the Vietnam War can be illuminated by the kind of narrative analyses we perform here, whether "historical" be understood as signifying a particular kind of narrative discourse or as the reality of events themselves, "what really happened."

It is therefore Mark Baker who articulates the wisest approach to the matter, suggesting something valuable about how those of us who were not in Vietnam — the typical reader of Vietnam War oral history is someone with no firsthand experience of war and often, as is increasingly the case, someone born after 1975 — are to listen to and "take" the accounts of those who were:

> Because of the personal equation, these accounts are commonly called war stories. It must be assumed that included here are generalizations, exaggerations, braggadocio and — very likely — outright lies. But if these stories were told within a religious framework, the telling would be called bearing witness. The human imperfections simply authenticate the sincerity of the whole. The apocryphal aspects have more to do with metaphor than with deceit. (xv)

In this book, then, we proceed from the axiom that everything said by the historical witness conveys a form of "the truth" even when the speaker is consciously or unconsciously lying; even the lies or misrepresentations point us in the direction of the underlying truths to which they indirectly refer or attempt to negate. With Marx, that is, we hold that "the phantoms of the human brain also are necessary sublimates of men's material life-process, which can be empirically established and which is bound to material preconditions" (75). Michel Foucault develops the implications of this kind of hermeneutic approach, which also reflects the influence of psychoanalysis on the interpretive and historical enterprise:

> one tries to rediscover beyond the statements themselves the intention of the speaking subject, his conscious activity, what he meant, or, again, the unconscious activity that took place, despite himself, in what he said or in the almost imperceptible fracture of his actual words; in any case, we must reconstitute another discourse, rediscover the silent murmuring, the inexhaustible speech that animates from within the voice that one hears, re-establish the tiny,

invisible text that runs between and sometimes collides with them. The analysis of thought is always *allegorical* in relation to the discourse that it employs. Its question is unfailingly: *what was being said in what was said?* (Foucault 27–28, emphasis added)

In his classic study of popular culture, Slavoj Žižek suggests that every narrative "scene" (whether of memory, literature, or cinema) is shaped and determined by latent forces. Hence, in his words, every "manifest imaginary scene . . . effectively holds within it the place of what this imaginary scene must 'repress,' exclude, force out, in order to constitute itself. It is a kind of umbilical cord tying the imaginary structure to the 'repressed' process of its structuration" (52). According to this way of reading, the typical oral testimony of the soldier can contain a primary, "repressed" content more or less recoverable by means of careful analysis (an analysis that, insofar as it takes narrative form, harbors its own latent dimension in turn). We are interested, that is, as much in the soldier's representation of his own history as in his — or anybody's — inability at times to comprehend and convey it narratively without telling distortions and evasions. Hence the term *"méconnaissance,"* as French psychoanalyst Jacques Lacan defines it (see *Aggressivity* and *Mirror*). *"Méconnaissance"* can be translated as "a failure to recognize," a "misconstruction," "a concept central to Lacan's thinking, since, for him, knowledge (connaissance) is inextricably bound up with méconnaissance" (Sheridan xi). In Freudian terms, *"méconnaissance"* belongs in that constellation of concepts including *repression, negation, denial,* and *disavowal,* modes of defense that consist in the subject's refusal to recognize the reality of an outrageous or traumatic perception — the reality, say, of his or her own nature, or of the real pressures converging upon him or her. In staging the scene of personal and cultural *"méconnaissance,"* the typical oral testimony can point to truths that escape the awareness of the speaking subject, even as the testimony, considered in its often rich narrative textuality, "knows" and tells more than the subject of the discourse consciously articulates. The speaking subject never fully masters what the speaking process brings to the light (or half-light) of language. A psychoanalytic approach to the study of oral narratives would thus focus on the ways in which insight and blindness interrelate and interact, probing into their complex and elusive relationship to the question of "truth" and to the historical realities they seek to represent.

"HE WANTED ME TO FEEL THE TRUTH, TO BELIEVE BY THE RAW FORCE OF FEELING"

"In any war story, but especially a true one, it's difficult to separate what happened from what seemed to happen. What seems to happen becomes its own happening and has to be told that way" (O'Brien 71). The issue O'Brien isolates here is not so much "what happened" as whether "what happened" can ever be *believed* by those who were not there. Thus O'Brien places in focus the question of an audience and a culture that may not know how to hear what the soldier has to say and which, out of this basic inadequacy, consigns all that strains credibility and credulity to the realm of "mythic truth."

> In many cases a true war story cannot be believed. If you believe it, be skeptical. It's a question of credibility. Often the crazy stuff is true and the normal stuff isn't, because the normal stuff is necessary to make you believe the truly incredible craziness.
>
> In other cases you can't even tell a true war story. Sometimes it's just beyond telling. . . . He wanted me to feel the truth, to believe by the raw force of feeling. (71, 74)[18]

Again it is Hemingway, in his classic story "Soldier's Home," who helps us to refocus the question of truth and veracity, not on what the soldier says, but on the pressures that lead him to shape his narrative in the way he does, and on the home culture's propensity to disbelieve him:

> At first Krebs, who had been at Belleau Wood, Soissons, the Champagne, St. Mihiel and in the Argonne did not want to talk about the war at all. Later he felt the need to talk but no one wanted to hear about it. His town had heard too many atrocity stories to be thrilled by actualities. Krebs found that to be listened to at all he had to lie, and after he had done this twice he, too, had a reaction against the war and against talking about it. A distaste for everything that had happened to him in the war set in because of the lies he had told. . . . His lies were quite unimportant lies and consisted in attributing to himself things other men had seen, done or heard of, and stating as facts certain apocryphal incidents familiar to all soldiers. Even his lies were not sensational at the pool room. His acquaintances, who had heard detailed accounts of German women found chained to machine guns in the Argonne forest and who could not comprehend, or were barred by their patriotism from interest in, any German machine gunners who were not chained, were not thrilled by his stories.
>
> Krebs acquired the nausea in regard to experience that is the result of untruth or exaggeration, and when he occasionally met another man who had really been a soldier and they talked a few minutes in the dressing room at a dance he fell into the easy pose of the old soldier among other soldiers: that he had been badly, sickeningly frightened all the time. In this way he lost everything. (69–70)

As the essays in this volume show, the soldier's relation to his own historical experience, mediated as it so often is by the oral historian or interviewer ("Oral history is practice and dialogue" [Portelli xvii]), is to be triangulated in a crucial sense: oral narrative implies not only the testimony of the participant in history and the agency of the historian/interviewer but also the consciousness and sensibility of that third party, the interpreting reader who, oscillating between the poles of identification and objectification, is called upon to bear witness and, in some sense, to enter into and extend the dialogue with which cultural memory perpetuates itself. In the introduction to *A Piece of My Heart: The Stories of Twenty-Six American Women Who Served in Vietnam,* Keith Walker recounts the process by which he came to understand his role not so much as an active interviewer but as an ideal listener, for whom attentive passivity and, indeed, what Keats called "negative capability," are paramount values:[19]

> I asked each of them to tell me about Vietnam (as much or as little as she was willing to recall), a little about how she got there in the first place, and then to follow up by talking about her life after coming home. For some, the memories came easily, but for others, recalling their experiences in Vietnam was a painful process. During many of the interviews there were long silences on the tapes. They are indicated in this book by a series of dots. But the dots can't possibly describe a moment when, at a dining room table late at night with tears welling in a woman's eyes, a sentence would drift away. There were times when the flow of a memory would take the person to such an unpleasant place that she would hesitate and then shift her trend of thought to avoid it. Some pauses lasted until the silence in the room became impossible to endure: during one woman's attempt to describe the scene in her hospital during the Tet offensive, there developed a pause of at least three minutes. I turned the tape recorder off.
>
>   And this was not an unusual incident. I found myself asking fewer and fewer questions; in fact, I made a serious point to interrupt only when a word or phrase was unclear. I became unwilling to influence the flow of recollection even if it meant that a degree of continuity or clarity might be sacrificed. There was a transformation taking place, a magical kind of presence reached by each woman at some point during our meeting, where past and present became one. (4)

The Vietnam War oral histories often take the form of confession and testimonial. Though often recording "everyday incidents of bravery, loyalty, and self-sacrifice" (Smith xii), the prototypical Vietnam War narrative is not one of heroic conduct; rather, it tends to be organized around some primal scene of death, mutilation, shameful conduct, helplessness, rage, and atrocity. In these cases, the material takes precedence over interpretations, and the only kind of appropriate response seems a sense of awe and stunned silence, a kind of listening "degree zero." Rifleman Jay Lazarin of the 25th Infantry Division went to the war in early 1967:

> My first combat operation came a few days later. . . . Within minutes, I saw my first casualties of the war; they were Vietnamese.
>   Lying under bushes at the tree line were a father and two children; all had

been hit by napalm. Their skin at various parts of their bodies was hanging off or, in the case of the badly burned girl, was dragging on the ground as they approached, the father gesturing with his two hands together in front of his face, as if in prayer. Myself and my "basic buddy" were told by my platoon sergeant to guard them as he motioned them to sit where they were. He and the rest of the platoon then started to search the tree line for other "Viet Cong."

I was horrified and curious at the same time; I couldn't keep my eyes off of them. I saw the damage that the napalm had done but didn't understand the mechanism that could cause such burns to still smolder as we sat opposite them. The children seemed to sleep but never cried. The father cried and continuously spoke to us and to himself. Neither I nor my buddy had any idea what he was saying. Through gestures, we offered him water, but he either didn't seem to understand or was not interested in our help. . . . We simply sat there for at least a half hour, listening to the sounds of men dropping grenades into bunkers and wells, firing shotguns at livestock, and then watching both the children die as the father vainly attempted to slap them both back to life as each one stopped breathing. I went for help after the first one seemed to go still. My platoon lieutenant came back with me and called a medic over the radio, who came as the father gasped for air in gulps, then fell over dead. Only then did we see that his entire back flesh had been completely burned through, exposing ribs and organs darkened from the burning. The medic looked at the children and walked away. He said nothing to us.

So, this was my first impression of the war itself. (Bergerud 237–38)

Our book is about learning to accept the oral narratives as significant documents in our understanding of the Vietnam War. Such oral testimony demands a special kind of receptivity and responsiveness that the following essays will attempt to embody and to enact.

In "Approaching a Truer Form of Truth: The Appropriation of the Oral Narrative Form in Vietnam War Literature," Jen Dunnaway inquires into the reasons why oral history has been treated as a particularly conducive mode for communicating the experience of the Vietnam War within the "fictional" literature that has emerged from this event. Specifically, Dunnaway examines oral narrative as a subject of appropriation by the diverse body of writing that has come to be known as Vietnam War literature, and suggests a number of reasons why the "war story" itself, however fragmented, embellished, or impressionistic, is portrayed in these works as having the capacity to convey the "truth" of the war experience more honestly and succinctly than formal prose fiction alone. Dunnaway focuses primarily on Tim O'Brien's *The Things They Carried,* Michael Herr's *Dispatches,* and Gustav Hasford's *The Short-Timers,* contextualizing these canonical literary works against the oral history collections of Mark Baker, Al Santoli, and Harold G. Moore. She addresses the synergistic relationship between fictional and non-fictional narratives, a relationship that, within Vietnam War literature, allows each of these forms both to complement and lend greater depth of meaning to the other. The major areas of emphasis included in this essay revolve around the problematic and multi-faceted concept of "truth" within Vietnam War literature.

"Concatenation and History in *Nam*" by Paul Budra argues that what makes the oral histories of the Vietnam War unique is the fact that they have appeared around an extensively documented historical event — perhaps the best documented conflict in history. Conventional narrative history has traditionally been perceived by the public as more objective, more penetrating, and more reliable than soldiers' firsthand testimony, but that has not been the case with the Vietnam War. Budra's chapter attempts to explain why that might be by examining the rhetoric, and especially the ideological rhetoric, of the Vietnam oral history as epitomized by one of the best known of these books, Mark Baker's *Nam* (1981). The rhetorical authority of *Nam*, Budra concludes, comes from two sources: the concatenation of short narratives that illustrate a general theme, and the primacy and authenticity of oral narrative, the witness experience.

Beginning with the premise that oral history is a mixed genre requiring consideration in a dialogic framework composed (at least) of ethnography, historiography, narratology, linguistics, and sociology, Kevin McGuirk contends that oral history bears equal consideration in the light of poetics. In " 'Disremembering, Dísmémbering': Poetics, and the Oral Histories of the Vietnam War," McGuirk reads oral histories by ex-combatants as a discourse more complex than what we know as normative prose. Poetics is pertinent in the first instance because the modern oral history represents the culmination of a post-Wordsworthian poetics of "a man speaking to men," the writing degree-zero of a romantic project. But oral histories by Vietnam veterans are not simply, in another famous phrase of Wordsworth, "emotion recollected in tranquility." Such histories gesture toward the unspeakable; hence, their discourse needs also to be approached "through the multiplicitous poetics of the twentieth-century avant-gardes," a poetics of trauma, rupture, and extreme experience, as it has been theorized and defined by such critics as Perloff, Damon, Felman, and McCaffery. The rich discursive complexity of these histories has not been fully revealed, McGuirk argues, owing to unexamined assumptions about the appropriateness of verse and prose to discourses of historical knowledge. In fact, these histories have the potential to represent a far more compelling and radically Wordsworthian "poetry" of the Vietnam War than the free-verse lyric typically assigned that label. Examining theorists of prose like Frye, Kittay, and Godzich, and writers associated with "Language" poetry, and enlarging the limited address to the poetics of oral history provided by theorists such as Tedlock and Portelli, McGuirk

interrogates the meaning and method of oral history collection and transcription. Finally, in a series of close readings of poems and oral testimonies,
as encountered in the poetry collection *Winning Hearts and Minds* and the
indispensable oral history compilations *Nam, Bloods,* and *A Piece of My
Heart,* McGuirk develops a poetics of Vietnam oral histories.

In "Talk, Write, Talk: Bobby Garwood, MIAs, and Conspiracy," Craig
Howes explores how oral histories have been used, and continue to be used,
as ammunition in the ongoing debate over missing-in-action (MIA) American soldiers in Vietnam. By exploring the conjunctions between confession
and conspiracy theory found in the many autobiographical and biographical
texts that provide conflicting versions of the experiences of former prisoner-
of-war Bobby Garwood, the chapter draws some conclusions about the provisional, unstable, highly politicized, and open-ended nature of personal and
conspiratorial narratives. Howes first describes what happened when the
subject of an oral history returns to America not only to find himself presumed dead, but also described by a variety of people, in print, as a defector
and a traitor. Robert "Bobby" Garwood, a Marine enlisted man who was
captured in 1965 and "released" in 1979, came home to court martial proceedings, largely based on the widespread and public declarations by other
returning American POWs of his defection over to the North Vietnamese
side. His initial legal defense, his subsequent "authorized" biography, his
sudden revisionist interview that declared firsthand knowledge of live American POWs after Operation Homecoming, and his frequent alterations and
elaborations of his story over the succeeding years, have made him a focal
point for conspiracy theorists, MIA/POW activists, movie directors, politicians, retired and penitent Vietnam vets, and government agencies and
bodies, including Congress. Howes explores how the phenomenon of Bobby
Garwood forces us to re-examine our notions of oral history, and particularly Vietnam War oral history, in the light of this individual's constant revision or reorientation of this history — changes increasingly provoked by
shifts in America's attitudes toward the war itself. Special attention is paid to
the impact of the Internet on the unfolding narrative, since MIA home pages,
Garwood debunking sites, and constantly updated or changing information
sources have only accelerated the transformations and contradictions in the
narrative.

Thomas Carmichael, in "Resolutely Other: The Vietnam War, Oral History, and the Subject of Revolutionary Socialism," examines oral histories of
the revolutionary Vietnamese subject. In *A Bright Shining Lie: John Paul
Vann and America in Vietnam,* Neil Sheehan quotes at length a May 1965
letter from John Vann to General Robert York, then commander of the 82nd
Airborne Division at Fort Bragg. Reflecting upon the political logic of the

intensifying war and American involvement in it, Vann writes, "the principles, goals, and desires of the other side are much closer to what Americans
believe in than those of the GVN" (Vann quoted in Sheehan, 524). Vann then
continues, "I am convinced that, even though the National Liberation Front
is Communist-dominated, that [*sic*] the great majority of the people supporting it are doing so because it is their only hope to change and improve their
living conditions . . . " (Vann quoted in Sheehan, 524). The imperative of
history is clear, as Vann puts it: "If I were a lad of eighteen faced with the
same choice — whether to support the GVN or the NLF — and a member of a
rural community, I would surely choose the NLF" (Vann quoted in Sheehan,
524). John Vann's remarks are telling, not only for what they say early on
about the folly of American policy in Vietnam or about Vann himself, the
themes of Neil Sheehan's great history, but also for what they suggest with
respect to American constructions of the Vietnamese who opposed them.

The oral history of the Vietnam War as it has appeared in the West has in
the main been the history of an American war, in which the Vietnamese, as
has often been observed, are figured inevitably as an Other projection. This
history has understandably endeavored to represent the private experiences
of American soldiers and other combat personnel engaged in a complex
negotiation of memory and trauma for an implied American audience. But
what is absent from the oral history of the Vietnam War in the West is any
real accounting of the subject in opposition, the subject of those great collectives that successfully stood against the American military, the Saigon regime
and its own military, and, before them, the exploitation and repression of
French colonial rule.

In "Oral History and Popular Memory in the Historiography of the Vietnam War," Van Nguyen-Marshall examines the complexities involved in
narrating the Vietnam War from a historian's point of view. She argues that
there remain many unresolved issues in both the written history and social
memory of the war. Her chapter focuses on three major zones of interpretation: (1) those expressing the points of view of U.S. scholars, (2) those of
Vietnamese civilians and ex-combatants in Vietnam, and (3) those of Vietnamese civilians and ex-combatants living abroad. Within each of the three
zones are competing voices trying to shape both written history and popular
memory. Drawing on her own experience of flight from a war-torn country in
1975, Nguyen-Marshall assesses what is at stake in the competing stories
within, and across, each of these major interpretive contexts.

In "Queering Vietnam: Katherine V. Forrest's Fictional Oral History,"
Priscilla L. Walton examines Teresa de Lauretis's recent work, *The Practice
of Love: Lesbian Sexuality and Perverse Desire,* arguing that it comprises a
re-evaluation of Freud's writings on sexuality, and moves to open a space,

working through Freud, for the theorization of lesbian desire. De Lauretis's discussion thus offers a means of analyzing the oral-in-the-written testimonials of sexuality and war. Given the "unspeakability" of homosexuality in war, even (or perhaps, especially) in oral histories, some of these testimonials must be articulated fictively, or as de Lauretis has argued, "reworked through fantasy . . . and then returned to the external world resignified." Katherine V. Forrest's *Liberty Square* performs such a rearticulation. A detective novel about a lesbian ex-Marine, turned LAPD cop, who has buried her ordeals in Vietnam, *Liberty Square* offers a venue ("fictitious," and thus "safe") for speaking the unspeakable. As it recounts the stories of gays and lesbians in Vietnam, and of the nurses, the novel explores how unspeakable stories can be spoken. Comprising a form of "oral history," if within a fictive venue, the narrative serves as the spoken history of its protagonists. *Liberty Square* thus becomes a vehicle for the examination of the combat experience of gays and lesbians, experiences that are often quite different from those of their heterosexual counterparts. Destabilizing the boundaries between fiction and history by impersonating oral history, then, *Liberty Square* is itself a testimonial to those whose stories have been written off. By writing those stories back in, the narrative offers an important commentary on the erasures of and in history, at the same time that it affords a form of fictive catharsis for its readers.

"*Bloods:* Teaching the Afroamerican Experience of the Vietnam Conflict" describes a course offered by William M. King, Professor and Coordinator of Afroamerican Studies at the University of Colorado, Boulder. The course focuses on Wallace Terry's *Bloods: An Oral History of the Vietnam War by Black Veterans* (1984) to provide a view of the war in Vietnam from an Afrocentric perspective. With special attention to two of the book's oral testimonies, King describes the manner in which his students come to grasp the potency of oral narrative to convey the subjective texture of the black military experience. The simple yet profound process whereby the students come to identify with these "Bloods," putting themselves in their places, is powerfully, pedagogically effective. The subjective narrative material of *Bloods* thus enables students to stretch their imaginations and their identities.

Michael Zeitlin's "The Things They Saw: Trauma and Vision in *A Piece of My Heart: The Stories of Twenty-Six American Women Who Served in Vietnam*" focuses special attention on the experiences of American military nurses who were positioned as the war's ultimate witnesses. Dealing with the shattered bodies of the wounded and the dead on a daily basis, these nurses were compelled to train their vision upon scenes of unimaginable horror. Zeitlin explores the testimonies of these witnesses in order to shed light on the psychoanalytic theory of trauma and thus to render that theory as anything but abstract. Witnesses to the suffering of American soldiers and, in many cases, Vietnamese civilians, and bearers themselves of terrible and often traumatic memories, these women enable us to grasp a measure of the war's staggering human cost. Reading their testimonies also enables us to ground the psychoanalytic theory of trauma within the living human subjects of contemporary history.

NOTES

1. It should be noted, however, that a sense of collective impotence, rage, and betrayal sometimes led to acts of fragging, in which American officers were assassinated in the field, typically during firefights, by soldiers in their own platoons. As James William Gibson notes, "Official fragging statistics exist . . . 126 in 1969; 271 in 1970; 321 in 1971 — for the army alone" (472). The phenomenon of "fragging" is one of the great "untellable" subjects of the Vietnam War.

2. In the shattering denouement of both novel and film, Joker, of course, also "walks the walk" with a vengeance, by becoming a killer.

3. In response to an increasingly more complicated and realistic recognition that the war cherishes no single moral center or "subject position," the Vietnam War oral history project has also come to include, as if moving out in concentric circles from the American infantryman's perspective, the experience of the American nurses and fe-male military personnel (some 15,000 women served in-country during the war) (see especially Walker, and essays by Walton and Zeitlin below), the testimonies of the wives and children of the dead soldiers, and, finally, the accounts of Vietnamese subjects, combatants and civilians alike (see the essays by Nguyen-Marshall and Carmichael below). Several works of Vietnamese first-person accounts, along with novels (e.g., Bao Ninh's *The Sorrow of War*), short stories, and memoirs, have already been published in English translation, including *Between Two Fires: The Unheard Voices of Vietnam* (1970), edited by Ly Qui Chung; *Viet Nam: The Unheard Voices* (1970), edited by Don Luce and John Sommer; *Portrait of the Enemy* (1986), edited by David Chanoff and Doan Van Toai; and a range of recently published and trans-lated works by Vietnamese writers (see Karlin). From a North American perspective, such material enables the work of contrast, comparison, and mutual recognition necessary to an ever-widening understanding of the Vietnam War.

4. On the theory and poetics of oral history as a narrative genre, the work of Alessandro Portelli remains indispensable: "What is spoken in a typical oral history interview has usually never been told in that form before. . . . The interview implicitly enhances the authority and self-awareness of the narrator, and may raise questions about aspects of experience that the speaker has never spoken or even seriously thought about. . . . This personal effort at composition in performance is supported by the use of socialized linguistic matter (clichés, formulas, folklore, frozen anecdotes, commonplaces) and by the example of genres derived from writing (the novel, auto-biography, history books) or mass media. These established blocks of discourse define secure paths in the uncharted territory of discourse, much like the invisible but rigid airways that guide airplanes in the fluid territory of the sky. . . . Between the fluid textual experiments and the frozen formulaic material. . . . we need to consider also the formulaic materials, the apparently formless connecting and supporting matter,

and the dialogic and directive role of the historian . . . we might define oral history as the genre of discourse which orality and writing have developed jointly in order to speak to each other about the past" (4–5).

5. "I returned home from Vietnam in March 1969. . . . But I was still an inarticulate teenager, confused and exhausted by my year in combat. There was no way that I could express what I had seen and knew to be true. So for ten years I said nothing. . . . Ten years later, in 1979, as if coming out of a shock-induced trance, I stopped running from my experiences there. I began interviewing and soul-searching with fellow veterans for an oral history of the war" (Santoli, *To Bear Any Burden* xix, xii).

6. Zalin Grant's *Survivors,* published in 1975, was the first in a coming wave of books featuring the voices of the American combat veterans. The most well known and influential of these books remains Mark Baker's *Nam: The Vietnam War in the Words of the Men and Women Who Fought There* (1981). Other notable collections addressed by the essays gathered in this book would include Al Santoli's *Everything We Had: An Oral History of the Vietnam War by Thirty-Three American Soldiers Who Fought It* (1981), Stanley Goff's and Robert Saunders's (with Clark Smith) *Brothers: Black Soldiers in the Nam* (1982), Wallace Terry's *Bloods: An Oral History of the Vietnam War by Black Veterans* (1984), Al Santoli's *To Bear Any Burden: The Vietnam War and Its Aftermath in the Words of Americans and Southeast Asians* (1985), Kim Willenson's *The Bad War: An Oral History of the Vietnam War* (1987), Harry Maurer's *Strange Ground: Americans in Vietnam, 1945–1975, An Oral History* (1989), James R. Wilson's *Landing Zones: Southern Veterans Remember Vietnam* (1990), Larry Engelmann's *Tears before the Rain: An Oral History of the Fall of South Vietnam* (1990), Otto J. Lehrack's *No Shining Armor: The Marines at War in Vietnam* (1992), and Ron Steinman's *The Soldiers' Story: Vietnam in Their Own Words* (1999). Some recent military histories, such as Lt. General Harold G. Moore (Ret.) and Joseph L. Galloway's *We Were Soldiers Once . . . and Young: Ia Drang— The Battle That Changed the War in Vietnam* (1992) and Eric M. Bergerud's *Red Thunder, Tropic Lightning: The World of a Combat Division in Vietnam* (1993), are based primarily on the authors' interviews with combat veterans. See Edwin Moïse's comprehensive on-line bibliography.

7. See Renny Christopher: "For thirty years, 'Vietnam' has, for most Americans, been the name of a war. That war has occupied a central place in American political and cultural discussion. The political positions that were laid out during the war along the spectrum from conservative to liberal, pro- and anti-involvement, have become entrenched in American cultural reworkings of the war. Few voices in the ongoing U.S. discourse on the subject acknowledge that Viet Nam is the name of a country" (1).

8. Allan Nevins, founder of the Columbia University Oral History Research Office, the world's major oral history archive, interviewed many of World War II's military elite. The Vietnam War oral history project has been carried out largely by "amateur" oral historians (though often professional journalists — e.g., Baker, Terry) and ex-combatants (e.g., Santoli, Lehrack), who have focused on gathering the voices of the ground soldiers.

9. In *Warring Fictions: American Literary Culture and the Vietnam War Narrative,* Jim Nielson castigates the "editors, publishers, writers, pundits, and professors who make up America's intellectual class" for promoting "a literature that favors individual lives over social relations" (6). Yet this binary is reductive and needs to be

deconstructed: "Though man is a *unique* individual—and it is just his particularity which makes him an individual, a really *individual* social being—he is equally the *whole,* the ideal whole, the subjective existence of society as thought and experienced" (Marx 76). See also Renny Christopher, who argues that "By focusing on narrow personal experience, or the 'grunt's eye view,' the larger framework of U.S. history and its neo-imperialism and of Vietnamese politics . . . are erased from the parameters of the narrative" (6). We take issue with this comprehensive definition and dismissal of the "grunt's eye view" throughout this book. The oral histories make clear that in war the individual life is the place where shattering historical forces converge. The fetishism of the heroic individual in various popular melodramas of war is "the ideological reflex and echo of this . . . process" (Marx 75). Finally, the grunts' narratives often reveal the kind of historical and political knowledge that Christopher's formulation would deny them.

10. One notes, for example, that massive venture undertaken in the 1930s, the Slave Narrative Collection of the Federal Writers' Project, whereby the testimonies of thousands of former slaves were recorded on audiotape.

11. America sent a conscript army to Vietnam made up primarily of poor white, African American, and Hispanic soldiers, each sharing what Jonathan Shay has called the "bad moral and demographic luck" of having been "U.S.-born in 1949, male, of a working-class family" (Shay 137).

12. See, in addition, Ehrenreich: "For my generation of historians . . . the history of war and warriors has taken second place to social history—the attempt to reconstruct how ordinary people have gone about their business, producing what they need and reproducing themselves. Reinforced by Marxism and later feminism, we have rejected the conventional history of 'kings and battles' for the 'hidden history' of everyday life, almost to the point of forgetting how much of everyday life has, century after century, been shaped by battles and dominated by kings or warrior elites" (xii).

13. Writes Martin Gilbert: "If each of the nine million military dead of the First World War were to have an individual page, the record of their deeds and suffering, their wartime hopes, their pre-war lives and loves, would fill twenty thousand books the size of this one. Individual suffering is not something that is easily conveyed in a general history . . . " (xxi). "[S]ome three million Americans would serve in Vietnam . . . more than fifty-eight thousand were to perish in its jungles and rice fields. . . . More than four million Vietnamese soldiers and civilians on both sides— roughly 10 percent of the entire population—were . . . killed or wounded. . . . It was a tragedy of epic dimensions" (Karnow 11).

14. Commander James B. Stockdale, a Navy pilot who flew over the scene at the Tonkin Gulf, was debriefed upon his return to the carrier *Ticonderoga* "by an intelligence officer, who asked if he had seen any enemy boats. 'Not a one,' Stockdale replied. 'No boats, no boat wakes, no ricochets off boats, no boat gunfire, no torpedo wakes—nothing but black sea and American firepower' " (Karnow 386).

15. The classic statement is, of course, Orwell's "Politics and the English Language": "In our time, political speech and writing are largely the defense of the indefensible. Things like the continuance of British rule in India, the Russian purges and deportations, the dropping of the atom bombs on Japan, can indeed be defended, but only by arguments which are too brutal for most people to face, and which do not square with the professed aims of the political parties. Thus political language has to consist largely of euphemism, question-begging and sheer cloudy vagueness. Defense-

less villages are bombarded from the air, the inhabitants driven out into the coun-tryside, the cattle machine-gunned, the huts set on fire with incendiary bullets: this is called *pacification*. Millions of peasants are robbed of their farms and sent trudging along the roads with no more than they can carry: this is called *transfer of population* or *rectification of frontiers*. People are imprisoned for years without trial, or shot in the back of the neck or sent to die of scurvy in Arctic lumber camps: this is called *elimination of unreliable elements*. Such phraseology is needed if one wants to name things without calling up mental pictures of them. Consider for instance some com-fortable English professor defending Russian totalitarianism. He cannot say outright, 'I believe in killing off your opponents when you can get good results by doing so.' Probably, therefore, he will say something like this:

While freely conceding that the Soviet regime exhibits certain features which the humanitarian may be inclined to deplore, we must, I think, agree that a certain curtailment of the right to political opposition is an unavoidable concomitant of transitional periods, and that the rigors which the Russian people have been called upon to undergo have been amply justified in the sphere of concrete achievement.

The inflated style is itself a kind of euphemism. A mass of Latin words falls upon the facts like soft snow, blurring the outline and covering up all the details. The great enemy of clear language is insincerity" (363–64).

16. See also, for example, Mailer: "[T]he American corporation executive, who was after all the foremost representative of Man in the world today, was perfectly capable of burning unseen women and children in the Vietnamese jungles, yet felt a large displeasure and fairly final disapproval at the generous use of obscenity in literature and in public" (63).

17. See especially White's essay "The Historical Text as Literary Artifact," in *Tropics of Discourse*, 81–100.

18. See Dunnaway's essay in this volume for a thorough discussion of O'Brien's distinction between "story truth" and "happening truth."

19. In this respect Walker rediscovers Freud's "fundamental rule" of psycho-analysis. For a concise summary see Laplanche and Pontalis (178–79).

WORKS CITED

Baker, Mark. *Nam: The Vietnam War in the Words of the Men and Women Who Fought There*. 1981. New York: Berkley Books, 1983.

Bergerud, Eric M. *Red Thunder, Tropic Lightning: The World of a Combat Division in Vietnam*. Boulder: Westview Press, 1993.

Browning, Christopher R. *Ordinary Men: Reserve Battalion 101 and the Final Solution in Poland*. 1992. New York: HarperPerennial, 1998.

Chanoff, David, and Doan Van Toai. *Portrait of the Enemy*. London: I. B. Tauris, 1986.

Christopher, Renny. *The Viet Nam War/The American War: Images and Representations in Euro-American and Vietnamese Exile Narratives*. Amherst: University of Massachusetts Press, 1995.

Chung, Ly Qui. *Between Two Fires: The Unheard Voices of Vietnam*. New York: Praeger, 1970.

Ehrenreich, Barbara. Foreword. *Male Fantasies*. Vol. 1: *Women, Floods, Bodies, History*, by Klaus Theweleit. Trans. Stephen Conway in collaboration with Erica

Carter and Chris Turner. Minneapolis: University of Minnesota Press, 1987. xi–
    xvii.
Engelmann, Larry. *Tears before the Rain: An Oral History of the Fall of South Viet-
    nam.* New York: Oxford University Press, 1990.
Fitzgerald, Frances. Introduction. *Between Two Fires: The Unheard Voices of Viet-
    nam.* Ed. Ly Qui Chung. xiii–xxiii.
Foucault, Michel. *The Archaeology of Knowledge and the Discourse on Language.*
    Trans. A. M. Sheridan Smith. New York: Pantheon, 1972.
Gibson, James William. *The Perfect War: Technowar in Vietnam.* Boston: Atlantic
    Monthly Press, 1986.
Gilbert, Martin. *The First World War: A Complete History.* New York: Holt, 1994.
Goff, Stanley, and Robert Saunders with Clark Smith. *Brothers: Black Soldiers in the
    Nam.* 1982. New York: Berkley Books, 1985.
Grant, Zalin. *Survivors.* New York: Norton, 1975.
Hasford, Gustav. *The Short-Timers.* New York: Bantam, 1979.
Hemingway, Ernest. *A Farewell to Arms.* 1929. New York: Macmillan, 1986.
———. "Soldier's Home." *In Our Time.* 1925. New York: Scribners, 1996. 67–77.
Herr, Michael. *Dispatches.* 1977. New York: Vintage, 1991.
Karlin, Wayne. "Hot Damn Vietnam: Twenty-Five Years Later, a Literature of Re-
    membrance." *Los Angeles Times,* Sunday, April 23, 2000, Book Review Section.
———. "The Man Who Stained His Soul." *Los Angeles Times,* Sunday, April 23,
    2000, Book Review Section.
Karnow, Stanley. *Vietnam: A History.* 1983. New York: Penguin, 1997.
Lacan, Jacques. "Aggressivity in Psychoanalysis." *Écrits: A Selection.* 8–29.
———. *Écrits: A Selection.* Trans. Alan Sheridan. New York: Norton and Norton,
    1977.
———. "The Mirror Stage as Formative of the Function of the I as Revealed in
    Psychoanalytic Experience." *Écrits: A Selection.* 1–7.
Laplanche, J., and J.-B. Pontalis, *The Language of Psycho-Analysis.* Trans. Donald
    Nicholson-Smith. New York: Norton, 1973.
Lehrack, Otto J. *No Shining Armor: The Marines at War in Vietnam—An Oral
    History.* Lawrence: University Press of Kansas, 1992.
Luce, Don, and John Sommer. *Viet Nam: The Unheard Voices.* Ithaca and London:
    Cornell University Press, 1969.
Mailer, Norman. *The Armies of the Night: History as a Novel, The Novel as History.*
    New York: Signet, 1968.
Marx, Karl. "Existence and Consciousness." *Karl Marx: Selected Writings in Sociol-
    ogy and Social Philosophy.* Trans. T. B. Bottomore. Ed. T. B. Bottomore and
    Maximilien Rubel. New York: McGraw-Hill, 1964. 67–87.
Maurer, Harry. *Strange Ground: Americans in Vietnam, 1945–1975: An Oral His-
    tory.* New York: Henry Holt, 1989.
Moïse, Edwin E. *Historical Dictionary of the Vietnam War.* Lanham, Md.: Scarecrow
    Press (Rowman & Littlefield), 2001.
———. *Vietnam War Bibliography.* http://people.clemson.edu/~eemoise/bibliogra-
    phy.html.
Moore, Lt. General Harold G. (Ret.) and Joseph L. Galloway. *We Were Soldiers
    Once . . . and Young: Ia Drang—The Battle That Changed the War in Vietnam.*
    New York: Random House, 1992.

Nielson, Jim. *Warring Fictions: American Literary Culture and the Vietnam War Narrative.* Jackson: University Press of Mississippi, 1998.

Ninh, Bao. *The Sorrow of War: A Novel of North Vietnam.* Trans. Phan Thanh Hao. Ed. Frank Palmos. New York: Riverhead Books, 1993.

O'Brien, Tim. *The Things They Carried.* 1990. New York: Broadway Books, 1998.

Orwell, George. *Collected Essays.* London: Mercury, 1961.

Portelli, Alessandro. *The Battle of Valle Giulia: Oral History and the Art of Dialogue.* Madison: University of Wisconsin Press, 1997.

Rottmann, Larry. *Winning Hearts and Minds: War Poems by Vietnam Veterans.* New York: McGraw-Hill, 1972.

Santoli, Al. *Everything We Had: An Oral History of the Vietnam War by Thirty-Three American Soldiers Who Fought It.* New York: Random House, 1981.

———. *To Bear Any Burden: The Vietnam War and Its Aftermath in the Words of Americans and Southeast Asians.* 1985. Bloomington and Indianapolis: Indiana University Press, 1999.

Shay, Jonathan. *Achilles in Vietnam: Combat Trauma and the Undoing of Character.* New York: Atheneum, 1994.

Sheehan, Susan. *Ten Vietnamese.* New York: Knopf, 1967.

Sheridan, Alan. Translator's Note. In Lacan, *Écrits: A Selection*, vii–xii.

Smith, Clark. Foreword. *Brothers: Black Soldiers in the Nam.* Ed. Stanley Goff and Robert Saunders. ix–xii.

Steinman, Ron. *The Soldiers' Story: Vietnam in Their Own Words.* New York: TV Books, 2000.

Sturken, Marita. *Tangled Memories: The Vietnam War, the AIDS Epidemic, and the Politics of Remembering.* Berkeley: University of California Press, 1997.

Terry, Wallace. *Bloods: An Oral History of the Vietnam War by Black Veterans.* New York: Random House, 1984.

Turner, Fred. *Echoes of Combat: Trauma, Memory, and the Vietnam War.* 1996. Minneapolis: University of Minnesota Press, 2001.

Walker, Keith. *A Piece of My Heart: The Stories of Twenty-Six American Women Who Served in Vietnam.* New York: Ballantine, 1985.

White, Hayden. *Tropics of Discourse: Essays in Cultural Criticism.* Baltimore and London: Johns Hopkins University Press, 1978.

Willenson, Kim. *The Bad War: An Oral History of the Vietnam War.* New York: New American Library, 1987.

Wilson, James R. *Landing Zones: Southern Veterans Remember Vietnam.* Durham and London: Duke University Press, 1990.

Žižek, Slavoj. *Looking Awry: Introduction to Jacques Lacan through Popular Culture.* Cambridge, Mass.: MIT, 1991.

2. Approaching a Truer Form of Truth
The Appropriation of the Oral Narrative Form in Vietnam War Literature

JEN DUNNAWAY

The Vietnam War story, the veteran's tale, has in recent years become something of a fixture within what Lauren Berlant has called the American "national symbolic" (5). The stories themselves — the fantastical, the ironic, the mundane, and the horrific — have come to form an integral part of the highly textured narrative fabric within which the American experience in Southeast Asia is wrapped, arguably surpassing even the war's official history in their ability to capture the collective national imagination. Tribute to the tenacity of the oral narrative form is its continuing prevalence in all forms of war-related media: the in-their-own-words ethos of the combat narrative has been integrated into everything from Hollywood cinema to poetry to historical documentary. In particular, the literary prose that has emerged from the Vietnam War is heavily influenced by this storytelling tradition in both form and content. What may seem initially like a pairing of dissonant elements — fictional literature on the one hand and the spontaneously told, *true* story of the grunt on the other — in fact represents a synergistic relationship in which each of these two forms contextualizes and lends a greater depth of meaning to the other.

Although I do not, for the purposes of this essay, assume the objective existence of a mutually exclusive binary between the oral narrative and the literary account, or even between fact and fiction, such binaries do indeed appear to inform the consumption of the works under consideration, particularly with reference to the reader's perception of truth. While literary accounts of the Vietnam War may explicitly draw attention to their own supposedly fictional nature, and even to the mechanisms by which they are fabricated, oral history collections are typically marketed under some variation of the phrase "The Vietnam War in the Words of the Men and Women Who Fought There" (Mark Baker's *Nam*), giving the sense of an objective and play-by-play re-enactment of combat and eliciting from many readers responses such as "This must have been what the war was actually like" (see, for example, customer reviews of Lt. Gen. Harold G. Moore and Joseph L. Galloway's *We Were Soldiers Once . . . And Young* on amazon.com). Thus, for the purposes of this essay, it is important to think of the oral history and the literary war narrative as generically distinct forms, even as various authors work to dismantle this distinction and delve into the many areas of overlap between them. It is this very cross-interrogation between the oral and the literary narrative that allows us to examine our own categorical assumptions about fact and fiction, and the criteria by which we determine what is and is not "true."

In this chapter, I will attempt to identify the ways in which the oral narrative functions around and within war literature, and examine how the literary appropriation of the oral war story, however fragmented, embellished, and impressionistic such a story may be, serves to convey the "truth" of the Vietnam War experience more compellingly than the more typically coherent structure of the literary narrative alone. Against the backdrop of the major oral history collections of Baker, Moore, and Al Santoli, the works I will consider over the course of this inquiry will include *The Things They Carried* by Tim O'Brien, a collection of interconnected vignettes unified by the overarching commentary of a purportedly fictional narrator who happens to bear the same name as the author; Michael Herr's *Dispatches,* which, though often classified as straight nonfictional autobiography, in fact represents a much more complex generic hybrid in which the overtly subjective "new journalism" of the 1960s is crosshatched with literary and mythic overtones; and *The Short-Timers* by Gustav Hasford, a novel loosely based on the author's experience as a military journalist, which formed the basis for Stanley Kubrick's 1987 film *Full Metal Jacket.* All three of these texts incorporate the oral narrative form to a greater or lesser extent into what is ostensibly a fictional literary framework, and in so doing each is imbued with a greater narrative power and immediacy while conveying the sense that, in O'Brien's words, "story truth is truer sometimes than happening truth" (203).

Within the context of Vietnam War literature, the notion of truth is mired in vagueness and contradiction. Reading works of this genre, one is immediately struck by the diversity of perspectives and by the many, many avenues by which one may arrive at truth. The oral narrative form in particular, by allowing the author to incorporate multiple subjectivities into the literary text, enables a deconstruction of the notion of a single and definitive truth that may be extracted from "the Vietnam War experience," a truth that may enable us at last to "make sense" of this ordeal and to rescript it along the lines of a comfortably coherent narrative. While Vietnam War authors tend to dismiss the possibility of extracting universal truisms from combat experience, they are nonetheless deeply concerned with achieving and conveying truth in their work. Tim O'Brien, especially, is engaged throughout his text in the task of self-reflexively delineating the process of achieving truth in his own narrative, even as that narrative unfolds. Particularly in the satirically titled "How To Tell a True War Story," this metafictional discussion of truth concerns to a large extent what truth is *not,* permitting his reader to infer only a vague and disunified working model of what truth *is,* a model that is perhaps highly appropriate given the fragmented and mosaic nature of the stories we are offered.

In "How to Tell a True War Story," O'Brien articulates the way in which truth in the combat narrative is a very different thing from factual accuracy; he tells us that "absolute occurrence is irrelevant" because "a true war story does not depend on that kind of truth" (89). Voicing a point of view echoed in both *Dispatches* and the oral history collection *Nam,* he shows us that truth is not a static construct that merely exists in reality, but is rather a fluid entity rooted in perception, language, interpretation, and imagination. It has been suggested that this tension between story and actuality represents a dilemma in O'Brien's mind, borne of his realization that "[h]e can tell no truth that is not already *contaminated* by its imaginative reconstruction" (Neilson 194, italics added). However, I would argue that O'Brien, in his consistent privileging of memory and narration over material fact, is suggesting instead that the wisdom reflected in the story that evolves out of an incident through the filter of memory and imagination is indeed *more* valuable than getting that incident "right" in a strictly factual sense, and that an overemphasis on "absolute occurrence" can even subtract from the truth the war story strives to convey. Similarly, Baker questions the assumed equation between physical reality and truth, both by addressing the question of inaccuracy directly and by proposing a more holistic and less absolute approach to narrative truth in his introduction to *Nam:*

> It must be assumed that included here are generalizations, exaggerations, braggadocio and — very likely — outright lies. But if these stories were told within a religious framework, the telling would be called bearing witness. The

human imperfections simply authenticate the sincerity of the whole. The apocryphal aspects have more to do with metaphor than with deceit. (xv)

Michael Herr goes a step further, pointing to the corrosive effect of rigid factuality on essential truth in his description of the accuracy-obsessed culture of combat journalism:

> The press got all the facts (more or less), it got too many of them. But it never found a way to report meaningfully about death, which of course was really what it was all about. . . . The jargon of Progress got blown into your head like bullets, and by the time you waded through all the Washington stories and all the Saigon stories, all the Other War stories and the corruption stories and the stories about brisk new gains in ARVN (the South Vietnamese army) effectiveness, the suffering was somehow unimpressive. (229)

"Death" and "suffering," the psychological reality of what the war experience is really "all about," somehow dissolve in the news media's soup of factual details; the most basic (and perhaps most disturbing) truths of the war are elided precisely through a myopic focus on tidy factuality, here described as the antithesis of wisdom, as something "blown into your head like bullets." Herr reiterates the positions of both O'Brien and Baker, suggesting here and throughout his work that truth does not arise from fact alone but from interpretation, residing more in consciousness than in physical reality.

Nor are truth and fiction posited in these works as mutually exclusive terms, as conventional understanding of the fact–fiction binary would indicate. By conspicuously subtitling his collection "A Work of Fiction," Tim O'Brien conscripts fiction as a very suitable agent of truth, in an ironic contradiction of the traditional association of fiction with invention and fabrication. Through his work, he asserts that even these latter elements have a place in the construction of truth; factual details are shown to be of a lesser consequence, and are indeed significantly malleable in the interests of the larger truth that the storyteller strives to convey. In "How to Tell a True War Story," O'Brien (as the narrator) recalls a soldier named Mitchell Sanders relating a fantastic story about a squad on a listening-post operation that encounters what appear to be the sounds of a Vietnamese rock concert emanating from the swirling mists of a deserted mountain. In the end, however, Sanders admits to the narrator that "last night, man, I had to make up a few things" (83), concerning the details, important ones, of his story. Nonetheless, the soldier asserts with undampened conviction that "it's still true" (84). Here O'Brien demonstrates the resilience of essential truth to the particulars of a given story; as in any mythology, the details are changeable in the service of truth, rather than the truth being a product of a set of details.

Describing the death of Curt Lemon, O'Brien is haunted not by the factual circumstances of his demise, of his having detonated a booby-trap at the same moment as when he stepped out into the sunshine, but by "the way the sunlight came around him and lifted him up and sucked him high into a tree full of moss and vines and white blossoms" (78). He emphasizes that this surreal death-by-sunlight, while impossible from a factual perspective, "represents the hard and exact truth as it *seemed*" (78), and it is *this* truth that O'Brien works to convey in his story. So much depends on "get[ting] the story right," on timing and modification, that the concrete or actual events of that moment become less important than the end result, the perfect rendering of the story that would allow the reader to "believe the last thing Curt Lemon believed, which for him must've been the final truth" (90).

It is for this reason that, as O'Brien later tells us, "story truth is truer sometimes than happening truth" (203). Though the perceptual, subjective truth of a moment in time, which in turn forms the story that is later told, may be at odds with the physical reality of that moment, it is the burning mental image of "what seemed to happen" (78) that for the storyteller and the audience becomes the most essential component of the event itself. In this way, the oral narrative achieves privilege over the factual occurrence that generated the narrative in the first place; the story envelops and replaces the very event it is describing, becoming in effect "truer than the truth" (89). In this sense, O'Brien would disagree with Walter Benjamin, who argued that "[e]ven the most perfect reproduction of a work of art is lacking in one element: its presence in time and space, its unique existence" and later, that "the presence of the original is the prerequisite to the concept of authenticity" (220). If story were merely a "reproduction" of the "original" event itself, it would follow that the spatial and temporal disintegration of the event within the mind of the storyteller, the distancing of the event from the individual through time and space, would contribute to a distinct *in*authenticity of the final product, which might not be found in print until thirty or more years following the incident itself. However, O'Brien's conception of authenticity in storytelling contends that retelling is not merely a mimetic exercise, that approximating the literal event as closely as possible is not the point. Instead, it is in the "reproduction" itself that authenticity is created; unlike Benjamin's "work of art," the original event is coded neutral, and it is only through the active construction of the story over time (and over many subsequent retellings) that it takes on authentic meaning, which is achieved by "adding and subtracting, making up a few things to get at the *real truth*" (O'Brien 91, italics added). In this way, the story exists in a realm outside of the parameters with which we are typically asked to define truth and authenticity; a story is not a static and straightforward "reproduction" of an event but rather its own dynamic that takes on independent life.

The balance between story-truth and happening-truth to which O'Brien introduces us leads into a larger discussion of the sources and directions of causality within the intricate web of the combat narrative. Specifically, he examines and then systematically dismantles the intuitive assumption that stories are generated by concrete, observable events and that this formulation is not reversible. Throughout *The Things They Carried,* he explores alternate means by which truth is arrived at, and it is through the oral narrative framework that he is able to do so. In "Sweetheart of the Song Tra Bong," O'Brien turns over his role of narrator to the field medic Rat Kiley, a character for whom "facts were formed by sensation, not the other way around" (101).

Kiley tells the story of a young medic named Mark Fossie who through a series of barely plausible logistical maneuvers succeeds in getting his high-school sweetheart and current girlfriend, Mary Anne Bell, to visit him in the war zone "up in the mountains west of Chu Lai, near the village of Tra Bong" (102). Once in-country, the All-American girl — "she had long white legs and blue eyes and a complexion like strawberry ice cream" (105) — undergoes an eerie transmogrification. She becomes more curious about the war, begins to go without makeup, and soon falls "into the habits of the bush" (109). She learns how to disassemble and operate an M-16. She wonders "what was behind those scary green mountains to the west" (106). She falls in with a contingent of Green Berets and goes out on night operations with them. "She wore a bush hat and filthy green fatigues; she carried the standard M-16 automatic assault rifle; her face was black as charcoal" (113). She becomes a killer and is utterly transformed by her experience: "At the girl's throat was a necklace of human tongues. Elongated and narrow, like pieces of blackened leather, the tongues were threaded along a length of copper wire . . ." (120). "And then one morning, all alone, Mary Anne walked off into the mountains and did not come back. . . . She had crossed to the other side. She was part of the land. She was wearing her culottes, her pink sweater, and a necklace of human tongues. She was dangerous. She was ready for the kill" (124–25).

With this introduction, and the fantastical and intensely felt story of Mary Anne Bell that follows, O'Brien further complicates his notion of truth beyond the fact–fabrication binary that he deconstructed in earlier sections. In "Sweetheart," the affective component of truth takes precedence over the story's literal authenticity; O'Brien employs the volatile figure of Rat Kiley to demonstrate that, for the storyteller, achieving truth lies in heating it up "to make it burn so hot that you would feel exactly what he felt" (101).

In the service of this *emotional* accuracy, whole events may be fabricated in order to convey the more primal truth of the affective environment. To assign authenticity to a story based on its sheer emotional impact, "to believe by the raw force of feeling" (81), is to allocate to the oral narrative an immensely powerful role in the determination of truth and untruth. Although Rat's emotionality and lack of credibility are established early and emphasized throughout his narrative, Mary Anne Bell is ultimately no less believable; the degree to which she has physically *materialized* is conveyed in the final lines of the story:

> She had crossed to the other side. She was part of the land. She was wearing her culottes, her pink sweater, and a necklace of human tongues. She was dangerous. She was ready for the kill. (125)

Thus, at the story's conclusion, we are shown a character who has evolved beyond the bounds of the narrative itself, having stepped out of Rat's story and into a space where she becomes unknowable and inaccessible to the narrator; with Mary Anne, O'Brien creates the sense of an escape, a figurative "crossing" from the realm of imaginary construct into that of physical reality. Despite the fairly obvious incredibility of the tale at face value, "Rat never backed down," and "swore up and down to its truth" (101), legitimizing and authenticating the account through the force of his conviction alone. Though the author never specifically attests to the authenticity of the tale, its very inclusion in this collection as a free-standing narrative, one told by someone other than the primary narrator, lends it a certain authorial independence; moreover, the thread of disbelief that runs through the story, manifesting itself as a periodic questioning of the premise and details by the soldiers who make up Rat's audience, is significantly excluded from the story's conclusion. Ultimately, we are left with the sense that Rat Kiley's story of Mary Anne Bell is among those we are meant to consider "true."

By thus establishing a complex hierarchy among affect, actuality, fact, and perception, O'Brien invites us to examine the kinds of truth we hope to crystallize from narratives of the Vietnam War. While the concept of truth within these narratives *does* confer a kind of essentialism, a primal sense of wisdom or irony or loss that can be expanded beyond the parameters of the story itself, he is quick to remind us that there are no absolutes or universals, and that ultimately, "true war stories do not generalize" (84). The kind of narrative truth we have become accustomed to expect, that which generalizes, encapsulates, and "indulge[s] in abstraction and analysis," is exposed as deindividuating and reductive, *un*true, a lie. As an example, the tension between Rat Kiley and Mitchell Sanders in "Sweetheart," regarding how a story *should* be told, serves to highlight our own expectations of the oral narrative itself and the kind of truth we can hope to obtain from it.

> Whenever he told the story, Rat had a tendency to stop now and then, interrupting the flow, inserting little bits of clarification and analysis and personal opinion. It was a bad habit, Mitchell Sanders said, because all that matters is the raw material, the stuff itself, and you can't clutter it up with your own half-baked commentary. That just breaks the spell. It destroys the magic. What you have to do, Sanders said, is trust your own story. Get the hell out of the way and let it tell itself:
>
> But Rat Kiley couldn't help it. He wanted to bracket the full range of meaning. . . .
>
> "The story," Sanders would say. "The whole tone, man, you're wrecking it."
>
> "Tone?"
>
> "The *sound*. You need to get a consistent sound, like slow or fast, funny or sad. All these digressions, they just screw up your story's *sound*. Stick to what happened."
>
> Frowning, Rat would close his eyes.
>
> "Tone?" he'd say. "I didn't know it was all that complicated. The girl joined the zoo. One more animal — end of story."
>
> "Yeah, fine. But tell it right." (116–17)

O'Brien, using Sanders's irritation to reflect the very discomfort with the oral narrative form that he anticipates in his own audience, dramatizes the way in which a true war story, with all its digressions, discontinuities, and rough edges, does not adhere to the same guidelines that govern the coherent and structured narrative, and that Sanders finds lacking in Rat's story. Michael Herr would agree:

> Sometimes the stories were so fresh the teller was in shock, sometimes they were long and complex, sometimes the whole thing was contained in a few words on a helmet or a wall, and sometimes they were hardly stories at all but sounds and gestures packed with so much urgency that they became more dramatic than a novel, men talking in short violent bursts as though they were afraid they might not get to finish, or saying it almost out of a dream, inno-cent, offhand and mighty direct, "Oh you know, it was just a firefight, we killed some of them and they killed some of us." (30)

Both authors strive to convey the fragmentation and incoherence that char-acterize the war story and that, though certainly not precluding interpre-tation, force us to employ a very different set of tools in order to determine meaning. As Herr points out, "[a] lot of things had to be unlearned before you could learn anything at all" (224). Mitchell Sanders, who throughout "Sweetheart of the Song Tra Bong," "How to Tell a True War Story," and "The Things They Carried," insists on "rules" or a "moral" for every story told (13–14, 20, 84, 122), represents the same over-cerebralized mode of narrative representation that we might reasonably expect to encounter not within the oral, but within the literary narrative form. By identifying this as a faulty approach, O'Brien suggests by extension that the model of truth from which we are working is similarly flawed and somehow fails to apply to the situation at hand. Ultimately, truth is determined not intellectually, but through "a quick truth goose" (38–39), the indescribable flash of authenticity that is inextricably rooted in visceral reality: "For a true war story, when truly told, makes the stomach believe" (84).

In the works of Herr, O'Brien, and Hasford, a distinct and inimical polarization is established between the official lines of the military and the informal discourse of the soldier. It is Michael Herr, as a civilian combat correspondent and thus as someone with experience in both realms, who maps out most succinctly the relationship between the two. His narrative is rife with ironic juxtapositions of official knowledge with the story of the grunt. The questionably low body counts offered to the press by the military following battles such as those of Ia Drang, Dak To, and Khe Sahn are countered by the speculative casualty estimates of those who were actually present; regarding the official three hundred American dead in the battles of the Ia Drang Valley, Herr writes, "I never met anyone who had been there, including officers of the Cav, who would settle for less than three or even four times that figure" (100). In this instance, the official figure does indeed appear to be the accurate one; in the opening pages of *We Were Soldiers Once,* Moore lists by name the 305 men reported killed in the Ia Drang. However, a sort of alternate truth is suggested in the informal discourse of the soldier, as documented by Herr; it is noteworthy that this discourse tends toward the cold, seemingly immutable world of statistics and numerical realities as an arena in which to meet and challenge the official history of the war. In *Everything We Had,* no editorial note or amendment accompanies the offhand assertion by Cavalry rifleman Thomas Bird that, in the battles of the Ia Drang, "The Cav lost about a thousand men. They were talking in terms of twenty-eight hundred NVA killed and about nine hundred to a thousand Cav" (42). The reality that this inaccuracy bespeaks is the experiential, visceral reality alluded to previously, reflecting the soldier's conviction that a battle experienced as so harrowing, one during which he witnessed mayhem to a degree unprecedented in this war, could not possibly have resulted in *just* three hundred and five dead: only a figure of nine hundred or more could accurately reflect "the hard and exact truth as it *seemed*" (O'Brien 78). Perhaps, in light of the pervasive and ever-contentious problem of doctored body counts during the

Vietnam War, it is less than astonishing that grunts would dare to offer differing estimates; certainly a vocal distrust of official numbers seems to form a convention in itself. As one soldier reflects,

> I don't know how it's possible to disguise thousands of deaths, but I believed there were thousands more Americans who died [in the war] than were reported. I saw it with my own eyes constantly. (Baker 128)

Still, for the figure of "nine hundred to a thousand" to stand unamended in a published oral history subtly invites a questioning of the very manner in which official numbers are arrived at. If estimates for the much more problematic total Vietnamese body count can vary by as much as a million, it follows that there is substantial room for error, and manipulation, in the ranks of the American dead as well. Significantly, it is the narrative of the grunt that suggests this possibility.

A feature of the soldier's casualty estimate is that it does not need explicitly to contradict the official figure in order to present a challenge to it. As with the estimate of "nine hundred to a thousand" American dead at Ia Drang, the official count is not cited or perhaps even known by the narrator. Instead, the inflated figure merely merges into the surrounding narrative, subversive in its nonchalance but certainly not unusual; it is but one entry in what is surely a considerable list of alternate body counts that do not fit existing official figures, but that perhaps more accurately reflect the subjective experience of a particular battle. It is from this experiential perspective, also, that the platitudes of military propaganda are cut down to size by the uncensored narrative of the grunt. Michael Herr shows General Westmoreland's famous "light at the end of the tunnel" speech withered by a single sardonic comment from one of the actual tunnel rats: "What does that asshole know about tunnels?" (49). Through such contrasts, Herr proposes an *inverse* hierarchy of credibility: "At the bottom," he tells us, "is the shitface grunt" (45), the smallest unit of warfare and the lowest point in the military power structure. And it is within the narrative of this individual, he argues, that the real truth of the war resides. To obtain any valid information,

> you had to leave the Dial Soapers in Saigon and a hundred headquarters who spoke goodworks and killed nobody themselves, and go out to the grungy men in the jungle who talked bloody murder and killed people all the time. (43)

While the privileging of the combatant over official sources of information is nothing new in itself, particularly with respect to the Vietnam War, it is a cliché that is borne out with remarkable consistency in both literary and oral narrative accounts. What is particularly interesting is the role that storytelling itself plays in usurping the official line as *the* definitive source of information; in *Dispatches,* it is always the rough, directly quoted words of the lowest combat infantryman which serve to undercut the meticulously engineered lies of the military spin doctor.

It can thus be said that the oral narrative functions within Vietnam War literature as a form of resistance; the war story itself acts as an agent to reclaim the very history that military discourse has worked so diligently to distort. Dale W. Jones relates the linguistic acrobatics of Herr's Military Assistance Command to George Orwell's principle of "political language," a code that employs "euphemism, question-begging and sheer cloudy vagueness" in "the defense of the indefensible" (quoted in Jones, 313). Or, as infantry medic David Ross explains, "anytime anything unpopular happened, they just changed the name of it" (Santoli 50). It is only through willful optimism and a calculated obscuring of reality, Orwell argues, that atrocity and the meaningless squandering of lives may be justified. In *Dispatches,* Michael Herr portrays the Command as being blinded by this type of insistent and collective self-delusion, hiding behind terms such as

> "discreet burst" (one of those tore an old grandfather and two children to bits as they ran along a paddy wall one day . . .), "friendly casualties" (not warm, not fun), "meeting engagement" (ambush), concluding usually with 17 or 117 or 317 enemy dead and American losses "described as light." (237)

Against the backdrop of the military's sterile and platitudinous rhetoric, the oral narrative of the grunt gains currency as perhaps the only reliable source of information. It is in this way that storytelling comes to form a system of resistance, the "unauthorized" narrative of the grunt subverting and replacing the officially sanctioned narratives of military and government institutions.

It can be said, too, that the armed forces recognize the subversive element of the oral narrative, if the military's unabashedly active role in the silencing of unofficial discourses is any indication. In *The Short-Timers,* Hasford demonstrates the ways in which the soldier, as early as boot camp, is brutally indoctrinated into silence. In one example, a young recruit named Philips begins to describe an eerie nightmare, apparently shared by a number of the others,

> Sergeant Gerheim's big fist drives Philips's next word down his throat and out of his asshole. Philips is nailed to the deck. He's on his back. His lips are crushed. (21)

Here Hasford dramatizes the silencing of the soldier's voice through his focus on the mouth, the very instrument of vocalization and communication, now described as "crushed" by the "big fist" of military authority. The brutality of the image underlines the fearful fanaticism with which this establishment works to suppress the exchange of unofficial information. A narrative that gives voice to the shared nightmare of the military reality, and the potential for subversive unity that such a narrative necessarily entails, is simply irreconcilable with the face of war that the military wishes to present.

The word of the soldier is feared and stifled precisely *because* it embodies truth. The grunts carry a certain narrative power borne of their proximity to combat, to the tangible realities of life and death from which the higher echelons of the military complex are conspicuously isolated. Again and again in these works, the combat infantryman is set apart, imbued with a distinct authority, and portrayed as one who holds the key to a "secret" truth that is inaccessible through the official narrative of the military. "Their secret," writes Herr, "brutalized them and darkened them and very often it made them beautiful" (109). This beauty translates to a special power that even the lowly and "expendable" grunt can wield over military superiors, pompous bureaucrats, and all others who think they know but haven't "heard the joke" (Hasford 126). Hasford's Animal Mother, one whom Herr would probably characterize as the quintessential "death-spaced grunt" (Herr 251), relegates a group of impudent rear-echelon "pogues" to disconcerted silence by simply smiling at them, "smiling like a man who knows a terrible secret" (39). In O'Brien's "How to Tell a True War Story," Mitchell Sanders describes a "fat bird colonel" who appears at base camp to badger the grunts for answers after they call in a costly air strike on a Vietnamese rock concert in the mountains.

> But the guys don't say zip. They just look at him for a while, sort of funny like, sort of amazed, and the whole war is right there in that stare. It says everything you can't ever say. It says, man, you got *wax* in your ears. It says, poor bastard, you'll never know — wrong frequency — you don't *even* want to hear this. Then they salute the fucker and walk away, because certain stories you don't ever tell. (82–83)

While O'Brien appears at first glance to suggest a complicity on the part of the soldiers in their own suppression of voice — a willful refusal to be heard even as the opportunity presents itself — it is made clear through the pettiness of military authority, as well as through the fantastical nature of the tale itself, that theirs is truly one of those "stories you don't ever tell." The colonel, concerned only that "they spent six trillion dollars on firepower" (82), is simply unworthy and underequipped to comprehend the full truth of the experience of war.

The secret knowledge of the soldier is thus paradoxically empowering. Though the suppression of the unofficial narrative is inextricably tied to disenfranchisement and painful silence, it simultaneously allows the soldier the opportunity to be raised to an almost mythic level of narrative power. Excluded from the official narrative of the war, the grunt is set free to become truly *self-authored* on his own terms. The irony in a story "you don't ever tell" nevertheless finding its way into the pages of a best-selling combat narrative, suggests a whole alternative network of information, one that has become an increasingly important element in our historical understanding of this period. The soldier's history, which Michael Herr pessimistically describes as a "secret history" (51) that has been lost in the convoluted and "cheer-crazed" jargon of the military (237), has on the contrary consistently evaded the forces of suppression, evolving into a formidable narrative voice that, as many now acknowledge, supplies some of the most valuable information on the war. Mark Baker writes,

> We must listen closely to the men and women who became both the victims and the perpetrators of the war, if we want to learn something real about this particular conflict, something real about the human spirit, something real about ourselves. (xvi)

Editors of oral history collections tend to promote the idea that the ability to experience and communicate the war as it truly *was* lies exclusively within the realm of those who were closest to it, and this principle has in turn been picked up by those authors who incorporate the oral narrative form into other genres. Michael Herr even suspects that the infantryman's immersion in the realm of the narrative "real" is the subject of a "half-hidden, half-vaunted jealousy" and a "furtive vicarious bloodthirsting" on the part of those who, far removed from the authentic experience of combat, fought the war only on paper (46). Like the "subjugated knowledges" that Michel Foucault identified as the domain of those individuals forming the lower echelons of a hierarchy (81), the unofficial discourse of the grunt provides a body of information that is perhaps ultimately more truthful and more resilient to bias and manipulation than the offerings of official sources. Despite the implicit and longstanding privileging of supposedly more concrete and verifiable forms of historical expression — the tactical accounts, the socio-political analyses, the memoirs of prominent contemporary figures — the power of the soldier's narrative vividly and truthfully to communicate the real war remains nevertheless undiminished.

Be this as it may, a prominent theme in all works considered here is that the experience of the Vietnam War is one that not only evades conventional language but also rarely finds a truly accepting audience even if it can be told. As door gunner Brian Delate suggests, the consequence is for many veterans a resigned silence regarding one's experiences:

> Before I went over I knew a couple of friends that came back. I asked, "What was it like?" and they didn't know how to explain it and I didn't know what I was asking. And when I came back I ended up being the same way. Almost mute. (Santoli 133)

To further complicate matters, it is this silence itself that is sometimes celebrated. Writing about Michael Herr, Marita Sturken points out that "The
mythic status of his book can be attributed to its depiction of the incommu-
nicability of the experience of the war" (87). Clearly, it would be a mistake to
assume that the abundant proliferation of oral histories and combat narratives that we enjoy today, and their evidently avid consumption by the public,
indicates that the problematic voice of the soldier has been comfortably rec-
onciled and assimilated. On the contrary, a distinct tension between what is
and is not said pervades the oral histories, suggesting that a degree of self-
censorship continues to shape these narratives; whether this restraint arises
from prevailing social norms, from the traumatic nature of the experience, or
from some other, more obscure motivation, is difficult to determine. Not surprisingly, the degree of disclosure in a given narrative is often a product of the
extent of the soldier's anonymity. Mark Baker does not identify his contributors at all, but merely separates each story from the last with a row of asterisks;
the apparent result is that his narrators are much more candid about describing their own participation in atrocity than are Santoli's, whose name, rank,
unit, area of operation, and dates in-country form the preface to each entry. In
many cases, these latter survivors tend to talk around the more unsettling
events in which they were involved, lapsing into evasive language or trailing
off into unresolved pauses. Unlike Baker's narrators, some of whom unabashedly confess to their enjoyment of death and killing (66, 75, 84, 135,
184) and to their participation in rape (65, 172, 191), torture (186, 196), the
mutilation of corpses (59, 65, 180, 192), and the killing and brutalizing of
civilians (65, 108, 179, 191, 192) and of other American soldiers (117), the
named and visible narrators of *Everything We Had* are more likely to describe
similar acts as being performed by someone else, as incidents to which they
themselves were merely the unfortunate and uncomfortable witnesses.

Conversely, in literary accounts of the Vietnam War, metaphors of absence, omission, and silence similarly abound, even in the works of contemporary authors such as Tim O'Brien, precluding any notion that all cards are
now on the table regarding the cultural reconciliation of this experience. One
of the most powerful of these metaphors is the tangible, even overbearing
presence of the dead in these works, not as merely inanimate corpses but as a
distinct narrative and imaginative force. Collectively, the dead form the cor-
poreal representation of the "secret history" itself, the unexpressed and permanently silenced narrative, the story that will never find a voice. Michael
Herr is familiar with the uncomfortable pressure of the dead; he describes
waking up one night with the eerie certainty "that my living room was full of
dead Marines" (261). Here, the dead constitute an absence so conspicuous
that it is felt instead as a tangible presence; like the mute, watchful corpses

whose presence torments Coleridge's Ancient Mariner, the silent dead function within the combat narrative as a powerful indictment of the forces that brought their end.

Then again, the dead are not always silent. Far from being excised from the narrative order, they are portrayed as having powerful lessons to communicate. Herr writes,

> After a year I felt so plugged in to all the stories and the images and the fear that even the dead started telling me stories, you'd hear them out of a remote but accessible space where there were no ideas, no emotions, no facts, no proper language, only clean information. (31)

The dead are thus associated with a certain purity of wisdom; for Herr, their story is simple and "always the same: it went, 'Put yourself in my place.'" (Or, in the words of Joker's cinematic counterpart in *Full Metal Jacket,* "The dead know only one thing: it is better to be alive"). In this regard, the narrative power of the dead rests upon what they have to tell us about the living. Sturken tells us that it is "The survivors of recent political events [who] often disrupt the closure of a particular history; indeed, history operates more efficiently when its agents are dead" (5). In war literature, however, the dead are both persistent and problematic in their disruption of official histories, providing a narrative realm within which terror, sorrow, and the yearning for life and light on the part of the living may be safely expressed through projection. "*A dead buddy's some tough shit,*" quips an unnamed soldier in *Dispatches,* "*but bringing your own ass out alive can sure help you to get over it*" (26). Rarely within these works is appreciation for life or gratitude for survival mentioned without a corresponding reference to the dead. In this way, the dead directly shape the oral narratives of the living, underlining by contrast the strong and essentially pacifistic life force that forms the undercurrent of these works.

However, the dead function within the combat narrative in more intricate ways than as mere reminders of the fragility of life; instead, the relationship between the living and the dead involves a complex dynamic of identification and communication, borne of the grunt's realization that death may very well be the next stage of his development. The result is a kinship with the dead that at times borders on tenderness:

> You look at the dried mud on the jungle boots of the Marine without a head and you're stunned that his feet look so very much like your own.
> You reach out. You touch his hand. (Hasford 102)

Often, this kinship translates into a sort of reverent and ceremonious treatment of dead bodies themselves, evident, for example, in the odd rituals by which the dead are purposefully reinstated into the narrative order of the living. In the final section of *The Things They Carried,* tellingly titled "The Lives of the Dead," the narrator recalls his induction into this ritual resurrection in the first days of his tour of duty. Encountering a "body without a name" (255), an old Vietnamese man lying dead amongst the ruins of a small village, members of the squad prop him up, shake hands, offer him C-rations, and finally propose a series of toasts to the man and his ancestors and descendants. While O'Brien himself balks at the strangeness of this interaction, and is overwhelmed by "that awesome act of greeting the dead" (256), he recognizes even so that this is a game that goes far beyond mere "mockery" (257). Talking to the deceased is one of the ways of "making the dead seem not quite so dead" (267), and of giving back the significance and individuality that the impersonal, mass death of war takes away. In *The Short-Timers,* Joker confesses that,

> After my first confirmed kill, talking to corpses began to make more sense than talking to people who had not yet been wasted. (129)

If the dead are essentially treated as living people, incorporated into the routines and rituals typical of company and conversation, then the dead are individuated; the "faceless responsibility and faceless grief" (O'Brien 203) felt for the mass of the war dead begins to be alleviated. Assigning the dead narratives of their own lends a significance to life as well as death, the oral narrative acting as a safeguard against the debasement of both that occurs in times of war.

The story itself is thus the crucial mechanism for reinstating the dead; through stories, the dead are able to exert a continuing presence, and are afforded a visibility and dimensionality that they were typically not allowed in life, where they existed within the military worldview as either anonymous civilians or expendable, interchangeable units of warfare. In "The Man I Killed," O'Brien constructs an entire life story for a young Vietnamese soldier whom he has killed with a hand grenade. The construction of this narrative is thorough and methodical, spanning the soldier's imagined childhood in My Khe, to his indoctrination into the Vietnamese tradition of patriotic resistance, to his education and first romance, and finally to his resignation to fulfilling his duty as a soldier, despite his desire for peace and his certainty that he will not last long in combat. Thus differentiated through the power of the story itself, the anonymous enemy dead, the "body without a name," becomes a living and three-dimensional entity. O'Brien argues that a story, which consists of "partly willpower, partly faith" (272), presents an opportunity to render the dead alive again; many years later, he can even envision an alternate ending for the tale of "The Man I Killed," one in which he simply allows the soldier to walk away unharmed:

> I'll watch him walk toward me, his shoulders slightly stooped, his head cocked
> to the side, and he'll pass within a few yards of me and suddenly smile at some
> secret thought and then continue up the trail to where it bends back into the
> fog. (150)

While the narratives constructed for the dead in their absence in no way
alleviate the wrong of their factual deaths, the writings nonetheless signify a
small gesture of hope on the part of the storyteller. O'Brien contends that the
lives of the dead can be preserved through stories; Rat Kiley, for instance,
continues to incorporate his friend Curt Lemon into his personal narrative
long after his death, and we learn that "[t]o listen to the story, especially as
Rat Kiley told it, you'd never know that Curt Lemon was dead" (268). In this
way, the ghostly presence of the once-living within the oral narrative signifies
a sort of idealism, an alternate pacifistic vision of the world in which the
meaningless deaths of both friends and strangers cease to occur. For O'Brien,
the imaginative realm in which he is able to speak to the dead is a place where
there are "no brain tumors and no funeral homes, no bodies at all" (273).
The drive toward life and peace is best reflected in the stories of the dead, a
created narrative realm in which "the dead sometimes smile and sit up and
return to the world" (255).

It is also worth noting that the narrative reinstatement of the dead is
another aspect of the resistance discussed earlier against the military's sterile
way of thinking about human life. As Michael Herr points out, the Command has an entire vocabulary that allows a glossing over of the reality of
death, in the same way that other unpleasant aspects of reality are distanced:

> Those men called dead Vietnamese "believers," a lost American platoon was
> "a black eye," they talked as though killing a man was nothing more than
> depriving him of his vigor. (43)

The wisdom the dead have to offer, like so many other aspects of the combat
experience, is clearly *not* accessible through the reality-obscuring rhetoric
of the institutions described in these works. Whereas Herr's Military Assistance Command and Hasford's *Stars and Stripes* (the American armed
forces' newspaper) are portrayed as entities that consider the dead only in
terms of loss or victory, the oral narrative itself becomes the mechanism
through which both storyteller and audience can come to grips with the
meaning of death on a personal level, a process that is contrary and perhaps
even inimical to military ideology and objectives. In this way, the oral narrative allows the storyteller to repopulate the conspicuous void left by official
sources: the narrative space formerly inhabited by the once-living.

In light of this, it is tempting to view the storyteller himself as something of a
heroic figure, a breaker-of-silences who establishes the sorely needed link

between "the World" and the true experience of the Vietnam War, one who at last gives a voice to the tales that would otherwise have been buried by the official discourse of the military, or even the distorting totalizations of the media. The figure of the heroicized storyteller is one that is variously embraced, undermined, rejected, and toyed with by the authors considered here, as the reader's natural tendency to localize authority within the source of narrative information is interrogated. O'Brien, for example, opens the final piece in his collection with the rhetorical but somewhat lofty proposal that "stories can save us" (255); his hyperbolic reverence for the value of the story (and, by extension, the storyteller) has led some to view him as preachy and moralizing, despite his explicitly anti-moral stance. At the other end of the spectrum, Hasford's Joker at one point quips bitterly that, as a Marine Corps journalist for the military's own *Stars and Stripes*, he has helped to "make the world safe for hypocrisy" (59).

As a civilian news correspondent with no particular agenda, Michael Herr is free to take a much more ambiguous position on his own craft, wavering between an adventuresome bravado and an almost apologetic humility. Some critics (Hellmann 155–56; Ringnalda 70) have pointed out that, at the outset of *Dispatches*, Herr implies a rather self-important connection between the reporter and the LURP (Long-Range Reconnaissance Patrolman), the task of each being, in essence, to brave the perils of uncharted territory in order to bring back crucial information. Dale W. Jones, for one, finds such first-person self-description "priggish and self-aggrandizing" at best, and at worst outright dishonest in its lack of appropriate narrative distance (314–15). However, such an interpretation fails to take into account Herr's seemingly endless capacity for self-irony; within every show of transparent machismo lies the very mechanisms by which such attitudes are undone. Not only do such overwrought comparisons imply a certain degree of self-mockery, but they are in addition countered by more sober reflections upon the correspondent's role, in which Herr acknowledges the extravagance of his earlier self-portraits. In "Colleagues," one of the final chapters of *Dispatches*, he chides,

> I could let you go on thinking that we [correspondents] were all brave, witty, attractive and vaguely tragic, that we were like some incomparable commando team, some hot-shit squadron, the Dreaded Chi, danger-loving, tender and wise. I could use it myself, it would certainly make a prettier movie, but all of this talk about "we" and "us" has got to get straightened out. (234)

Jones is correct to suggest that there is indeed much room for self-aggrandizement on the part of the storyteller within the domain of the oral narrative. The appointed (or self-appointed) storyteller, as the locus of communication for perhaps a large number of individual stories from a variety of sources,

fills a crucial role whose nobility is easy to over-inflate. This is especially
the case for Herr and O'Brien, who unlike Hasford do not go out of their
way to categorically undermine this role in ways that make them look truly
bad. However, the various ways in which all of these authors play with the
heroicized and self-heroicized elements of the storyteller betray the true complexity of the relationship between this figure and his craft, and cast a pro-
foundly self-conscious gaze upon the role of this storyteller within, specifically, the chaotic landscape of the Vietnam War.

The representation of the storyteller's subject matter is a large issue with
which both Herr and O'Brien struggle. Within these works, even the most
positive associations between storytelling (or reporting) and truth are tempered by a corresponding fear of *mis*representation — of individuals, of the
narratives of those individuals, and of the events in which the storyteller
stood as either a witness or a participant. It is important to note here that, in
these works, the central consciousness of the main participant-observer represents a hybridization of the storyteller of the oral tradition and narrator of
the literary, producing a necessarily fragmented metanarrative that must
incorporate both this subject's own experience and the multiple subjectivities
of those around him who contribute to the narrative tapestry. Because of the
candid authenticity that the oral narrative confers, and its grounding in the
world of *real people* rather than purely fictional "characters," the incorporation of this form into the literary text entails a pressing drive to get
these stories *right,* to represent the multiple storytellers in good faith and "in
the interests of truth" (O'Brien 182). As a result, the price of the narrator-
storyteller's privileged position is in many cases an inordinate burden of guilt
and hauntedness, borne of the imperative not only to relate truthfully one's
own experience, but also to give voice to that of others who may lack the
means to do so, representing these other, external subjectivities both fairly
and faithfully.

Tim O'Brien is especially attuned to the high stakes of truth, and approaches the problem of representation from a deeply personal perspective.
In "Notes," the narrator recounts a letter he received from his former squad-
mate Norman Bowker, in which he requests after an extensive preamble that
O'Brien write a story about *him,* "a guy who feels like he got zapped over
there in that shithole. A guy who can't get his act together and just drives
around town all day and can't think of any damn place to go and doesn't
know how to get there anyway" (179). The story that resulted from this
exchange, O'Brien tells us, was an earlier version of "Speaking of Courage,"
the preceding piece in *The Things They Carried* for which "Notes" provides
the explanatory background. The central crisis of "Speaking of Courage" is
indeed a crisis of representation, depicting the way in which Bowker, now

returned from Vietnam, comes up hard against the impossible-to-articulate experience of loss. In the story, his perpetual orbit around the lake in his father's car suggests a parallel circling of the truth itself, dramatizing his verbal and psychic paralysis as he considers all things he "would have said" (161) to a variety of imagined listeners. When he discovers he cannot even communicate his story to the tinny, disembodied voice emanating from the intercom box at the local drive-in restaurant, Bowker realizes that he "could not talk about it and never would" (172). His later appeal to O'Brien, to represent him in his absolute inability to represent himself, constitutes a final and desperate effort to be heard, to have his story out at last before the world: "I'd write it myself," Bowker tells O'Brien, "except I can't ever find any *words*" (179, italics added). By seeking this representation-by-proxy, positing O'Brien as the means through which his experience will be articulated, Bowker places upon him the onerous responsibility to introduce him into the narrative realm from which he finds himself excluded by virtue of his own paralysis.

Inevitably, O'Brien fails in this endeavor; he sends Norman Bowker the first published version of "Speaking of Courage." And, "Eight months later, he hanged himself" (181). O'Brien had initially expressed reservations about his work:

> Something about the story had frightened me—I was afraid to speak directly, afraid to remember—and in the end the piece had been ruined by a failure to tell the full and exact truth about our night in the shit field. (181)

By placing this personal failure of representation alongside Bowker's suicide, O'Brien demonstrates all that can be lost by failing to achieve the "full and exact truth." Though it is unreasonable to conclude that the death resulted directly from Bowker's dissatisfaction with the story, the causal relationship is implied through the terse proximity of these two elements in the text. Ultimately, Bowker was suffocated by his own silence, his inability to be heard either through his own initiative or through an appointed storyteller; he remains silent even in death, having taken his own life quietly and unremarkably without so much as leaving a note. With the second, stronger version of "Speaking of Courage," the one that appears in this collection, O'Brien hopes at last to "mak[e] good on Norman Bowker's silence" (181). However, Bowker himself obviously no longer exists either to affirm or to attack his own portrayal in the revised "Speaking of Courage"; his absence is used to pose the question of whether any representation of a person outside of the narrator's immediate consciousness can be absolutely fair or truthful, suggesting an interesting possible reason for O'Brien's insistence that *The Things They Carried* is a work of "fiction." As an object in art or fiction can never be absolutely realized but only approximated, the figures that appear in even the "true" accounts of the Vietnam War are by necessity somewhat fictionalized, regardless of whether these figures ever existed as real people.

In *Dispatches,* Michael Herr defines his relationship to representation in the relatively more impersonal world of combat journalism. Though he shares with O'Brien the drive to achieve truth in representation, the nomadic nature of his profession creates a difficulty in establishing the causal effects of representation or misrepresentation that lie within the interpersonal sphere. However, in his later chapter "Colleagues," Herr moves away from the purely experiential aspects of the Vietnam War to a more self-conscious assessment of his own role within it, and of the nature of his interaction with the many oral narrative "texts" with which his work brings him into contact.

Clearly, Herr prides himself in his immersion in the world of unofficial discourse. He spurns the daily military press briefings known as the "Five O'Clock Follies" (105), fumbles through tedious interviews with high-ranking officials (156–58, 231), and scoffs at the journalists who are mystified that he ever finds anything to talk to grunts about (30). He feels keenly his responsibility not only to report accurately, but also to represent truthfully those who have no other outlet. However, there are some formal aspects of his work that call into question the validity of his mode of representation; concerns have been raised regarding Herr's refusal to identify any but a few of his speakers, and the omission of names and particulars cited as a means by which to compromise his credibility. The niceties of identification are thus posited as a crucial factor in conferring a certain groundedness in reality, and, at least in this view, truth. The inclusion of a name permits a connection between the narrative and the external world, providing the skeptic with a specific person who could conceivably be looked up in a directory and called upon to confirm the verity of Herr's account.

However, *Dispatches* does not attempt to adhere to the formula of the more structured oral histories, such as *Everything We Had,* in which a speaker's particulars form the preamble of each contribution; the work does not, as O'Brien would say, "depend upon that kind of truth" (89). Instead, the sometimes disembodied patchwork of oral narratives over which Herr presides strives to capture the sound and the feel of combat. As with Mark Baker's policy of anonymity, Herr's refusal to document sources does not detract from his credibility, but rather enhances the sense created by *Dispatches* of a primal and spontaneous language taken directly from the source, suggesting a direct interface with war at the most guttural level. Herr's narrative style is best described by analogy to the Soldier's Prayer, which as he explains,

came in two versions: Standard, printed on a plastic-coated card by the Defense Department, and Standard Revised, impossible to convey because it got translated outside of language, into chaos — screams, begging, promises, threats, sobs, repetitions of holy names until their throats were cracked and dry, until some men had bitten through their collar points and rifle straps and even their dog-tag chains. (60)

Herr reproduces the sound of the Standard Revised in his own narrative, creating in *Dispatches* a sort of linguistic pandemonium in which single phrases, italicized scraps of dialogue, free indirect discourse, "pop grunt mythology" (74), popular song, and second- or third-hand war stories combine and intersect under the most incongruous of circumstances, and in which the focus shifts without warning between scenes, characters, even regional dialects ("Got me one hunnert 'n' fifty-se'en gooks kilt," drawls one Texan [190]). When speakers *are* identified, it is often merely a nickname or the phrase on a soldier's helmet that differentiates storyteller from listener. The result of these techniques is a kaleidoscopic montage of voices and images that situates itself decidedly outside of the formalities of literature and even the conventions governing the presentation of oral histories. Presenting his material in this way, Herr opens up a realm in which the trappings of civilization fall away, and in which constructs such as personal identification are hardly the issue.

Still, it is the feedback he obtains in the field that Herr uses to measure the success of his representational endeavors.[1] He is attuned to the special and often curious ways in which members of the press are treated by combatants, whose reactions range from reverence to disgust. Whichever the case, the correspondent is instantly and almost universally recognized as the medium of vocalization — the narrator–storyteller — "And always," writes Herr of the grunts,

they would ask you with an emotion whose intensity would shock you to please tell it, because they really did have the feeling that it wasn't being told for them, that they were going through all this and that somehow no one back in the World knew about it. (220)

In this way, Herr is faced with the responsibility of releasing scores of combatants from silence, and with the suffocating possibility that the thwarted communication of every soldier in the country rests upon his words. Though he does not spell out as explicitly as O'Brien what he does with this responsibility, he is keenly attuned to the ramifications of misrepresentation in a similar way, but on a larger scale. Herr works throughout *Dispatches* to distance himself from certain types of journalists while at the same time remaining aware that he too bears the collective responsibility for the prevalent representations of the war that are manifest in the news media at large. "You guys're reporters, huh?" accuses one Marine. "Boy, you really get it all fucked up" (214). He also describes how every correspondent will eventually hear "one version or another of 'My Marines are winning this war, and you people are losing it for us in your papers' " (244). While Herr ostensibly tends to make light of such accusations, and takes care to explain that his reception by grunts in the field is more often supportive than hostile, the shadow cast by the misrepresented soldier contributes to a creeping self-doubt that heavily informs his reflections on his own role in the war. At times, Herr seems to come close to agreeing with the feelings of those grunts

> who preferred not to be in your company, who despised what your work required or felt that you took your living from their deaths, who believed that all of us were traitors and liars and the creepiest kinds of parasites. (221)

Still, the morosely apologetic tone that causes "Colleagues" to read at times like a confessional is periodically interrupted by gropings toward self-justification:

> All right, yes, it had been a groove being a war correspondent, hanging out with the grunts and getting close to the war, touching it, losing yourself in it and trying yourself against it. I had always wanted that, never mind why, it had just been a thing of mine, the way this movie is a thing of mine, and I'd done it; I was in many ways brother to these poor, tired grunts, I knew what they knew now, I'd done it and it was really something. (220)

Ultimately, however, "the war still offered at least one thing I had to turn my eyes from" (219), the pure and unmitigated hatred of the misrepresented soldier:

> You would feel it coming out to you from under a poncho hood or see it in a wounded soldier staring up at you from a chopper floor, from men who were very scared or who had just lost a friend, from some suffering apparition of a grunt whose lip had been torn open by the sun, who just couldn't make it in that heat. (222)

Like Norman Bowker's suicide for O'Brien, it is this clean, impersonal loathing which for Herr is the most unredeemable consequence of his work, and which makes him falter most perceptibly in his belief that he is "telling it" right. In a broader sense, the silent loathing of the failed narrator–storyteller represents the psychic deficit created by the unvoiced narrative, the figurative hole that volatile information burns into the psyche for want of a viable outlet. The hatred borne of the silenced narrative is as tangible as the presence of the dead discussed previously, and it is this omitted, absent *presence* from which the distinct overtones of sorrow in *Dispatches,* and particularly in the section "Colleagues," seem to originate. If anything, Herr's guilt stems from his inability, within the limitations of his profession, to represent *more* thoroughly, more deeply, and in ways that would allow the soldier to feel that his story was in fact being heard. In his day-to-day work, however, he must simply endure his own complicity in the fact that in the back of every column of print you read about Vietnam there was a dripping, laughing death-face; it hid there in the newspapers and magazines and held to your television screens for hours after the set was turned off for the night, an after-image that simply wanted to tell you at last what somehow had not been told. (233)

In *The Short-Timers,* Gustav Hasford takes an even less optimistic stance on the possibility of truthful representation. Through Joker, we are allowed a firsthand look at the ways in which military-sanctioned sources of information are manipulated and even falsified. As a reporter for the Marine Corps' own *Stars and Stripes* — "You ever hear any news in the *Stars and Stripes*?" asks one veteran. "The only good thing in *Stars and Stripes* was the Sergeant Mike cartoon" (Santoli 29) — Joker in fact directly contributes to one of the many channels of official military discourse discussed previously. Making no pretense of objectivity, Joker seems to revel in the self-reflexive phoniness of military journalism, and even takes a sort of self-undermining mock-pride in the role he plays in the military's systematic campaign of misinformation:

> The article I actually write is a masterpiece. It takes talent to convince people that war is a beautiful experience. Come one, come all to exotic Viet Nam, the jewel of Southeast Asia, meet interesting, stimulating people of an ancient culture . . . and kill them. Be the first kid on your block to get a confirmed kill. (45)

In addition to writing bogus, upbeat articles, Joker is also sent on a farcical photography assignment to collect "atrocity photographs" as a means of demonstrating the cruelty of the Viet Cong (126). Arriving at the mass grave only to discover with disappointment that "There are no corpses with their hands tied behind their backs," he sets up the shots for his colleague Rafter Man by assembling a Vietnamese "family" from the bodies of the civilians, then tying the corpses' limbs together with demolition wire. "As a final touch," he says, "I wire the dog's feet together" (127).

With this ghoulish show of journalistic dishonesty, Hasford simultaneously dramatizes both the need for and the impossibility of unadulterated representation. By portraying Joker as an intelligent man with a sensitivity to contradictions, one who sports a peace button on his uniform while wearing a helmet inscribed with the words "Born to Kill," but one who nevertheless becomes incorporated with unnerving ease into the "propaganda machine" of the Marine Corps (61), Hasford demonstrates the inherent malleability not only of information itself, but of those persons who are posited as authoritative narrative sources. He also pays special attention to the consequences of such misrepresentation on a microcosmic level; Joker's thinly veiled disillusionment with military institutions, his refusal to accept a promotion to sergeant, and his tenuous and dissonance-producing position as one who has "made the world safe for hypocrisy" (59) point to the wider unease within American culture regarding the validity of the information we are given, and the extent to which we are invited to become complicit in the undermining and falsification of authentic narratives. Although Hasford's specific commentary is apparently aimed at institutionalized deception by the military, his message has repercussions in the larger discussion of narrative truth. As Joker's editor, Captain January reiterates Aeschylus' classic adage in what sounds more like an order than a reflection: "[i]n war, truth is the first casualty" (61).

Thus throughout all three of these works, the narrator–storyteller maintains a turbulent and often contradictory relationship to truth, one the often culminates in the rejection of the idea that ultimate authenticity may ever be attained through this or any mode of representation. As Mark Baker tells us of the narratives he has collected for *Nam:*

> This book is not the Truth about Vietnam. Everyone holds a piece of that puzzle. But these war stories, filled with emotion and stripped of ambition and romance, may bring us closer to the truth than we have come so far. (xvi)

If it is the uncensored narrative of the grunt, the raw material of the oral history, that offers the truest glimpse of the war experience, it is unsurprising that Hasford's Joker, mired in the cynical falseness of military journalism, ultimately comes to locate truth solely in the bluntest machinations of war, denying by implication any intersection between truth and humanity: "Guns tell the truth. Guns never say, 'I'm only kidding.' War is ugly because the truth can be ugly and war is very sincere" (98). While Herr and O'Brien do not share Hasford's nihilism, the suggestion that the truth is "ugly" is echoed by both authors in their respective works (Herr 98; O'Brien 87). A recurring concern in both Vietnam War literature and oral history is that of a public ill-prepared for this ugly truth. The need for not only a receptive audience, but for a receptive *culture,* contributes to a guarded caution on the part of the narrator, giving rise to the conflicting tendencies both to delineate the truth explicitly and to rein it in to some degree so that its full impact is cushioned. The oral narrative functions within this dynamic as the medium through which the "secret history" of the Vietnam War may be brought to light, while the voicing of individual narratives through the literary metanarrative of the narrator–storyteller is crucial in making the truth of war palatable through the personalization and individuation of this secret history. Ultimately, the appropriation of the oral narrative into formal literary discourse mirrors a larger reinstatement of the truth into the collective cultural narrative surrounding this event. It suggests an emerging willingness on the part of American culture to recognize and legitimatize the lost narratives of the Vietnam

War, to raise them to a well-deserved position of esteem within the war's larger historical narrative. By "telling it" in the soldiers' own words, these authors begin to alleviate the wrong of the suppression of the oral narrative both during the war and beyond, and in turn help to ensure that this wrong will not be repeated; in the words of Michael Herr, "Not much chance anymore for history to go on unselfconsciously" (44).

NOTE

1. It is important here to keep the modes of representation distinct. While the soldiers Herr encounters in the field are obviously not reacting to *Dispatches* per se, or even specifically to Herr's pieces for *Esquire,* but to the more diffuse representational body which constitutes the news media, Herr nonetheless at times seems to take responsibility for the media in its entirety, translating the grunts' criticism of their representations therein into a studied critique of his own work.

WORKS CITED

Baker, Mark. *Nam: The Vietnam War in the Words of the Men and Women Who Fought There.* New York: Berkley Books, 1981.

Benjamin, Walter. "The Work of Art in the Age of Mechanical Reproduction." *Illuminations.* Ed. Hannah Arendt. New York: Schocken Books, 1968.

Berlant, Lauren. *The Anatomy of National Fantasy: Hawthorne, Utopia, and Everyday Life.* Chicago: University of Chicago Press, 1991.

Foucault, Michel. *Power/Knowledge: Selected Interviews and Other Writings, 1972–1977.* Ed. Colin Gordon. New York: Pantheon, 1980.

Hasford, Gustav. *The Short-Timers.* Toronto: Bantam Books, 1979.

Hellmann, John. *American Myth and the Legacy of Vietnam.* New York: Columbia University Press, 1986.

Herr, Michael. *Dispatches.* New York: Avon Books, 1977.

Jones, Dale W. "The Vietnams of Michael Herr and Tim O'Brien: Tales of Disintegration and Integration." *Canadian Review of American Studies* 13:3 (Winter 1982): 309–20.

Moore, Lt. Gen. Harold G., and Joseph L. Galloway. *We Were Soldiers Once . . . and Young: Ia Drang—The Battle That Changed the War in Vietnam.* New York: Random House, 1992.

Neilson, Jim. *Warring Fictions: Cultural Politics and the Vietnam War Narrative.* Jackson: University Press of Mississippi, 1998.

O'Brien, Tim. *The Things They Carried: A Work of Fiction.* Toronto: McClelland & Stewart, 1990.

Ringnalda, Donald. "Unlearning to Remember Vietnam." *America Rediscovered: Critical Essays on Literature and Film of the Vietnam War.* Ed. Owen W. Gilman, Jr., and Lorrie Smith. New York: Garland Publishing, 1990.

Santoli, Al. *Everything We Had: An Oral History of the Vietnam War by Thirty-Three American Soldiers Who Fought It.* New York: Ballantine Books, 1981.

Sturken, Marita. *Tangled Memories: The Vietnam War, the AIDS Epidemic, and the Politics of Remembering.* Berkeley: University of California Press, 1997.

3. Concatenation and History in *Nam*

PAUL BUDRA

If the Vietnam War was, for North America, the first television war, it rapidly became, after the American withdrawal, a war of print. Told and retold in books, newsletters, and specialized magazines, the war generated a publishing industry unlike that which followed the other American conflicts of the twentieth century. The differences are in part due to the ideological confusion that surrounded the war; they are in part due to the technology of the war: the electronic media ensured that, for the first time in military history, there was a transcript of the speech of a representative cross-section of *all* ranks of combatants engaged in a war. It is not surprising, then, that the Vietnam War has generated a unique (though subsequently imitated) publishing sub-genre: the oral history.

This should be qualified: oral history did not begin with the American experience of the Vietnam War. In fact, it is one of the oldest techniques of history writing. Classical historians such as Herodotus and medieval chroniclers such as Bede interviewed witnesses of events they recounted.[1] But through most of modernity oral history was considered a secondary, at best supplementary, form to political and legal history. It was used when there was no, or little, written history; for example, following the hierarchy of data set out by Leopold von Ranke in the nineteenth century, it documented when there were no documents. It was distrusted by traditional historians because it did not provide the three qualities that they seek in sources: fixed form, precise chronology, and multiple witnesses of specific occurrences. It only became an organized scholarly activity in 1948 with the launching of the Oral History Project at Columbia University, and did not become a widely recognized sub-discipline until the 1960s. Then an interest in social history, the work of such historians as Jan Vansina on the oral traditions of Africa, and the wide availability of the portable tape recorder made oral history a growth industry. Alex Haley's hugely popular *Roots* (1976) introduced oral history to a mass audience. There are now journals, societies, and conferences dedicated to oral history; there are ongoing theoretical arguments over its providence and techniques; there are professional and amateur practitioners.[2]

The fact remains, however, that oral history is still used primarily when no written record of events exists. What makes the oral histories of the Vietnam War unique is, first, the fact that they have appeared around an extensively documented historical event, perhaps the best documented military conflict in history. Beginning in 1975 with Zalin Grant's *Survivors,* a flood of these oral histories of the war has emerged, creating a Vietnam literature that uneasily straddles the boundaries between narrative and collocation, testimony and interview, history and recollection, while raising disturbing questions about authorship, authenticity, colloquialism, appropriation of voice, myth-making, and tropics of discourse. And these histories do not simply seek to supplement the more conventional narrative histories; they attempt to confound those traditionally privileged texts. Their aim is to "bring us closer to the truth than we have come so far" (Baker xvi). In other words, they are presented as more real than anything produced by standard historical methods. This dialectic between the historical modes was not necessary with previous conflicts. As rhetorical critic Philip Wander has shown, conventional narrative history has traditionally been perceived by the public as more objective, more penetrating, and more reliable than soldiers' first-hand testimony (Hansen 4). This has not been the case with the Vietnam War.

The second trait that makes oral histories of the Vietnam War unique is that some of the most popular of these histories eschew the generally acknowledged protocols and formats of oral history itself as they have been defined by theorists such as David Henige and Paul Thompson.[3] The interview processes in these books tend not to be documented; the names of the witnesses may not be given nor the questions asked of them; they contain no record of attendant document research. And, as Alessandro Portelli has noted,

> at the core of oral history, in epistemological and in practical terms, lies one deep thematic focus which distinguishes it from other approaches and disciplines also based on interviewing and fieldwork, such as anthropology, sociology and folklore: the combination of the prevalence of the narrative form on the one hand, and the search for a connection between biography and history, between individual experience and the transformation of society, on the other. (25)

But many of the Vietnam oral histories avoid both narrative and the drawing of connections between their witnesses' experience and socio-political forces. In so doing, they create a very different form of oral history that necessitates an original rhetoric and criterion of authenticity. In this chapter, I will begin an examination of the rhetoric of such Vietnam oral histories by analyzing one of the best known of these books, Mark Baker's *Nam* (1981).

Baker, a journalist and professional writer who did not serve in Vietnam, interviewed some 150 veterans for his book. The interviews of veterans in *Nam* are broken into bits, some pages long, some only sentences long, and collected into chapters that organize them thematically and, to some extent, chronologically. The book contains four large sections — "Initiation," "Operations," "War Stories," and "The World" — that give a general scheme to the anecdotes. Each of these sections is divided into two chapters. So the "Initiation" section is divided into chapters "Ask not . . . " and "Baptism of Fire"; these contain anecdotes of enlistment, boot camp, and first engagement in Vietnam. Each chapter is prefaced by a short journalistic rumination by Baker. Once into the oral history proper, there is nothing to mark or distinguish the individual anecdotes. The names of the speakers are not given; dates of events being described may or may not appear in the individual narratives, but they are not supplied by Baker, so the chronological orientation is erratic. The book, then, is different from many of the other oral histories of the war that do present their interviews as monologues assigned to individuals. Instead, "*Nam* attempts the reconstruction of a collective, and therefore anonymous, experience" (Portelli 35).

How does Baker establish a rhetorical authority without the authenticating apparatus of orthodox historical discourse, indeed, *against* such an apparatus? The rhetorical authority of *Nam* comes from two sources: the concatenation of short narratives that illustrate a general theme, and the primacy and authenticity of oral narrative, the witness experience. Let us look at the question of concatenation first. This sort of structure, the collection of short, illustrative non-fiction narratives into compendia, is not overly common in contemporary non-fiction writing but is a form that dominated the middle ages: this is the exemplary mode. A recognized rhetorical strategy since the time of St. Gregory, the exemplary mode uses short, usually historical, narratives to illustrate a *sententia* or moral, often concatenating many (sometimes hundreds) of exempla to prove the point. The exemplum collection, then, is paratactic, that is, conceptually underdetermined. It is aggregative rather than analytic; more mimetic (it marks out specific data as a field of inquiry) than consistently diegetic (it does not necessarily provide a narrative or argument). If an argument does appears, it does so in framing devices such as marginalia, highlighted sententia, or some sort of narrative introduction such as a dream vision. In the most interesting cases there is no formal argument at all and the discourse's diataxis (the combination of the mimetic and the diegetic) emerges from induction: meaning manifests itself in the teleology implicit in the accumulated examples. This is why medieval works that employed the exemplary mode were often so long: the more examples, the more exempla, the stronger the inductive argument.

The mode has been unpopular since late modernity because, as John Burrows notes, such literature condemns itself to an ancillary role as the servant of the moral, political, or religious beliefs of its age (Scanlon 29). This often makes for very dull literature. It does, however, make for interesting ideological positioning. As Larry Scanlon has argued, "the exemplum's specificity as a discursive form cannot be narrative, because its narrative does no more than illustrate or confirm this principle which is completely sufficient without such illustration or confirmation" (4). That means "the exemplum's specificity as narrative is defined precisely by its constant movement between the historical and the textual. . . . The exemplum illustrates a moral because what it recounts is the enactment of that moral" (33). Exemplum does not merely confirm moral authority, in Scanlon's view, but reproduces it (5). This is very effective if the authority that is being reproduced is hegemonic, if there is sufficient ideological certainty that the illustrated moral may pass as moral law. So, in the Middle Ages, an argument by exempla on the power of God to punish tyrants or on the fickleness of women (two favorite topics) could reproduce authority without irony or qualification. An oral history like Studs Terkel's *The Good War,* about the American involvement in World War II, may be the modern equivalent. As the title indicates, it takes as a given that the American experience of that conflict, whatever its complexities, can be morally circumscribed by the "epochal victory over fascism" (8). But the same cannot be done to America's experience of the Vietnam War. That was a war of attrition, a war of upper military echelon incompetence and Pentagon dishonesty, a war without borders, without a visible enemy; a war of untrustworthy allies; a war of disillusionment, despair, and defeat. What pattern, what ideology, can be inferred from the exempla of this conflict?

Tellingly, Baker does not provide traditional diegetic material to explicate the teleology of his concatenated interviews: there is no formal argument or narrative. His ruminations in the chapter introductions are general, even sweeping, reflections on moral ambiguity. So in the introduction that prefaces the chapter containing anecdotes of war atrocities Baker speculates that "No eighteen-year-old kid went to Vietnam thinking, 'Oh boy, now I'm going to be evil.' But most of them met their darker sides face to face in that war" (168). When he describes encounters with individual veterans in these passages, the veterans are stripped of names and details, becoming amalgams: Everyvets. This is what he says at the beginning of the book:

> I told the veterans I had no intentions of forging a political document honed on guilt and condemnation. Nor was I interested in glorifying war and the soldier's lot. I just wanted to record what they could remember about the intersection of their lives with the Vietnam War and the consequences of that experience. (xiv)

What Baker does, then, and I think he does this more successfully than many of the other editors of oral histories about the Vietnam War, is to use the exemplary mode not to articulate and manifest a moral truism, that synecdoche for ideological hegemony, but rather to break ideological certainty through contrast and generate disorientation through eclectic juxtaposition. We can find examples of such juxtaposition in early modern exemplary models too, especially in annal histories. Annals were eclectically inclusive, paratactic recordings of events, great and insignificant. As the exemplary mode moved away from the paratactic towards the hypotactic (in which elements are logically subordinated one to another), argument was foregrounded; the more obvious the argument, the less the exempla relied on concatenation and the more the work as a whole relied on narrative, leading to an eventual transformation of the annals into modern narrative history.

Baker, in a conscious stylistic move, reasserts the medieval parataxis to model ideological uncertainty, invoking the annal history before it evolved into narrative. Absent, of course, is the hope that a pattern will emerge when sufficient material is collected. Indeed, Baker assumes the opposite, and while other editors of Vietnam oral histories have limited their fields of inquiry — to the Africanamerican experience of the war, the POW experience, specific companies — Baker is careful to avoid overt preselection, thereby making the possibility of teleological emergence all the more slight. Baker *does* impose a type of coherence on the anecdotes by arranging them in rough order: as mentioned, the first section of the book contains anecdotes of enlistment, boot camp, and first days in Vietnam. The last section contains anecdotes of return to "The World," the United States. Implied, then, is the span of enlisted soldiers' service: one year, thirteen months for Marines. But lacking is the sense of teleology through accumulation that the exemplary mode traditionally manifests. We get a beginning and an end, but the exempla in between cannot be wrought into pattern. This is not to say that there is chaos: order is sometimes apparent in contrast. In trying to represent the diversity of the Vietnam experience, Baker concatenates the most radically different ex-

periences together, so a story of the enlistment of an inner-city petty criminal
may be followed by a story of a medical school prankster:

> I got into the Marines because the army wouldn't take me. I was seventeen,
> hanging out in the neighborhood in Brooklyn with nothing to do. I knew I had
> to go to court sooner or later for some shit I was into. The Army recruiter
> didn't even want to look at me since they didn't get involved with court
> problems or seventeen-year-olds. Forget the Navy and the Air Force. They
> had intelligence tests and I didn't have any . . .

> I was in Johns Hopkins Medical School at the time. As a prank, somebody cut
> one of the fingers off the cadaver I was working on and kept it. When I went to
> turn in the cadaver, I couldn't account for the finger . . . A week later I had my
> draft notice. They turned me right in to the Board. (6–7)

At other times he uses the weight of accumulation to imply a pervasive-
ness of experience. In the chapter "Victors," he concatenates stories of atrocities, creating the suggestion of constant and ubiquitous brutality. The group-
ing of veterans' stories about returning home suggests a universal experience
of alienation:

> I didn't know how to act, didn't know what kind of clothes to buy, didn't like
> long-haired people, didn't like nothing. I carried a gun on me. People seemed
> to be messing with me all the time. Hey, I'd seen enough of that fighting shit.
> I didn't need that. You get back though and they say, "I see you made it all
> right. Big fucking deal." Some fucking ass asked me, "How come you didn't
> get killed."

> When I came back about six of us were walking through the airport and
> a girl — maybe eighteen or nineteen, about the same age as me really — she
> asked me how many women and children did I kill. I told her, "Nine. Where's
> you mother at?" (246–47)

But as a whole, the paratactic structure of the book suggests that the individual experience of the war, discontinuous and ambiguous as it was, or perhaps
because it *was* discontinuous and ambiguous, is itself the synecdoche for the
American experience of the war. So the teleology that *Nam* manifests is a sort
of anti-teleology, anti-pattern. Baker's rejection of the coherence of narrative
or even chronology is made commensurate with the subjective experience of
a diffuse and baffling war.

This all makes a certain historical sense. It is difficult to generate something as simple as a closed chronology of America's experience of Vietnam;
the Americans left on March 29, 1973, but when did they arrive? When they
officially entered the war? When they first sent advisors to the area? When
they blocked the election of 1954? And the individual soldier's experience of
the war was discontinuous: boot camp, a year in the field, "an environment
that was unpredictable, ephemeral, and claustrophobic" (Hansen 236), then

a plane ride back home. While in previous conflicts it may have been true that "having been in the war is the most immediately tangible claim for having been in history" (Portelli 26), the nature of the warfare in Vietnam worked against the realization of such master narratives. Many units operated in isolation; breakdowns in military hierarchy and operations planning, as well as the existence of covert operations into neighboring nation states, meant that many soldiers had no idea of their place in an over-all strategy; the narratives provided by the Pentagon and political leaders were untrustworthy, a fact that came home to the American public with the publication of *The Pentagon Papers* in June and July of 1971. And, as James William Gibson has suggested, "the experience of contemporary warfare evades theoretical formulation because of the exponentially multiplied killing power of technological weapons: the analytical appropriation of the warrior's knowledge has its limits" (quoted in Hansen 223). Napalm destroyed the ability of the soldiers who deployed it to contextualize their own actions.

At the same time, the desire to structure according to priorities the remembered subjective experience over the totalizing narratives of academic or even journalistic history marks these works as resolutely postmodern. It is hard to imagine a more obvious example of Jean-François Lyotard's benchmark of the postmodern condition — the rejection of totalizing narratives (xxiv) — in history writing than a work like *Nam*. It also signals the presence of paranoia, one of the by-products of the conflict and, perhaps, one of the hallmarks of the postmodern "age of conspiracy" (Don DeLillo, quoted in Pinsker 624). Because *The Pentagon Papers* proved to the American public that the American military had lied about the engagement in Vietnam, and because, from very early in the conflict, journalists were uncovering information that contradicted official reports, a pervasive cynicism emerged around the war. This would find its most popular image in a series of movies about the rescue of abandoned American prisoners-of-war from behind communist lines. In films like *Good Guys Wear Black* (1977), *Uncommon Valour* (1983), *MIA* (1984), and *Rambo* (1985), the rescuers work against the American government that wants the POWs forgotten. An oral history like *Nam* contains a similar distrust of authoritative discourse. Its strategy of rejecting the various protocols of conventional and oral history while asserting a primacy of the veterans' experience as a conduit to the "truth" is the historiographical equivalent of Rambo's refusal to let the American government dismiss the forgotten POWs as "ghosts."

Put another way, Elizabeth Tonkin, in a discussion of her work on African oral history, argues that "Memory is even sometimes treated [by traditional historians] as if it is pre-historical, a distinction which sits all too neatly with traditional versus modern, primitive versus civilised and oral versus literate — all dichotomies which, in practice, are balanced unequally in favour of 'us,' not 'them' " (Tonkin 119). The experience of the Vietnam War has created an analogous dichotomy between the veterans, whose memories of the conflict are protected as the defining element of their identity politics, and any authority — political, military, academic, or journalistic — that would question those memories. To apply the terms of Tonkin's formulation, the veterans and the writers such as Baker who record their memories are desperate to be "them."

But both the rhetorical authority of the exemplary mode and the postmodern historiographic implications of the inductive technique are offset by the witness format. The first-person narratives, recounted in colloquial language, give the book its other source of rhetorical authority, a sense of veracity and primacy that Baker is happy to exploit. Speech, as unmediated expression, is privileged by the writer Baker over writing. The book begins with an epigraph, apparently the uncredited words of one of the vets: "You want to hear a genuine story?" Note the emphasis on *hear*, as opposed to *read*. In the last of the chapter prefaces, Baker addresses the reader this way:

> You'll find a Vietnam vet much more easily than you think. Try to get him to tell you about his experience if you are genuinely interested. Once he starts talking, just keep your mouth shut and listen. You both may learn something about that particular conflict, about the human spirit, about yourselves. At least it won't be another waste of time. (271)

Note the emphasis on orality, on passive attendance to memory rather than analytic engagement with history. In the words of Michael Frisch, a theorist of oral history,

> oral history can be understood as a way of bypassing historical interpretation itself, avoiding all the attendant elitist and contextual dangers. It seems to provide a way to communicate the past more directly, to be presented with a somehow purer image of the past. (74)

The authority of orality is paradoxically heightened by Baker's refusal to name the vets who are speaking. Their voices, undifferentiated by textual clues, are disembodied. This anonymity engenders authority by raising the journalistic to the oracular. At the same time, this anonymity, combined with the concatenation, means that we experience a community of voices, a discussion; we're overhearing the babble of the survivors. This discontinuity acts, in part, as a metaphor of the American cultural memory of the war, a memory that was shaped by television: the Vietnam War, because of its media representation, became a war of sound bites, of first-person witnesses, of sixty-second stories, of images rather than narratives. This in part explains the predominance of oral discourse even in conventional narrative accounts of the war. Voiceover narration is a cliché of Vietnam War movies. As mentioned at the outset, the presence of the portable tape recorder and the electronic media journalists in the fields of Vietnam gave the record of that conflict the potential to be less mediated than that of previous wars. It wasn't written, it was broadcast, and the Pentagon had not yet learned to control and spin the media the way it did during the Gulf War and the war in Iraq. It may, however, have had a premonition of the force of recorded history. General William C. Westmoreland, at the height of the American engagement in Vietnam, asked the Army War College and Military History Research Collection to begin interviewing

> retired senior Army officers with respect to their lives, careers, and the events in which they participated, the positions of responsibility that they held and their views on problems as they saw them then and now. (Barnard ii)

The mandated focus of this project on senior staff officers may have been an attempt to control the oral record of, at least, the army.

The other point here is that the voices that defined the war for America were, quite early on, in conflict; the stateside peace movement offered sound bites, demonstrations, and interviews, that contrasted those offered by political authority as well as those offered by soldiers and journalists in the field. We may want to ask the following question: was ideological breakdown responsible for the proliferation of conflicting voices, or did the conflicting voices precipitate the ideological breakdown? Either way, the reifying of these contradictions in texts like *Nam* means that the rhetorical authority of these texts is very different from that of the exemplary mode they recall. While traditionally the concatenation of exempla supported a specific ideological utterance, here we have a heteroglossia: the diverse voices of *Nam* cannot articulate a single viewpoint and yet they stand as a community. The tension between the two rhetorical authorities — the anti-narrative, parataxis of the concatenated exempla, and the anti-history resonance of polyvocal orality — is not resolved. This irresolution, and the dialectical strategies of authority that *Nam* employs (anti-narrative, anti-history), ensures that the Vietnam oral history eschews closure. Remember Baker's admonition that we go out and find vets to listen to, to continue the process. Anecdote becomes antidote. As J. T. Hansen has argued, the public was grossly misinformed about combat after the first two world wars and as a result many soldiers went to Vietnam with "expectations [that] were an imaginative projection, based on their nations' lingering memories of World War II, especially those in the popular media. Vietnam veterans still feel humiliated by their naïve belief in John Wayne movies" (Hansen 236). *Nam* and books like it refuse to be co-opted into an analogous process of myth-making.

NOTES

1. For a brief overview of premodern and early modern uses of oral history, see Henige, 7–17.

2. For an overview of the growth of oral history in the twentieth century, see Starr, 4–26.

3. See Henige, especially 23–105, and Thompson, 91ff. The amount of space that these theorists dedicate in their books to the processes of oral history is indicative of their concern for systematizing, and therefore authenticating, the discipline, a concern ignored by writers such as Mark Baker.

WORKS CITED

Baker, Mark. *Nam: The Vietnam War in the Words of the Men and Women Who Fought There*. New York: Berkley, 1981.

Barnard, Roy S. *U.S. Army Military History Research Collection: Oral History*. Special Bibliographic Series 13. Carlisle Barracks, Pa.: U.S. Army Military History Research Collection, 1976.

Frisch, Michael. "Oral History and *Hard Times*: A Review Essay." *Oral History Review* 7 (1979): 70–79.

Hansen, J. T., A. Susan Owen, and Michael Patrick Madden, eds. *Parallels: The Soldier's Knowledge and the Oral History of Contemporary Warfare*. New York: Aldine de Gruyter, 1992.

Henige, David. *Oral Historiography*. London: Longman, 1982.

Lyotard, Jean-François. *The Postmodern Condition: A Report on Knowledge*. Theory and History of Literature 10. Minneapolis: University of Minnesota Press, 1979.

Pinsker, Sanford. "America's Conspiratorial Imagination." *The Virginia Quarterly Review: A National Journal of Literature and Discussion* 68.4 (1992): 605–25.

Portelli, Alessandro. "Oral History as Genre." *Narrative and Genre*. Ed. Mary Chamberlain and Paul Thompson. Routledge Studies in Memory and Narrative. London and New York: Routledge, 1998. 23–45.

Scanlon, Larry. *Narrative, Authority, and Power: The Medieval Exemplum and the Chaucerian Tradition*. Cambridge and New York: Cambridge University Press, 1994.

Starr, Louis. "Oral History." David K. Dunaway, and Willa K. Baum, eds. *Oral History: An Interdisciplinary Anthology*. Nashville: American Association for State and Local History, 1984. 4–26

Terkel, Studs. *"The Good War": An Oral History of World War Two*. New York: Pantheon, 1984.

Thompson, Paul. *The Voice of the Past: Oral History*. Oxford: Oxford University Press, 1978.

Tonkin, Elizabeth. *Narrating our Pasts: The Social Construction of History*. Cambridge Studies in Oral and Literate Culture 22. Cambridge: Cambridge University Press, 1992.

4. "Disremembering, Dísmémbering"

Poetics and the Oral Histories of the Vietnam War

KEVIN MCGUIRK

I have wished to keep the reader in the presence of flesh and blood.

—Wordsworth 335

. . . sometimes they were hardly stories at all but sounds and gestures . . .

—Herr 35

Nowadays, you can often spot a work
of poetry by whether it's in lines
or no; if it's in prose, there's a good chance
it's a poem.

—Bernstein, "Of Time" 215

My somewhat per-verse assertion: the "best" "poetry" of the Vietnam War lies, not in the official verse, but in the oral histories as told "by the men and women who fought there" (Baker), which are found in numerous published collections, in the tapes of the Winter Soldier Investigation, and in every utterance, gesture, and performative sound that re-members the dismembering force of the Vietnam War. If oral history is a mixed genre, it requires consideration in a dialogic framework (Portelli 3) composed (at least) of ethnography, linguistics, discourse analysis, narrative theory, as well as historiography. Adding another consideration, I contend that oral history bears consideration in the light of poetics.

A poem, it might be said, is whatever a given poetics constitutes as such. I do not wish to claim, then, as Dennis Tedlock once did, that "oral HISTORY *is* POETRY" (my emphasis). My concern in this essay is to frame the oral histories of the Vietnam War with the history and potentials of poetics to offer a vantage point on oral history — "talking the talk," as the editors of this volume put it — as a discourse other than what we know as prose. Prose is writing exclusively; oral history is not. Poetics is pertinent here, in the first instance, because oral history is the culmination of a post-Wordsworthian poetics of "a man speaking to men," the writing degree-zero of a romantic project. While I think that this idea is worth elaborating in its own right (i.e., that oral history, and not the contemporary "Wordsworthian" free-verse lyric, is the true descendant of Wordsworth's radical poetics) and that a scholar's argument could be propounded to show this, I want ultimately to propose the view that oral histories of the Vietnam War in particular should be refracted through the multiplicitous poetics of the twentieth-century avant-gardes.[1]

One reason Wordsworth is not enough is that although the war was largely fought by the "common man" of middle America — farmboys of the midwest, Brooklyn streetkids, Arkansas good ol' boys, Africanamericans from all over — he was thrust into a Deleuzian landscape,[2] an overdetermined, de-centered modern environment remote from "the permanent forms of nature" whose impress, Wordsworth argued, were the founding structures of a wholesome sensibility. A commonplace of discourse on the war is the romantic fall into experience: decent young men of the heartland return from their year-long "tour of duty" as both traumatically alienated and alienating; and this topos is crucial to Wordsworth, as it is to romantic culture generally. But casting it into the nightmare mold of Vietnam experience demands a virtual change of terms: in place of Nature's age-old push from the kingdom of childhood into the poignant bewilderments of adulthood, comes some fundamental perversion of the Human wrought by History. As one vet interviewed by Wallace Terry put it:

> I went to Vietnam as a basic young man of eighteen. Before I reached my nineteenth birthday, I was an animal. When I went home three months later, even my mother was scared of me. (236)

In the twentieth century, it is the avant-garde's "language of rupture" (Perloff, *The Futurist Moment*), the "accidenting" of form to meet the accidenting of history (Felman and Laub), that has provided some minimal metonymy of history in the testimony of broken form itself. What Marjorie Perloff calls the "futurist moment" of the early second decade of the twentieth century accomplished not merely a passive mimesis of "the horror," not just a less illusioned realism, but an activist, material intervention in the structures (semiotic, ideological, performative, social) that purported to hold "common" sense in place. As Perloff argues, this meant a pointed address to a fundamental binary — prose versus poetry — which, in imposing mutually defining and regulating norms, directed discursive practice toward equally self-limiting poles. Prose is linear, transparent, general, goal-driven, natural (as is evident in realism, journalism, scholarship). Poetry is sensuous, opaque, immediate, useless, artificial (as in Swinburnian lyricism, aestheticism). As Northrop Frye puts it,

> Very early in our education, we are made familiar with the distinction between verse and prose. The conviction gradually forces itself on us that when we mean what we say we write prose, and that verse is an ingenious but fundamentally perverse way of distorting ordinary prose statements. (17)

As a dynamic and unstable genre, with no necessary written form, oral history provides a fruitful occasion for considering the ways in which prose and verse are deployed passively or actively to produce meanings about the war experience.

Frye's discussion of what he calls "the associative rhythm" gives an immediate sense in which the prose–verse binary is breached by a rhythm that can be identified with neither one nor the other but is found in both. The associative rhythm is marked by paratactic syntax, filler phrases, non-linear exposition, idiomatic shorthand — very much what I take "talking the talk" to mean. Spoken utterance is not necessarily associative in its rhythms, since the patterning of prose can impose itself upon the speech of educated individuals, especially on certain occasions. Collections like Harry Maurer's *Strange Ground,* a history of the war in the usual sense, but conducted through interviews with Americans who worked in Vietnam (not just soldiers) between the early 1940s and the 1970s, is largely talk marked by literate protocols: hypotactic syntax, periodicity, what Frye calls prose control. It is worth noting that its speakers even get a *Paris Review*-style introduction that bestows upon them something like an author-function.

By contrast, collections like Mark Baker's *Nam* and Wallace Terry's *Bloods,* which are histories of *the experience* of war, mostly from the point of view of very young draftees, are highly associative. If the associative rhythm can be found in Whitman as well as Sterne, I think it's fair to versify a passage from *Bloods* that is distinguished formally by what is usually (in the age of prose) identified as a poetic device — anaphora:

> I still cry.
> I still cry for the white brother that was staked out.
> I still cry because I'm destined to suffer the knowledge that I have taken
>   someone else's life not in a combat situation.

I think I suffered just as much as he did. . . .
I still have the nightmare twelve years later. . . .
I still have the nightmare.
I still cry.
I see me in the nightmare, I see me staked out. (257)

If Frye is right, this is *not* prose.[3] Is it "poetry," then? Frye's account is primarily descriptive; it doesn't tackle thorny practical and ideological issues suggested by non-literary modes like oral history that have no essential text. Which would distort the actual speaking less: the "artifice" of verse, or the normativity of prose? There is no "right" answer, especially if "right" entails assumptions about the essential nature of poetry or prose. *Poetry is not a positivist category.* Indeed, what it is, and what it increasingly proposes in its postmodern phase — against the essentializing definitions of later romanticism — is a performative investigation, a "radical artifice," as Perloff's title has it, in the business of discovering the nature of discourse. As Charles Bernstein, the contemporary "Language" poet and theorist, puts it: "All writing is a demonstration of method; it can assume a method or investigate it" ("Writing" 226).

I do not aim, then, to make common cause between Futurists splattering sound poetry (cf. Marinetti "The Siege of Adriannopolis") and farm boys and ghetto boys telling about "walking point." Though both the Futurist "language of rupture" and the "radical artifice" of contemporary Language writers have some bearing here, I'm interested also in points of resonance between the American poetics of the Vietnam era itself and the oral histories of the war. Here there are, I think, two, in some ways antithetical, tendencies bearing upon the oral history of the war.

First, there is the populism that proclaims poetic utterance as natural right of the common person, or poetry as not unlike the natural discourse we might call "talking the talk." This has its roots in Wordsworth, but I'm thinking especially of the "talk-poet" (not Wordsworth's "a poet . . . is a man speaking to men" but "a poet is a man on his feet, talking"), David Antin's notion of "Human Poetics" ("Talking to Discover" 451). Antin opposes a human poetics, on the one hand, to what usually goes by "poetry," that is,

> *an unnatural language act going into a closet so to speak sitting in front of a typewriter [. . . .] and it's so unnatural sitting in front of a typewriter that you don't address anyone [. . . .] the whole problem of our literate and literal culture has been to some extent the problem of the dislocated occasion. (Talking at the Boundaries 56)*

On the other hand, he is wary of the exoticism suggested by the Ethnopoetics movement led by his friend Jerome Rothenberg, and Dennis Tedlock, because Ethnopoetics might mean in effect "not Human Poetics but Poetics of

the Other" ("Talking to Discover" 451). Oral history has significant resonance with both Antin's concerns and the more anthropological concerns of
Ethnopoetics.

Second, there is a poetics "in extremis," where the substance of the poetic
is the poetic ruptured, enraptured, stretched, bent, and broken around extreme experience. This looks back to Futurism, to Dadaism, and slightly
later, to Antonin Artaud, and it contributes to the emerging genre of performance art. The poet-theorist Steve McCaffery summarizes the aims of sound
poetry by quoting Foucault: "to restore words to the noises that gave birth
to words, and to reanimate the gestures, assaults and violences of which
words now stand as the now silent blazons" (*Close* 164). Not only the performance, but the "ambient theories" of the 1970s (Kristeva, Deleuze, Lyotard), he notes, emphasized somatic ruptures and flows, "the body [-as -pro-
cess] as both a conceptual and actual preoccupation in art and performance"
(*Close* 168).

That such extremities became the focus of avant-garde activity suggests
how the "common" extremity of the grunts, who formed the literal avant-
garde of the U.S. military, had invaded consciousness at home and demanded
an altogether different sense of immediate or common experience than that
offered by Wordsworth. Such art, like that of the Dadaists and Futurists, was
in part a form of testimony to the symptoms of disease that society at large
insisted were of the kind termed "false." The American people found it very
difficult to accept that the My Lai massacre was not an aberration, and that
many American deaths occurred because of strategic ineptitude or cynicism,
friendly fire, or fragging of officers. Given the numbing unaesthetic horror
of the grunts' stories, impinging upon the reader more horrifically than
any performance — like a veritable flooding of the Real, of what cannot be
gainsaid by art, into discourse — one might well conceive an oral history of
the grunts' experience partaking of the same impulse described by Foucault.
This would seem particularly apt since oral history's relative freedom from
literature's generic directives, as well as the policing by a critical establishment, would allow it to admit the "barely suppressed scream" which, as
C. D. B. Bryant claims, is "the voice of Vietnam literature" (quoted in Lawson 363).

Oral history, however, has observed its own decorums, or rather those of
scholarship (history, the social sciences) and journalism. These direct the
historian to purvey the *reasonable* truth contained within discourse and not
the unreasoned truth or testimony of the material discourse itself. Hence, we
have standard prose as the standard mode of transcription. In this connection, the comments of Sylvia Molloy on the autobiography of a nineteenth-
century Cuban slave are suggestive:

the *Autobiographia* as Manzano wrote it, with its run-on sentences, breath-less paragraphs, dislocated syntax and idiosyncratic misspellings, vividly por-trays that quandary—an anxiety of origins, ever renewed, that provides the text with the stubborn, uncontrolled energy that is possibly its major achieve-ment. The writing, *in itself,* is the best self-portrait we have of Manzano, his greatest contribution to literature; at the same time, it is what translators, editors and critics cannot tolerate. (quoted in Beverley 99)

If this is true for written work, how much more so for the infinitely more nuanced, textured, multi-dimensional material of oral history. If a "scream," as McCaffery notes, "can never be a social contract" (*Close* 171), the task remains, then, to register "the scream," by some metonymy of presentation, some material trace of the real. Begin, perhaps, by revoking the contract issued by Wordsworth to an impossibly straight-shooting "man speaking to men" and revise it for the vet twisted by extremity. Then incite a "poetical history" that includes everything from sound and gesture, to the transparent middle register of record privileged by scholars and journalists (as well as by mainstream poetry), to political analysis.

Such a discourse will perforce be experimental, an avant-garde of oral history. But how do you sustain attention to the strategies of poetry, and justify it to a culture where the natural is identified with the transparent, the serious with the formally conservative, and both with the normative: that is, with prose? The only solution might be to make a claim proleptically to a discourse beyond the aesthetic/non-aesthetic divide. Maria Damon's forging of connection between avant-garde poetics and social marginality takes po-etry as cultural practice rather than literary work, and is the best promise I know for a postliterary poetics. In a remarkable sentence near the end of her book *The Dark End of the Street: Margins in American Vanguard Poetry,* she speculates that

[t]he grimaces and cries of crack-addicted infants and the halting honesties uttered by Persons with AIDS in the privacy of their hospice-sponsored sup-port groups may constitute the "real" avant-gardes of postliterary contempo-rary poetry, the front-lines of undreamed-of expression. (241)

In this not-quite postliterary moment, then, "avant-garde" might be glimpsed as not only or even primarily a critical term for the art-world an-tics of an urban vanguard, but a name for the troubled, stubborn, demotic soundings issuing forth from the "tour of duty" of those abjected not through Art but through History: the grunts "walking point," the LURPs on recon, the avant-gardes of the American military. In this ambiguated place between a "human poetics" and "radical artifice," I invoke Hopkins's "disremember-ing, dísmémbering" force not just for *his* peculiar agony of self in extremis, but to indicate that I proceed under the sign of the unrealized and perhaps unrealizable poetics figured in his prescient, prosodic consciousness of the inadequacy of a normative poetics, not to mention a normative prose, to twentieth-century extremity.

So why not the poetics of *Vietnam poetry,* the verse of soldier poets upon which is bestowed the honorific *poetry?*

In 1972, three vets published a collection of poems by soldier poets, which they titled ironically *Winning Hearts and Minds,* or *W.H.A.M.* They brought out the collection under their own imprint, *1st Casualty Press,* because it had been rejected by forty publishers. Giving minimal attention to authorship (poets' names appeared only under their poems, not in the table of contents), the editors presented a book *for use.* The "Note to the Reader" that followed the poems outlined six ways in which "this book can be properly utilized" (Barry 118), summarizing them in verse:

> *Read it aloud*
> *Recopy it*
> *Dramatize it*
> *Give it as a gift*
> *And sing it!*
> *Poetry is a human gift.*
> *Use it.*

W. D. Ehrhart, one of the best-known soldier poets, recalled in 1990 not work by poets, but "artless poems, lacking skill and polish," by veterans "hurt" into poetry, which nevertheless "collectively had the force of a wrecking ball"(313). But Basil Paquet, one of the editors of *W.H.A.M.,* remembers differently. If the book sold well, the critical response was dismaying: "The thing that the book's reviewers most admired about it was — in separate poems as well as collectively — the lyric voice of these beautiful, young poet Americans who could depict the war experience" (86).

But if it's use-value that counts, not cultural capital, why care what the reviewers, the custodians of culture, have to say? Any evaluation of the success of the anthology *in the editors' own terms* would have to be based on an ethnography of reception and use — field work, not aesthetic judgment. What is interesting, however, is that, notwithstanding Ehrhart's account of the poems as "artless" (too harsh a judgment, I think), their mode remains art-writing, the poem as a thing set apart, rather than a social practice. Reviewers recognize the signals. "Official Verse culture," as Charles Bernstein calls it, affirms exactly what Paquet points up: the single voice uttering lyrically burnished truths of experience.

Despite the distinguished work of poets like Ehrhart, Bruce Weigl, or Yusef Komunyakaa (who has only recently written about the war), and despite the inalienable right of vets to the form-giving, consolatory, perhaps therapeutic exercise of verse-writing, especially the re-membering task of lyric poetry, Vietnam poetry *as a public practice* is hampered by the particular limitations of postromantic literary lyric, specifically the lyric of the 1960s and 1970s. Committed to demotic values, such poetry eschews overt rhyme, abstract language, and intellectualization, promoting subjective reflection through imagistic presentation ("show, don't tell") and closure in tentative epiphanies. This is what Charles Altieri calls the "scenic mode." A poem in the scenic mode, he writes, "places a reticent, plain-speaking, and self-reflective speaker within a narrative scene evoking a sense of loss. The poet tries to resolve the loss in a moment of emotional poignance or wry acceptance that renders the entire lyric event an evocative metaphor for some general sense of mystery about the human condition" (10). Thus:

> The first salvo is gone before I can turn
> But there is still time to see the battery
> Hurl their second load of fire into the night.
>
> The shells arc up,
> Tearing through the air like some invisible hand
> Crinkling giant sheets of cellophane that line the stars.
>
> The night waits, breathless.
> The far horizon erupts
> In pulsing silence. (*W.H.A.M.* 16)

Of more particular interest here is the rhetoric of such a mode, its peculiar public privacy, or what Charles Olson called "the-private-soul-at-any-public-wall" (239). As Jerome McGann writes, the rhetoric of the lyric is "a rhetoric of displacement" in which "the audience is not addressed directly" (123). The lyric norm, as Frye puts it, echoing John Stuart Mill, is for the poem to be "preeminently the utterance that is overheard" (249). Moreover, in fronting an unnamed, generic, overheard speaker, the lyric invites simple identification, "as if the reader were not being placed under the power of [a particular] writer's rhetoric" (McGann 123), instead of encounter with real and confounding expressions of a vet's experience in the person of the vet or what is frankly a substitute version with its own distinct materiality.

The reasons for the development of this overheard *I* in poetry are complex, but they are closely related to the romantic discovery of subjectivity set in relief against an objective background. The contemporary lyric, as John Koethe observes, presents us with an *I* at the center of a stage construed as a field of force and threat, an objective circumstance against which subjectivity emerges as pathos or power stabilized within the frame of the poem. Not surprisingly, the Vietnam lyric, taking up the predominant pathos of the genre, finds a keynote in the pathos of unshakable memory. The chief objective circumstance for the Vietnam vet writing poetry is the horrific experience haunting him:

> Seven winters have slipped away,
> the war still follows me.
> Never in anything have I found
> a way to throw off the dead. (Franklin 276)

Given the characteristic evasion of objective context in lyric, subjectivity in lyric gets concretized, not through relations with its real empirical grounds but as, in Paquet's phrase, the "lyric voice" beloved of reviewers. The purity of such a voice derives from its privacy and inwardness, its freedom from rhetorical constraints, and the absence of material responsibility to any grounds outside the speaker's imputed subjectivity.

I want to emphasize that this absence does not suggest any evasion of responsibility on the part of the poet *as empirical person* toward his experience or her telling of it. The point is that the logics of genre, as many writers have attested, can hijack the course of any piece of writing. How does the lyric encourage evasion of the grounds of utterance? In technical terms, the lyric poem finds its relative freedom from situational restraint (occasion) in its reliance upon a restricted set of what linguists call *deictics*. *Deixis* means "pointing," and refers to those elements of utterance that ground language in time, space, and person. At a conference not long ago, I heard a speaker claim for poetry the virtue of "located speech," since it had always been *positioned* speech, grounded in the primary deictic, the pronoun *I*. Poetry has not found its validity, then, in general, decontextualized "truth." But the issues are complex, since lyric relies upon a limited set of deictic terms calls *shifters* (*I, you, here, there, then, now*) that, without further corroboration of specific persons, places, and times, are simply elements of language that produce a subjectivity effect as well as generic time–space. These are the ingredients for that old chestnut of literary value, the "concrete universal."

What distinguished the phase before prose's hegemony in the modern epoch, according to Godzich and Kittay, is a shift in how texts, especially texts of knowledge, locate themselves. In oral contexts (and theoretically poetry retains a residue of this orality, but only in the sense of "song"), the figure of the *jongleur* grounded knowledge in the space of utterance. Knowledge was communal, rhetorical, agonistic — closely linked to the living realities of gesture, space, temporality, and sound (Ong). In contrast, prose, aspiring to an ideal transparency, develops as deictic-free, not positioned in (and therefore compromised by) specific time, space, and person. Certainly literary prose has played around with this, but it still remains that one does not need to know a novelist's own grounding in the writing in order to follow the novel. We may have the fiction, say, of a *narrator* writing in a bathtub, but not the novelist, and the novel as the dominant form of modernity exemplifies in literary discourse what is characteristic of what we know as literature as such, a written mode that does not need such grounding to make sense. Semiosis, as Jed Rasula observes, replaces deixis in literary reading (*Poetics*).

Despite a conventional emphasis upon sincere expression (Wordsworth: "poetry is the spontaneous overflow of powerful feelings" [344]), literary poetry relies on certain protocols of internal control, notably irony.[4] If connections are implied rather than explicitly stated ("slipping away" played off against "throwing off" in the example above), the lyric is characterized by a kind of symbolist wit. Here is Paquet's "In a Plantation":

> The bullet passed
> Through his right temple,
> His left side
> Could not hold
> Against the metal,
> His last "I am" exploded
> Red and grey on a rubber tree.

Note the lines that emphasize natural phrasing, the flat apparently literal exposition that discovers its double meaning as if by accident. That "I am" is at once the naturalistic "I am — " of utterance choked off by death, and the "I am" of the Cartesian self-presence, which is denied literally by a bullet and figuratively by the war. The poem is a witty play upon the fragility of subjectivity. Is it about Vietnam, too? Only the rubber tree locates the poem with any specificity.

Despite the implied breakdown of subjectivity (not just a specific soldier's death but a general condition), the lyrics locate themselves at the familiar crossroads of pathos and power, a site that promotes a preoccupation with the poet's own potency. The wit of symbolism makes the poem's moves themselves the contents of the poem. Noting that symbolism "tends to deflect all attention from external event back to the poet's essentially romantic imagination," Cary Nelson recalls that "what the war called into question, for poetry, was precisely this ability of language to transcend anything . . . the whole medium of public utterance becomes a mode of deception, and not even poetic utterance is innocent" (9). The wit of lyric is not only (as Adorno might have implied) an affront to the inassimilable reality of experience; it is also a way of outmaneuvering experience.

Again, this is not to question the sincerity of the poet's motivation, nor the empirical person's sense of responsibility. What it means is that lyric poems may speak more to each other, and look like each other, than they do to particular empirical experiences. If, as Koethe adds, one aspect of the objective circumstance the contemporary poet deals with is the legacy of poetry itself, to get beyond mere echoing of other poems, a poem cannot simply, however skillful the craft, take on new experience and hope to represent its specificity (72). If the poems of *W.H.A.M.* are indeed artless, it is in this. Drenched in generic imperatives that it is only dimly aware of, the poetry of the Vietnam War advances into a field that makes a work *automatically* intertextual in the most basic sense: its goal of Wordsworthian plain-speaking is compromised by what are now Wordsworthian conventions.

In this connection, Jonathan Holden makes a case for the postmodernism of verse from the 1970s against Marjorie Perloff's judgment, in 1978, on the preponderance of "conservative, instant Wordsworth" (quoted in Holden 112). Confessing that he was at first disheartened by the apparent force of Perloff's critique, Holden rallies to explain how verse of the 1970s is postmodern, not in the qualities of "irreducibility" promoted by Perloff and exemplified for her in John Ashbery, but in a different form of accounting for poetic circumstance, specifically

> in a changing rhetorical contract between poet and reader. Less and less are poems offered as personal testimony whose prime test is sincerity and authenticity. Although such a contract, after the stultifying impersonality of late-modernism, once seemed to place a too heavy demand on a poet to scour his own experiences for authentic "material." Recoiling from the demands of testimony, yet still committed to poetry that treats of the self, a poet may now find himself resorting to forms that resemble extended hypotheses instead of testimony, poems that invite the reader to "suppose" and that then proceed to spin a mythology. (136)

With this account, Holden effectively complicates the rather simple, not to mention polemically strategic, opposition assumed by Perloff between theoretically naïve lyric and sophisticated postmodern poetics. But why "recoil from testimony"? As if a soldier needed to "scour" his experience for authentic "material." The experience of the war imposes itself.

If straight lyric poetry is less canny than Holden's "let-us-suppose" postmodernism, both aspire to exactly what, as Nelson notes, the war called into question: the transcendence of circumstance without fully tabulating the costs of that transcendence. Koethe's argument suggests that the most valid poetry will be that which fully takes account not only of experience but of the very mode in which it constructs a space. Holden's notion begins to look rather simple set next to the lineated agonistics of Creeley, Antin's talk-poems, the searing self-questioning of Rich's Vietnam era poetry; or, on the other side, the dynamic, unstable genre of oral history.

If Wordsworthian poetry, instant and preponderant, seems limited as a social practice, it is interesting to think that Wordsworth's key claims and ambivalences have evolved not in the conservation area called literature, but in a discourse moving in the currents of social and political history: oral history. Not surprisingly, advocates of Wordsworthian lyric poetry have typically seen the avant-garde, with its *dis*-membering strategies, as some kind of inhuman threat to the "truth" of common experience. At the same time, their somewhat reactionary claim over a reified "ordinary" has been underwritten largely by the demoticized but not fundamentally altered realm called Art. Indeed, its inadequacy to extremities like war, not to mention its disdain for the very common, if souped-up, media and consumer environment of the postwar United States, suggests how Platonic its Idea of the ordinary is. Oral history is the real avant-garde of Wordsworthian poetics.[5]

Wordsworth's "Preface" made a seminal contribution to what might be called cultural poetics of the ordinary, a field that developed in the nineteenth century. The democratizing potentials of such a poetics have borne rich fruit, but went hand in hand with the less obviously happy campaign against not only the artifice called rhetoric, but also the artifice of art itself. What could the eventual effect be except to sideline and trivialize art? While Wordsworth's poetry seems quite evidently metrical now as well as highly rhetorical, Wordsworth's aim was strikingly different from its predecessors in that he sought a mimesis of the mind as it actually worked as the rememberer of past emotions. Blank verse would be deployed as a flexible means for tracing and regulating the spontaneous movements of the mind in reflection; "pleasure in numbers," as he puts it, tempers the pain that inevitably accompanies the direct expression of emotion (343). Metrics appears in the *Preface* almost as an afterthought, something effectively extrinsic to the definition of poetry itself, and providing merely technical support for the primary business of expressing feeling. As feeling becomes the chief value of nineteenth-century poetics, the *sine qua non* of poetry, the line is easily dropped to allow more direct access to that feeling particularly as it is embodied in "voice." During the same period, developments in empirical sciences and in journalism demand prose to get direct access to data and knowledge. Without intrinsic materiality, poetry is left without material defense. Wordsworth, unwittingly colluding with nineteenth-century positivism, teeters blindly over a theoretical precipice beyond which lies the endless vista of prose. Poetry (as in phrases like "the poetry of life") becomes, as Roland Barthes noted long ago, substance instead of attribute, "carr[ying] its own nature within itself" (54), something "inside" and ontologically prior to a material text itself. The line, "that material thing," has posed problems ever since to poetics (except in discussions that are really about "craft"). In its postromantic, phase poetics has said little of the line, focusing instead on the more nebulous qualities of image and "voice." The line stands for an indefensible artifice. In fulfilling Wordsworth, then, poetry is left to abandonment, where it is invented anew (newness being the American insistence at least since Whitman) or revolves, vestigially, in the little space of feeling prescribed by Wordsworth.[6]

A poetics-to-be of oral history, built in the space of abandonment, would have to function outside the economy of art. This would not entail, however, discounting the methods of aesthetic reading, nor the aesthetic qualities of the stories themselves. Portelli, generous in his understanding of oral history, puts it this way:

> What do we, as historians, do with the aesthetic project of many narrators, with the beauty incorporated in so many of the stories we hear? Do we, as purveyors of truth, expunge these features from our work (thus, of course, maiming the authenticity of the document), or do we recognize them as also *facts* in their own right, to be acknowledged and used? (19–20)

Portelli's terms here are classical, premodern. Beauty remains a consideration, but not one I think particularly important to modern poetics, or to modern experience, like the experience of men in Vietnam. (The "beauty" Tim O'Brien admits in his superb "How to Tell a True War Story," a fictional meditation on the impossibility of straight telling, is presented consciously as unlikely, even perverse, within the modern environment of the war.) The oral histories typically bring neither beauty nor dignity nor formal wholeness, but speak an experience of degradation and a language of terrible inexpressibility.

With Wordsworth as a starting point for a poetics of oral history, we can find implicit poetics in the introductions of oral historians. "A man speaking to men," the poet speaks "in a selection of language really used by men" (339), composing within the intense memory-field Wordsworth calls, in the famous phrase, "emotion recollected in tranquility" (335). This is exactly the field of the oral rememberer, a field opened by the questions of the historian–interviewer, although these are almost always elided in publication. In the introduction to *A Piece of My Heart,* Keith Walker explains the sense of the space of oral history that emerged as he conducted interviews:

> I found myself asking fewer and fewer questions . . . I became unwilling to influence the flow of recollection even if it meant that a degree of continuity or clarity might be sacrificed. There was a transformation taking place, a magi-

cal kind of presence reached by each woman at some point during our meeting, where past and present became one. (4)

Mark Baker, the editor of *Nam,* proposes to "just let the vets speak." His volume is a testament to the primacy of experience and the irreducible authenticity of having been there:

> What happened in Vietnam? What did it look like? How did it smell? What happened to you? Vietnam veterans know firsthand the statistics, the heroism, the evil and the madness. They are the ones qualified to look inside the casket and identify the body for what it is—a dead boy killed in a war, who had a name, a personality, a story all his own. (12)

Baker's emphasis on the soldiers' *own* stories is belied somewhat by the overall organization of anonymous stories into one narrative (more on that later), but both volumes are motivated by a more or less Wordsworthian desire to hear common truth and a faith in the validity of the direct expression of the individual's experience, not through public rhetoric, but through reverie and sharing. Accordingly, Baker pointedly disclaims political interest (his claim to monetary *interest* is asserted as a guarantee of ideological *disinterest*): "I had no intention of forging a political document honed on guilt and condemnation" (13). But why *not* forge a political document, and why is it assumed that such a document will be "honed on guilt and condemnation"? The answer is that only experience rings true, is most transparently available, in direct unproblematic testimony without commentary or significant editorial or material framing. Verse, needless to say, will not be considered.

That seems simple, but it becomes rather complicated once we consider some mechanics and the materiality of this unstable discourse. Questions about transcription must come up in dealing with oral history, even when verse is not an option (Where to punctuate? Spell phonetically or "correctly"? Paragraph where? Walker uses ellipses to mark pauses in the narration). The practical questions are important, but they need to be considered under the larger question of materiality, or method. To speak of materiality in contemporary criticism is to consider the formal as well as literal material elements of discourse as bound up with larger questions of ideology, as embodying specific and overdetermined ideological dispositions. This goes well beyond the creative writing sense of, say, craft, that is the focus of much mainstream reflection on lyric poetry, as well as beyond the positivist assumption, more pertinent to questions of transcription, that there can be an iconic correspondence between, for example, SHOUTING and bold print. It is the avant-garde that has primarily directed us to materiality, to the ways in which non-semantic elements of discourse produce meaning, in part by breaking it, and they have done so in response to extremities and atrocities like the Vietnam

War. The legacy of twentieth-century poetry is its tenacious attempt, more radical than that of Wordsworth, to find a way of recording, of manifesting in a different materiality, what Susan Howe calls "the stutter in American literature" (67). A twentieth-century poetics must be an "a-poetics," since it is not a study of objectively existing forms and modes, positively known through typologies or a menu of critical approaches, but a homing in on gaps and ruptures, possibilities and abjections, stressing the *making,* not *aesthesis*, restoring the basic sense of *poesis,* a continuous making and re-making and unmaking responding to the extraordinary, unpredictable pressures of twentieth-century reality.

Portelli takes into account the possibilities of non-normative transcription (though not the possibility or appropriateness of avant-garde experimentation). He tells the story of how he once wished to transcribe a small portion of an informant's history in verse, that of Dante Bartonini, "a singer, a poet, and a storyteller" (20) who had fought against the Fascists. Introducing his partisan songs with a brief historical narrative, "[t]he hieratic tones, the carefully timed pauses, the solemn rhythm, conveyed to the story the quality of epic poetry" (20). Portelli first presents the passage in free verse, "follow[ing] the rhythmic quality of the voice" (22). But he presents another verse version also. This time he centers the twelve lines on the page, and capitalizes the first letter of each line — this in order to underscore how Bartonini "projects [the Resistance] into a special epoch in the past, and suggests we commemorate it" (22). (Portelli's publisher, incidentally, would not finally allow the verse to stand.)

Portelli indicates that in producing the free verse transcription he followed "Tedlock's instructions" (22). In 1973, having made a pact with David Antin, who had begun to publish his own "talk-poems" in alternative format, a pact "that we would never again allow our own words — even our critical discourse — to be published in a prose format"(Tedlock 107), the anthropologist/ethnopoeticist Dennis Tedlock produced a conference talk in verse on the subject of verse transcription. It opens directly with its provocative thesis:

POETRY is ORAL HISTORY
and oral HISTORY
is POETRY. (109)

This is followed by an argument for the usefulness and appropriateness of verse transcription. The argument is illustrated in part with examples from Zuni storytellers and in part with Tedlock's own lineated transcription of his talk. Tedlock's claim is valuable, but he reduces the issue to sensitive and accurate transcriptions of oral discourse. (Portelli's rendering of Bartonini's speech as "a verbal icon to the Resistance" (22–23) actually goes beyond "Tedlock's instructions"; deploying conscious artifice, where the dominant aesthetic of the 1960s favored the natural and the transcription of the natural using the typed page as score, he produces a more sophisticated, dialogic writing than Tedlock's method could possibly yield.) For Tedlock, writing is still just frozen speech (to be thawed in performance), stored information.

Thus Tedlock advances what is essentially a mechanics, not a poetics, of transcription. Certainly this is useful. Prose, as he rightly points out, is a limited medium for recording oral discourse. It cannot register pauses, pitch, volume — and ignores the whole physics of utterance. (What about ellipses, italics? These breaks in normative prose dispose it toward the poetic.) Shake-spearean actors, like readers of the iambic line generally, can use the meter to guide performance.[7] But Tedlock's method demonstrates a superficial sense of what form is.

Whatever Paul De Man accomplished, and even if we demur before his austere negations, he made clear how thoughtlessly positivist much criti-cism is, and how subtle the incommensurable relations between rhetoric and form. Consider Tedlock's own thesis, with its totalizing equation. As it is rendered above, the thesis is structured rhetorically as a chiasmus: two halves of the statement mirror and balance each other. Chiasmus formally rein-forces the relationship of equality that Tedlock is proposing. The *this equals that*, however, is put awry by lineation. Tedlock is working in two different systems: the rhetoric tries to *form* the content of the statement to produce meaning transparently, but the lines dislocate the exact mapping of form onto content. The lines are merely notations, iconic to performance, external format not intrinsic form.[8] To fully consider material elements as more than instrumental, we need to attend to the historical baggage of form itself.

"It was crazy"; "I don't know who I was." Most of the oral histories of the war by Americans testify to the deep sense of dislocation and trauma felt by vets on a fundamental level and the extreme difficulty of relating their experi-ence. The question becomes not just what is the best mode for representing that experience (verse or prose), but whether the difficulty itself should be rendered, its awkwardness and opacity.

If what threatens the subject and exceeds representation produces the sublime, the twentieth century was characterized by a perverse sublime deter-mined by historical extremity. As Elaine Scarry has written, pain, whether physical or psychological, cannot speak itself (4). If inexpressibility was a commonplace of romantic discourse, the avant-garde takes it to the verge of bliss and wrenches it to accommodate not sublime nature, in its "permanent forms," but what Shoshana Felman, following Mallarmé, terms "accident."[9]

Registering the full implications of free verse as then conceived (in the 1890s) in its unpredictability, since its rhythms do not console with a tale already told, Mallarmé introduces free verse to the Anglo world by declaring that "a violence has been done" to poetry. As Felman puts it, "[a]s the testimony to an accident which is materially embodied in an *accidenting of the verse,* poetry henceforth speaks with the very power — with the very unanticipated impact — of its own explosion of its medium" (19). The medium must explode because the accident *"pursues the witness . . .* the witness is 'pursued,' that is, at once compelled and bound by what, in the unexpected impact of the accident, is both incomprehensible and unforgettable. The accident does not let go: it is an accident from which the witness can no longer free himself" (23).

Felman argues that testimony to such accident is a central twentieth-century form of discourse, and the resonance here with the "accident" of Vietnam — what in any civil or natural order should not have happened — is powerful. Poetry, in this context, in becoming commensurate with its own modern situation, gathers meaning as a break with normative prose (and normative Victorian verse) and an exploration of alternative representation. It offers, then, its own important testimony, not just in what it says but in its material form:

> By its very innovative definition, poetry will henceforth speak *beyond its means,* to testify — precociously — to the ill-understood effects and to the impact of an accident whose origin cannot be properly located but whose repercussions, in their very uncontrollable and unanticipated nature, still continue to evolve *even in the very process of the testimony.* (21–22; second emphasis mine)

O'Brien's "How to Tell a True War Story" exemplifies the point *poetically.* In trying to relate a wartime incident, the death of a young soldier playing catch with a hand grenade, the narrator discovers that he cannot do it, he cannot find the right register, he cannot even tell exactly the sequence of events. Thus the story becomes a dialectical, probing movement, circling back and retracing the ground, between avid retelling and reflection on its impossibility. The linear plotting of narrative breaks off repeatedly, giving way to, or being made into, a component in a rhythm of recurrence (Frye) and exposition by increments. White spaces between narrative "assays" abound. Thus, during the process of testimony itself, the story continues to evolve.

But that is literature, a space in which O'Brien is free to investigate the mode itself, without any call to truth. Oral histories have a different purpose, tied to truth-telling. How far can a history stray toward the "poetic"? In *Against Literature,* John Beverley poses a question that could be central to any consideration of the politics of discourse: "are there experiences in the world today that would be betrayed or misrepresented by literature as we know it?" (69). Beverley's discussion of Latin American *testimonio,* a form of oral history inflected toward political testimony, suggests interesting ways to consider relations between the literary and non-literary. *Testimonio* produces not only a powerful "truth-effect" but a *"trace of the real"* (82). Moreover, as "a demotic and dynamic form, not subject to critical legislation by a normative literary establishment" (71), it marks a signal departure from the economy of art, forced by a certain pressure of reality, of extremity, upon narrative form. It is this precise material contact between artifice and the real, between form and content — not form containing, resembling, or providing a window on content — that makes of transcription not a question simply of the best *this* representing an objective *that,* but a complex and necessarily open problematic.[10]

A major accomplishment of the aesthetic ideology has been to promote a literature that occludes the literal material reality of history. Poetry after the romantics, pursuing a "prosody of natural speech," beats a retreat from the agonistic space of rhetorical utterance and contingent selves that characterizes the oral realm in favor of the "lyric voice" of what Matthew Arnold called our "best self." Beverley suggests that *bildungsroman,* the narrative of an individual's gradual transcendence of circumstance, is the model for literary subjectivity. Subjectivity, as Koethe suggests of the lyric, is won *against* objective circumstance. (Suggestively, Hugh Kenner called James Joyce's *bildungsroman A Portrait of the Artist as a Young Man* an extended lyric). Poetry's social role, in Arnold's account, will be to lift our best self above our "every-day selves [by which] we are separate, personal, at war" (95), by providing a point of view in the permanent passions of humanity from which we might view the puny gestures of personal and political interest. The truth-effect Beverley claims for *testimonio* is derived, I think, in large part from *not* doing this, by instead remaining tethered to circumstances, and presenting a speaker who identifies with his community, and on the micro level by keeping all those pointings outside the utterance itself that are covered by the concept *deixis.* The oral story, openly transcribed by a literate interlocutor, refuses in-itselfness, constantly pointing outside itself, grounding utterance in material locations and social context above which the speaker does not presume to rise.

Yet oral histories, *as published texts,* typically evade these material elements. And the more oral histories are produced as relatively disembodied linear narratives by singular speakers, ungrounded in specific historical locales and specific situations of utterance, the more they collude in making best selves out of materially grounded and bodied historical ones. As Portelli notes, "the tendency prevails to efface the historian's presence both from the field situation and from the published text, in the attempt to create the fiction that the informant is speaking directly to a reader [or to nobody, like a lyric poet or writer], and — just like a book — would have spoken in the same way to anyone." Portelli adds that *"personal exchange* becomes a *public statement"* (32). In fact, however, it becomes something else, that peculiar floating public privacy of the literary lyric.

If the Futurist moment has passed, the practical and ideological need of the kinds of innovation initiated by the avant-garde has not. I have mentioned the commonplace of the fall into experience. The story America tells itself over and over, most notably in Hollywood, is that the little guy is dignified, even heroic. His fall can be redeemed, if you just give him a hearing. In a curious sense, this too goes back to Arnold and behind him, Wordsworth (though American culture has waived the need of what Arnold privileges as Culture). Oral histories exemplify this move, especially when they are rendered as monologues in prose, void of materializing features that situate utterance. Caught in some still point of reflection ("emotion recollected in tranquility"), the best self of the most unredeemable talker gets forwarded, just as in the denatured lyric poem. Oral histories promote the illusion of a free-standing Wordsworthian speaker in control of memory. In Vietnam, however, as Herman Rapaport has argued, making a Deleuzian point, the normalizing structures of real/unreal, self/other, good/bad get exploded in the thousand plateaus of Vietnam (145).

Should verse be applied? One problem, certainly not addressed by Tedlock, is the aesthetic legacy of poetry, the meta-physical baggage it still carries from its symbolist phase. It is the power of this legacy that puts poetry in question after Auschwitz. For decades, art was on probation in a postwar era dominated by grim forms of realism in fiction and strict, unambitious formalism in poetry. But now in this almost postliterary moment, all device is up for grabs, all is conceded to the logos-at-large, the form-giving activity that is human itself: *poesis*. The real avant-gardes of such a moment, as Damon suggests, will not be identified through the categories of art, but will stand at the edge of experience and scarf whatever means they need to embody it verbally. Democratizing art turns out not to mean, as the Arnoldians thought, exposing everyone to Mozart and Wordsworth, or giving prosodic tongue to every mute, inglorious Milton, but recognizing a pluralized field in which everyday poesis gets called by its proper name. To think of mainstream verse, then, as the official or only poesis of the Vietnam War is to read a radical condition not merely of theoretical "becoming" (Deleuze), nor of the subject on trial (Kristeva), but of the "disremembering, dísmémbering" (Hopkins) of the soldier's very self as containable within the timid frame of the Wordsworthian free verse lyric. The oral histories of the young men — LURPS on recon, grunts walking point — beg a more flexible poetics, one that might include "even in the very process of the testimony" (Felman) (which is in significant part the editor/transcriber's), the strenuous fragmentations of the avant-garde. But the point, finally, is that oral history is not simply either prose or poetry. As Robert Dale Parker puts it, "oral story," when pressed, "multiplies into more than any method of reproduction can discover or contain" (163).

CONCLUSION: *NAM*

Nam is the history that's stayed with me most, that's given me bad dreams. If any oral history resonates with the abjection and delirium of 1970s art and society, it's this. Talk about the body-in-process — the body made (becoming-soldier); the body unmade — pulverized, sick, tortured, dismembered; the body dead. Matter as meat is its nexus. "Je est un autre" is its psychology. I ought to argue now that the continuities postmodern poetics claims with body as sound, not just signs but the non-semiotic noises of cries, laughter, screams, grunts — poetry as displaying radical materiality — should promote in work like this some registration in the materiality of verse of the material experience where language meets bodily existence, where History is a matter of what bodies do to other bodies. And yet there is something in the flattened, anti-idealizing pose of *Nam* that, in fronting what's most gross and horrific, turns its own non-art prose to a statement of bloated disgust, a stylistic despondency before bodies reduced to meat.

So yes, Baker sets out to record the horror beyond ideological agendas, to tell it, tough-guy wise, like it is. The sensationalism of bloody testimonies, the broken lives, the violent deeds, may throw utterance into surreality and moral vertigo without contesting prose norms one iota, blundering forth where no "art," as Paquet's experience of reviewers reveals, may tread without compromising all securities, all vestments of chosen form. Neither vet nor peacenik, Baker is too noirishly jaded to claim either ideal disinterest, or idealizing interest. For one thing, he's out to make a buck. But he's too facile in throwing up this facade, and proceeds to organize the words of his broken heroes as a redemptive narrative of a generation. Scattering each speaker's individual narrative across thematic sections, Baker charts a journey from innocence to experience, from the banality of induction to the full-blown terror of sublime dislocation in the Nam, on to (he implies) some kind of healing in the telling. The stories are searingly personal, but the speakers remain unnamed, fragmentary, possessed only of roughened stories and partial understanding. In narratological terms, "story" overwhelms "discourse." No exemplary self coheres, emerges. No "best self" returns from the Nam. The poetic device of a ragged, irregular refrain — "it was crazy" — melds the self together. And the prose hits something beyond the simply normative:

stylistically banal compared to the horror it records, lacking the stimulus of
any occasion beyond Baker's "assignment," giving way before the reader as
readily as a McDonald's burger to his teeth. McCaffery's curious and brief
riff on "The Line of Prose" is suggestive here:

> We have come to think of this inertia, this non-appearance of the value of the
> line [since "prose has never petitioned the line as a sign of value"] . . . as the
> product of rationalist forces (specifically the classic sense of language as a
> neutral ground), yet this refusal to engage in valorization might serve a de-
> constructive "end" and unmask that metaphysical strain in poetry which
> demands a self-fulfilling presence, a parousial meaning and significance in-
> voked inside the dream of recovering through the written mark, a body with-
> out writing. ("Line" 198)

Poetry is often taken as a negation, and transcendence, of the prosaic, of the
banal. In *Nam* we have poetry negated—a *negative poetry* occasioned by a
refusal to redeem except by the most clichéd plotting, a disgust with the
metaphysical trace carried in every hint of hifalutin' "Poetry."

APPENDIX: TWO "POEMS"

First, in prose:

*We were going single file through his rice paddies, and the farmer started
hitting the lead track with a rake. He wouldn't stop. The TC went to talk to
him, and the farmer tried to hit him too, so the tracks went sideways side by
side through the guy's fields, instead of single file. Hard On, Proud Mary,
Bummer, Wallace, Rosemary's Baby, the Rutgers Road Runner, and Go Get
Em—Done Got Em went side by side through the fields. If you have a farm
in Vietnam and a house in hell, sell the farm and go home.*

*In the Nam you realised you had the power to take a life. You had the power
to rape a woman and nobody could say nothing to you. That godlike feeling
you had was in the field. It was like I was a god. I could take a life, I could
screw a woman. I can beat somebody up and get away with it. It was a
godlike feeling that a guy could express in the Nam.*

Next, in verse:

A BUMMER

*We were going single file
Through his rice paddies
And the farmer
Started hitting the lead track
With a rake*

He wouldn't stop
The TC went to talk to him
The farmer
Tried to hit him too
So the tracks went sideways
Side by side
Through the guy's fields
Instead of single file
Hard On, Proud Mary
Bummer, Rosemary's Baby
The Rutgers Road Runner
And
Go Get Em — Done Got Em
Went side by side
Through the fields
If you have a farm in Vietnam
And a house in hell
Sell the farm
And go home

IN THE NAM

> *In the nam*
> *you realised*
> *that you*
> *had the power*
> *to take*
> *a life, you*
> *had the power*
> *to rape a*
> *woman,*
> *and nobody*
> *could say nothing*
> *to you*

> *(that godlike feeling you had was in the field*

po8 ɒ sɒm ı ǝʞıן sɒm ʇı)

> *i could take a life*
> *i could screw a woman*
> *i can beat somebody up and get away with it*

> *it was a godlike feeling that a guy could express in the nam*

What does lineation perform in each case? Is one version "better" than the other? Does lineation aestheticize, or at least introduce an aesthetic element where apparently there was none? Is it possible to theorize such a move so that lineation doesn't appear as an appropriation by art?

In "A Bummer," aesthetic strategy is determinedly modest. Lineation paces reading

> slows down
> the build
> up
> to
> epiphany

The wry, bitter advice given at the end of this poem emerges from a flat presentation of "fact." The poem eschews emotional coloring, minimizes obvious signs of artifice, and thereby "earns" its bleakly laconic judgment. Asserting its allegiance to demotic values ("a bummer"), it forestalls accusations of aesthetic indulgence.

The poem "in the nam" is angled awry. Its speaker relishes a memory of destructive power. The subject-position is unsympathetic, and identification with an overheard speaker isn't invited. The grammar is unreliable, shaky, shifty even. This seems genuinely demotic. On one hand, the speaker embraces the subject-position as his own; on the other, he distributes agency among "grammatical persons" ("I," "you" [demotic for "one"], "a guy"). The lineation radicalizes presentation, omitting punctuation; ignoring stanza integrity; breaking units of offensive detail; deploying the space, including turning the weird utterance of godlike feeling upside down to visually transmit the vertiginous position at odds with the humanistically self-reflexive position of a lyric speaker. It presents the speaker, not just the content, the irony.

The wrestle with words is satisfied with the lyric formula (and there's doubtless something therapeutic in "getting it right"), but if "poetry" is to be used in dealing with such topics as Vietnam, why not exploit its potentials?[11]

NOTES

1. I mean "avant-garde," an overdetermined concept anyway, in the most general sense. I include the historical avant-gardes, what Marjorie Perloff calls "the futurist moment," but also the ongoing explorations, by poets primarily, of the nonnormative in discourse.

2. See Herman Rapaport's tour de force essay, "Vietnam: The Thousand Plateaus," which addresses the question, "How does the [American] 'unit' disarticulate, dematerialize, frag" in the "rhizomic landscape" of Vietnam? (137).

3. Frye: "The irregular rhythm of ordinary speech may be conventionalized two ways. One way is to impose a pattern of recurrence on it; the other is to impose the logical and semantic pattern of the sentence. We have verse when the arrangement of words is dominated by a recurrent rhythm and sound, prose when it is dominated by the syntactical relation of subject and predicate" (21).

4. Irony is something like "intratextual deixis," where one meaning is "grounded" in an other. Interestingly, Antony Easthope locates the "founding moment" of modern discourse, specifically the hegemony of iambic pentameter in poetry, in the dominance of transparency as the chief value. A transparency-effect is achieved by a "separation between words and the reality they might refer to . . . 'form' (signifier and means of representation) came to be radically distinguished from 'content' (signified and the represented)" (94). Irony becomes a basic and unremarked figure of control, one which, in relating two elements, both within an utterance, keeps signified and signifier related but separate from each other.

5. For a trenchant critique of the ways in which American poetry about the Vietnam War leans toward "pithy vignettes of 'authenticity,' " see Rasula on Carolyn Forché's anthology of "poetry of witness," *Against Forgetting*. While Forché writes that "Extremity demands new forms or alters older modes of poetic thought," this formulation, Rasula notes, "is abandoned when it comes to the selection of American poetry" (300). "To read her selection of Vietnam war poetry," he says, "is to be astonished at the prospect that she (and maybe even her selected poets) are unaware of the extraordinary verbal ballistics of Michael Herr's famous *Dispatches*—a book of 'prose' that deftly exposes most poetry about Vietnam as conceptually and semantically retrograde" (301).

6. It is only with the recent Language movement that poets have wholly embraced artifice. This has meant turning to prose not as a supplement supporting and explaining the artifice of verse, but as itself an artifice, an ideological donné to be exploited, occupied, and *contaminated* by poetry.

7. Easthope's reading of the iambic line is pertinent here. The iambic line does not involve us dialectically but imposes a specific form of reading that comes off as natural while depending on ideological values. The line as conceived by Tedlock similarly imposes a specific, positivistically "natural" form of reading.

8. Robert Dale Parker's recent critique of Tedlock suggests that what is really motivating him is the desire to throw the weight of capital that poetry possesses in mainstream culture behind the oral performances of indigenous people in order to legitimize them.

9. If Tedlock, as an anthropologist, is dealing primarily with traditional stories, more or less achieved, if still evolving, the modern oral history is about "accident," the assault upon what is customary, what is traditional, upon what sustains communal or tribal life. Its forms, then, will be wracked, uncertain, stumbling, discovered perhaps for the first time in sharing with an oral historian.

10. Since prose gradually emerged as hegemonic in modernity, it has insisted upon an appearance of normativity, and it is in the nature of the normative to appear natural, given. In such a scheme, poetry obviously occupies the position of an Other, the non-normative, and it is here, I think, that the virtue of poetics as the wide-open discourse of the non-normative appears. Now, Easthope's brief for the normative force of iambic pentameter is really about the way in which the poetic conforms and adapts to modernity's imperatives and participates in the construction and regulation

of a bourgeois subject. Maria Damon's version of literary history is strikingly at odds since it leaps from Plato and the founders of western philosophical discourse to a contemporary American situation in which poetry figures as the marginalized, the abandoned. At any rate, what this double and complicitous tale of poetry and prose suggests is that prose is best understood, in a master-slave relation, from the point of view of the poetic. This is implicit in Stephen Fredman's book on "poet's prose," a form of discourse that is essentially poetry's critique of hegemonic prose from within, a guerrilla attack using the weapons of poetry to expose, deform, and erode prose's apparently natural status and its hegemonic power.

11. "A Bummer" is verse, a poem from *W.H.A.M.* (7); "in the nam" is prose lifted from *Nam*.

WORKS CITED

Altieri, Charles. *Self and Sensibility in Contemporary American Poetry.* New York: Cambridge University Press, 1984.

Antin, David. *Talking at the Boundaries.* New York: New Directions, 1976.

———. "Talking to Discover." In *Symposium of the Whole: A Range of Discourse toward an Ethnopoetics.* Ed. Jerome and Diane Rothenberg. Berkeley: University of California Press, 1983.

Arnold, Matthew. *Culture and Anarchy.* 1869. Ed. J. Dover Wilson. Cambridge: Cambridge University Press, 1986.

Baker, Mark. *Nam: The Vietnam War in the Words of the Men and Women Who Fought There.* New York: Quill, 1982.

Barry, Jan, Larry Rottman, and Basil T. Paquet, eds. *Winning Hearts and Minds: War Poems by Vietnam Veterans.* Brooklyn: 1st Casualty Press, 1972.

Barthes, Roland. "From *Writing Degree Zero.*" 1953. *A Barthes Reader.* Ed. Susan Sontag. New York: Hill & Wang, 1987. 31–61.

Bernstein, Charles. "Of Time and the Line." In Frank and Sayre, eds. 215–16.

———. "Writing and Method." *Content's Dream: Essays 1975–1984.* Los Angeles: Sun & Moon, 1986. 217–36.

Beverley, John. *Against Literature.* Minneapolis: University of Minnesota Press, 1993.

Damon, Maria. *The Dark End of the Street: Margins in American Vanguard Poetry.* Minneapolis: University of Minnesota Press, 1993.

Deleuze, Gilles, and Felix Guattari. *Anti-Oedipus: Capitalism and Schizophrenia.* Vol. 1. 1974. Trans. Robert Hurley, Mark Seem, and Helen R. Lane. New York: Viking, 1977.

Easthope, Antony. *Poetry as Discourse.* London: Methuen, 1982.

Ehrhart, W.D. "Soldier Poets of the Vietnam War." In Gilman, ed., *America Rediscovered.* 313–31.

Felman, Shoshana, and Dori Laub. *Testimony: Crises of Witnessing in Literature, Psychoanalysis, and History.* New York: Routledge, 1991.

Frank, Robert, and Henry Sayre, eds. *The Line in Postmodern Poetry.* Urbana: University of Illinois Press, 1988.

Franklin, Bruce, ed. *The Vietnam War in American Stories, Songs, and Poems.* Boston: Bedford-St. Martin's, 1996.

Fredman, Stephen. *Poet's Prose: The Crisis in American Verse.* New York: Cambridge University Press, 1980.

Frye, Northrop. *The Well-Tempered Critic.* Bloomington: Indiana University Press, 1963.

Gilman, Owen W., Jr., and Lorrie Smith, eds. *America Rediscovered: Critical Essays on Literature and Film of the Vietnam War.* New York: Garland, 1990.

Godzich, Wlad, and Jeffrey Kittay. *The Emergence of Prose: An Essay in Prosaics.* Minneapolis: University of Minnesota Press, 1987.

Herr, Michael. *Dispatches.* New York: Knopf, 1977.

Holden, Jonathan. *The Rhetoric of the Contemporary Lyric.* Bloomington: Indiana University Press, 1980.

Hopkins, Gerard Manley. "Spelt from Sybil's Leaves." *Poems and Prose.* Ed. W. H. Gardner. New York: Penguin, 1963. 59.

Howe, Susan. "Susan Howe." *Postmodern Poetry: The Talisman Interviews.* Ed. Ed Foster. Hoboken, N.J.: Talisman Publishers, 1994.

Koethe, John. "Contrary Impulses: The Tension between Poetry and Theory." *Critical Inquiry* 18.1 (Autumn 1991): 64–75.

Kristeva, Julia. *Revolution in Poetic Language.* 1974. Trans. Margaret Waller. New York: Columbia University Press, 1984.

Lawson, John. "Telling It Like It Was: The New Fictional Literature of the Vietnam War." In Gilman, ed., *America Rediscovered.* 363–81.

Maurer, Harry. *Strange Ground: Americans in Vietnam, 1945–1975 — An Oral History.* New York: Henry Holt, 1989.

McCaffery, Steve. "The Line of Prose." In Frank and Sayre, eds. 198–99.

———. "Voice in Extremis." *Close Listening: Poetry and the Performed Word.* Ed. Charles Bernstein. New York: Oxford University Press, 1998.

McGann, Jerome. "Private Poetry, Public Deception." *The Politics of Poetic Form: Poetry and Public Policy.* Ed. Charles Bernstein. New York: Roof Books, 1990. 119–47.

Nelson, Cary. *Our Last, First Poets: Vision and History in Contemporary American Poetry.* Urbana: University of Illinois Press, 1981.

O'Brien, Tim. "How to Tell a True War Story." *The Things They Carried.* 1990. Toronto: McClelland & Stewart, 1991.

Olson, Charles. "Projective Verse." 1950. *Collected Prose.* Eds. Donald Allen and B. Friedlander. Berkeley: University of California Press, 1997. 239–49.

Ong, Walter. *Orality and Literacy: The Technologizing of the Word.* London: Methuen, 1982.

Paquet, Basil. In *Facing My Lai: Moving Beyond the Massacre.* Ed. David L. Anderson. Kansas City: University Press of Kansas, 1998.

Parker, Robert Dale. "Text, Lines, and Videotape: The Ideology of Genre and the Transcription of Traditional Native American Oral Narrative as Poetry." *Arizona Quarterly* 53.3 (Autumn 1997): 141–69.

Perloff, Marjorie. *The Futurist Moment: Avant-Garde, Avant-Guerre, and the Language of Rupture.* Chicago: University of Chicago Press, 1986.

———. *Radical Artifice: Writing Poetry in the Age of Media.* Chicago: University of Chicago Press, 1991.

Portelli, Alessandro. "Oral History as Genre." *The Battle of Valle Giulia: Oral History and the Art of Dialogue.* Madison: University of Wisconsin Press, 1997. 3–23.

Rapaport, Herman. "Vietnam: The Thousand Plateaus." In *The 60's, without Apology.* Ed. Sohnya Sayres et al. University of Minnesota Press, 1984. 137–47.

Rasula, Jed. *The American Poetry Wax Museum: Reality Effects, 1940–1990*. Urbana, Ill.: NCTE, 1996.

———. "The Poetics of Embodiment: A Theory of Exceptions." Ph.D. dissertation, University of California-Santa Cruz, 1989.

Scarry, Elaine. *The Body in Pain: The Making and Unmaking of the World*. New York: Oxford University Press, 1985.

Tedlock, Dennis. *The Spoken Word and the Work of Interpretation*. Philadelphia: University of Pennsylvania Press, 1983.

Terry, Wallace. *Bloods: An Oral History of the Vietnam War by Black Veterans*. New York: Ballantine, 1985.

Walker, Keith. *A Piece of My Heart: The Stories of Twenty-Six American Women Who Served in Vietnam*. Novato, Calif.: Presidio, 1985.

Wordsworth, William. "Preface to *The Lyrical Ballads*." *Criticism: The Major Texts*. Ed. Walter Jackson Bate. New York: Harcourt Brace Jovanovich, 1970.

5. Talk, Write, Talk
Bobby Garwood, MIAs, and Conspiracy

CRAIG HOWES

*There are times when I've been places or I've said
things or done things that I don't remember.*

—Robert Garwood[1]

John F. Keener has called Lee Harvey Oswald "the central figure in a narrative with no center," standing "at the collision point" of "biography, or the
story of a 'lone gunman,' and conspiracy, or 'the plot to kill the President'"
(303). As usually understood, biography takes "individual volition as its
causal determinant," assuming that life events, even if presented out of order,
have a "sequential itinerary." Conspiracy does something different. It sub-
merges the individual life "into an historical narrative whose various human
components are indistinguishable, indistinct, and sometimes missing" because "a larger conspiratorial Truth" requires "sacrificing the specificity, fa-
miliarity, and immediacy of biographical narrative" (303–304). And finally,
in the "sublime conspiracy," not only does individual volition dissolve "as a
viable means of understanding our world," but even the notion of the force
directing events "disseminates from a human group into a profound conspiratorial melange" (305). Or as Richard Hofstadter puts it, sometimes "History *is* a conspiracy" (Keener 304).

If, as Sanford Pinsker claims, the Kennedy assassination is "the 'mother'
of contemporary conspiracy theory" (621),[2] the story of the Vietnam War's
Missing in Action was among her first born, and the figure often standing "at
the collision point" between biography and conspiracy is Robert "Bobby"
Garwood. In 1993, when I wrote about Garwood in my book *Voices of the*

Vietnam POWs, I focused on his contacts with other captives and on his status as the White Cong—an American GI accused of crossing over to the enemy. Though I mentioned his unexpected 1979 return from Vietnam, and his prominence in the MIA controversy, I simply noted that over time his story had shifted "in its emphasis, details, and revelations," and I concluded that whatever else might come to light, "I suspect Robert Garwood will have the last word" (230). As for the larger controversy, I raised it only to excuse myself from discussing it. Though some MIAs may have been POWs, I could only write about Garwood, because like "the men themselves, their stories remain MIA" (7). I am returning to him now to explore how his "story" complicates the assumptions of oral history, and how the sublime conspiracy narratives that have absorbed this story deal with these same assumptions. What follows, therefore, will be a series of narratives—historical, conspiratorial, technological—within narratives, deployed variously in ever unfolding configurations that increasingly, I suspect, will be the way the "story" of the Vietnam War will be told.

Garwood's story comes in a mind-boggling variety of forms. Movies, congressional hearings, debriefings—official and unofficial, voluntary and involuntary—court martial transcripts, group histories, newspaper and magazine articles, memoirs, Web sites, *Playboy* interviews, reports to the Assistant Secretary of Defense, pilfered and posted e-mail, public speaking engagements, legally mandated confessions of duplicity, faxes, phone calls, electronic lists, rumor—on and on. All of these, however, agree that Marine Private Robert Garwood disappeared on September 28, 1965, ten days before he was to leave Vietnam, and that on March 22, 1979—thirteen and a half years later, and six years after all American POWs had supposedly returned—he resurfaced in Hanoi, and then came home. The controversy rages over what happened in between, but before heading into the "conspiratorial mélange," it might be helpful to map out at least three of the timelines running through this story. First, there's the biographical chronology of Garwood himself, stretching from his birth, on April 1, 1946, to this moment of writing, since he is very much alive. The two most important dates in this chronicle are those of his capture and return. Other red-letter periods include the time he spent with other American POWs between mid-July 1967 and late 1969, his 1980–81 court martial, his claim in 1984 that he had seen live POWs in Vietnam after 1973, and the 1997 publication of Monika Jensen-Stevenson's *Spite House: The Last Secret of the Vietnam War.*

The second timeline records the order in which the many Bobby Garwood stories have appeared. Two POWs paroled in January 1968 were the first to tell his story, followed by more POWs released in November 1969, and then by those who returned in early 1973. Each POW was officially debriefed — providing an oral history, though a classified one. Many POWs then published memoirs dealing with Garwood, or participated in group oral histories that discussed him, or gave interviews to the compilers of John G. Hubbell's authorized history *P.O.W.* (1976). Some POWs did all three. All of these versions were produced before Garwood reappeared, and many POWs repeated their stories under oath at the hearings and eventual court martial that found him guilty of collaboration in 1981. Since Garwood did not testify, his own version of his captivity therefore became public years after accounts by people who assumed he would never return, or who told them as part of his trial. This second timeline runs from those first POW debriefings in 1968 to the 1983 publication of Winston Groom's and Duncan Spenser's authorized biography *Conversations with the Enemy: The Story of PFC Robert Garwood,* the first substantial narrative that claims to tell the story from Bobby's point of view.[3]

The third timeline maps out Garwood's steady absorption into the POW/MIA conspiracy narratives. Although activists were understandably interested in him from the moment he reappeared, he publicly entered this realm in late 1984, when he announced that he had personally seen American POWs in Vietnam after Operation Homecoming. Tracing this chronology up to yesterday requires following Garwood into so many corners and onto so many public platforms that any coherent account is virtually impossible. But Monika Jensen-Stevenson's *Kiss the Boys Goodbye* (1990) and *Spite House* (1997), POW Frank Anton's memoir *Why Didn't You Get Me Out?* (1997), and Joe Schlatter's Internet postings on Garwood are clearly important, and so are a number of government and activist events.

Though these three timelines dovetail from 1979 on, when he came home, found out what people had been saying about him, started talking himself, and found new friends in the world of POW/MIA activists, I will discuss these narratives in the order they first occurred. Bobby Garwood will therefore begin as a text, become a voice, then turn into that chameleon-like figure who now haunts an ever-expanding oral history of war.

GARWOOD BEFORE GARWOOD — THE WHITE CONG

Second-hand information about Garwood started filtering back to military intelligence from the moment of his capture. First listed as an "unauthorized absence," his status was changed to "missing" on November 4, 1965. In December, soldiers found "Fellow Soldier's Appeal," a pamphlet signed by Garwood that urged U.S. troops to go home. He was then listed as "presumed captured." Over the next seven years, released South Vietnamese prisoners, paroled Americans, and finally the POWs returning during Operation Homecoming in 1973 all supplied first-hand information. Four books dealing with Garwood were published before he returned. Memoirs included *A Hero's Welcome* by POW James Daly (1975) and *We Came To Help* (1976), which tells the story of Monika Schwinn and Bernhard Diehl, two captured German nurses. The product of well over three hundred interviews, John G. Hubbell's *P.O.W.: A Definitive History of the American Prisoner-of-War Experience in Vietnam, 1964–1973* (1976), gives a detailed account of Garwood. Zalin Grant's *Survivors* (1975) is, however, the key text, because it records the shared experience of those POWs who knew Garwood in captivity.

As Winston Groom would note in his 1983 biography, though these stories came from "foot soldiers, a warrant officer, a doctor — from blacks, whites, from Hispanic soldiers," and even from two foreign nationals, all agreed that "Garwood had chosen to give his allegiance to the enemy, and in this he was alone, separate from other prisoners" (320). Debriefers started hearing this story in January 1968, when two paroled Marines, Luis Ortiz-Rivera and Jose Agosto-Santos, reported that Garwood had participated in a "liberation ceremony" in May 1967, but then refused to leave "for reasons of 'conscience,'" and "officially crossed over" to the enemy.[4] With a new Vietnamese name and a commission in the North Vietnamese Army, he was "'a POW now working with the VC'" (Schlatter, *Case* I).[5] Returning South Vietnamese prisoners confirmed this account in February 1968, and eighteen months later, additional paroled Americans described Garwood as wearing a Ho Chi Minh button, carrying an AK-47 rifle, and bragging about fighting beside the Viet Cong against American troops. These debriefings did not lead to a change in Garwood's status, but the Marine POW screening board recommended that if he ever returned, he should be read his rights under Article 31 of the Uniform Code of Military Justice (*Case* I). Given the circumstances, it is not surprising, then, that some officials were relieved when Garwood did not return during Operation Homecoming (Grant 154).

The published accounts were equally damning. Although Bernhard Diehl would not personally "condemn" Bobby, there was no doubt in Diehl's mind that Garwood was "a deserter." He carried a .45, "his bulging pockets were filled with everything from drugs to plastic explosives," and his "whole outfit bespoke the liberation fighter" (Schwinn 83–84). According to Hubbell's *P.O.W.*, "Big nice-looking, well-fed Bobby Garwood was hard to believe, but he was real, a living breathing traitor who had taken up arms on behalf of the enemy and had no compunctions about helping to hold American troops in vile captivity" (401). The POWs interviewed for Zalin Grant's *Survivors* agreed. Tom Davis "thought he was a mixed-up guy," but "had to accept him as a Vietcong" (115). Frank Anton called him a "rifle-toting turncoat," and ultimately so did author Grant, who titled one section of his group history "The American Vietcong."

While some POW witnesses at Garwood's court martial were telling their stories in public for the first time, others were on their third or fourth round. These proceedings produced sixteen volumes of records, including 3,833 pages of transcripts (*Case* IV). The testimony was devastating. Ortiz-Rivera described the liberation ceremony, and Garwood's refusal to leave. Frank Anton said that Garwood lived apart, had a weapon, acted as a guard, and carried a picture of Ho Chi Minh. The Bobby who helped three Vietnamese guards escort Gus Mehrer to the camp had a carbine and hand grenades. He later told Mehrer that he had broadcast anti-American propaganda, fought against U.S. forces, and "had some sort of intimate relationship with a Montagnard female." Even easygoing Ike McMillan said that Garwood "interrogated prisoners of war" and informed on the POWs to their captors (*Robert Garwood, POWs and the USG* 1). Given under oath over eleven months, all of this testimony led inevitably to Garwood's conviction for serving as a guard, interpreter, camp mole, and interrogator (*Case* IV).

This gathering of debriefings, interviews, testimonies, memoirs, and oral histories, offered by individuals who knew Garwood during a two-and-a-half year period of his thirteen-and-a-half year stay, and who assumed they would never see him again, is his first history. When Bobby did reappear, these witnesses repeated their stories in court. After all his appeals had been rejected, what remained, then, was the story of a convicted deserter and collaborator. This narrative's central premise — that Garwood crossed over — led investigators from the start to look for signs of the deserter. In 1969, the Marine Corps had the CIA conduct a graphological analysis of some captured documents. The report confirmed that the handwriting was Garwood's. It also claimed that the writer displayed the same "lack of emotional stability, low sense of responsibility and loyalty, and the need for security" that had been noted in his pre-capture personnel reports (*Case* I).

John F. Keener draws on Richard Hofstadter to identify such retroactive constructions as the lifeblood of human conspiracy — an account with "a 'distinctly personal' enemy and 'decisive events' which are 'the consequences of someone's will' " (304). Collaboration is the conspiracy here, and the "distinctly personal" enemy is Garwood himself. The interpreter simply demonstrates how the "decisive events" — the rejected liberation ceremony, Garwood's actions toward the POWs — are "the consequences" of his will. His court martial and all the courts of appeal decided they were. End of story. Guilty.

But imagine for a moment what would happen if Lee Harvey Oswald suddenly came back from the dead today, and offered to explain what *really* happened in Dallas. And now assume that he had a reputation for lying about himself, that his own fate would depend on the kind of story he told, and perhaps most importantly, that he was familiar with everything written or filmed about the Kennedy assassination since November 22, 1963. This basically was Garwood's situation when he began to tell his own story.

GARWOOD ON GARWOOD

When Bobby Garwood stepped back into the narrative in 1979, circumstances kept him from supplying his own version. His first problems were legal, although even before he left Hanoi, people he had never met began protecting his interests. Dermot G. Foley, an attorney with ties to the National League of Families, a POW/MIA organization, told the Marines that there should "be no discussion whatever with him (PFC Garwood) respecting his experiences or his conduct in Vietnam until or unless he has had an opportunity to meet and fully consult with his family and me" (*Case* III). Ironically enough in retrospect, Bobby's four hours of initial debriefing were therefore restricted to questions about other possible live POWs. (He said he hadn't seen any.)

For the next two years Garwood remained silent, as his attorneys and then his authorized biographers presented a story of his captivity that refuted those versions presented at his court martial or already in print. In a pattern that will recur endlessly, then, anyone telling the Garwood story, including Bobby himself, has to deny or explain away the damning details already circulating. Presented at his court martial, the first such revision argued that psychological and physiological problems caused his observed behavior in captivity. As Winston Groom describes it, the lawyers tried "to present Garwood as a lifelong survivor from a deprived background, imprisoned longer than any other U.S. solider, a man who had simply done what he had to stay alive; and to intensify the evidence about Garwood's headaches and head injuries" (351).

But even while being prosecuted, Garwood was preparing to break his own silence. Within months of his return, he had hired a literary agent, signed a book contract with Putnam's, and begun "long, secret sessions with the tape recorder" and Winston Groom, his assigned biographer (9–10). In a foreshadowing of things to come, however, when Groom drew on these sessions to rough out the draft for a *Playboy* interview, Garwood's legal team decided that even the existence of the tapes threatened their case. He was therefore instructed to write a letter that claimed he was drunk during the tapings, which he had considered only "bull sessions" anyway. When the court martial began, all such sessions stopped. The *Playboy* interview appeared only in July 1981, after his conviction. The full-length biography, *Conversations with the Enemy: The Story of PFC Robert Garwood,* was released in 1983.

Groom and Garwood jointly held the copyright: in addition to refuting charges of collaboration, and his lawyers' and psychiatrists' claims of mental incompetence, the book was also supposed to make Bobby some money. Though his sentence had been quite lenient — a dishonorable discharge, basically — he lost some $150,000 in back pay. In the introduction, Groom claims that despite the delays, disagreements, and "obscure, bitter, and self-serving" nature of many participants' recollections, Bobby's personal involvement in the project ensures "that this telling is as close to the truth of the Garwood matter as it is humanly possible to get" (10–11). "And so what is Garwood?" Groom asks, "A traitor? A patriot? A hero? Or simply an unfortunate, trying to make the best of a horrible and impossible situation?" Though the "only thing for certain is that Bobby Garwood was a survivor," Groom's thesis is actually quite simple (394). Bobby was not mentally ill, but his childhood, military experience, and early captivity can account for what his fellow POWs saw between 1967 and 1969, and his treatment over the following ten years accounts for his behavior when he came home. Garwood is therefore the product and the victim of his environment and global politics. To know his past is to understand him, and ultimately to forgive him.

Groom presents Garwood's Indiana childhood as something worthy of Faulkner or Flannery O'Connor: "A roustabout father, a strict grandmother, a crippled Uncle Buddy suffering 'from some sort of dimly understood palsy,' and a 300-pound stepmother who seemed 'to be literally drowning in excess weight' were the important people in Garwood's life. His mother had fled" (Howes 222).[6] This background explains why Bobby has always coped by letting others control him — "his father, his stepmother, his grandmother, the juvenile court, the Marine Corps, the Vietnamese, or most recently his squadron of lawyers" (Groom 66). As a result, the life of this "innocent, yearning to be free," follows the course of a billiard ball. He becomes a Marine to escape his family and a juvenile detention home. He is captured, supposedly after a firefight, when he gets lost after being ordered to pick up a Marine officer near Da Nang. His interrogator's lessons on the politics of the war baffle Bobby, and being forced to witness a session of Russian roulette straight out of *The Deer Hunter* between two condemned South Vietnamese POWs terrifies him. In response, Garwood vows to "live through every day simply to get to the next in the faith that some day the war would end, and there would be no more reason to keep him" (61).

This strategy of "go along to get along" received welcome, but eventually disastrous support from Army Captain William F. "Ike" Eisenbraun, the first

American POW Bobby met. Although Ortiz-Rivera and Augosto-Santos had some brief contact with Ike before his death, and other U.S. prisoners heard about him from POW Edwin "Russ" Grissett, who would also die in captivity, no one who returned had really known Eisenbraun. Beginning with Groom's version, virtually all sympathetic accounts therefore portrayed Ike as a mentor whose lessons unintentionally created most of Garwood's later problems. Ike taught him how to survive in the jungle, and Bobby was a good student. Ike said Bobby should learn Vietnamese, so he did. And Ike ordered Bobby to "do whatever the VC tells us to do. Don't piss them off" (82). So both men wrote antiwar statements to get their names out, and sought parole through good behavior. Thus Eisenbraun was not just Bobby's "comrade in arms, friend, leader, officer in charge, almost a father, almost the father he never had," but also his alibi (87). Garwood's language and jungle skills, and his apparent friendliness with his captors, can now be seen as evidence that he had followed his commanding officer's orders.

Before he died, Eisenbraun ruefully but accurately predicted that the other Americans would misinterpret Garwood. " 'We got eyes,' " one POW said. When people start dying, " 'you're eating at the guards' kitchen, and you don't see none of the guards starvin' to death' " (188–89). Garwood was silent, but he knew the real story. His captors now kept him separate most of the time — hence his apparent freedom to come and go at will — to discredit him with the other POWs. His supposed privileges, his new Vietnamese name, and those forced duties that made it seem like guarding or interrogating have the same purpose. As for his good health, it was due to Eisenbraun's lessons on how to eat "insects and wild herbs and roots," and his own talent for catching rats (187–88). But this adaptability, the key to his survival, proved to be his most damning crime. " 'You been here so long you've turned into a gook,' " POW Dennis Hammond, who did not survive, supposedly told him, " 'You don't sit, you squat, you chew that red shit, you dress, eat, walk, carry things like one of them' " (178). Anticipating this reaction, Eisenbraun told Garwood that " 'You gotta try to find ways to help the others, Bob,' " but warned that he couldn't let them drag him down to their level of weakness (153–54). Whatever his intentions, though, Bobby did realize that as a "white Caucasian, AK strapped to his back, black pajamas, sandals, beard," he did appear to be "the worst of a hippy, a grunt, and a gook, all rolled up in one' " (178).

Offered at a time when military debriefings, publications, and a court martial had already declared him a collaborator, this is Garwood's defense — and given the undeniable horrors of captivity, it's a pretty plausible explanation. What must be remembered, however, is that Garwood and Groom had the prosecution's case in their hands. As a result, Bobby's defense is almost too complete: " 'The Vietnamese forced me to,' he seems to say, 'and Eisenbraun, my senior officer, ordered me to. But actually I didn't do anything at all, many other POWs did the same or worse, and anyway, I was only trying to help!' " (Howes 227) The biography's proportions suggest that it is above all responding to specific charges. Of its 411 pages, 170 describe Garwood's life before he met the first POW who testified against him. Sixty-five cover his two-and-a-half years of contact with surviving POWs. Forty more deal with the court martial. Less than eighty pages, therefore, retell his experiences from 1969 to 1979 — by far the longest phase of Bobby's captivity, and what Groom significantly calls the "The Lost Years." And a further note: although Garwood recalls hearing rumors about French POWs working "over the hill," *Conversations with the Enemy* does not mention any other American POWs in Vietnam after 1973.

In response to other versions of the story, an oral history — the archive of Garwood interviews that Groom held over four years — has therefore been shaped into a highly focused, polemical history. The argument finally rests on the issue of character. The Garwood emerging from his authorized biography is no traitor, but a passive, not especially bright, young man who adapts to his surroundings by following the path of least resistance. His occasional successes lead others to mistake his naïveté for calculation, and his good nature for a cunning mask. In a world of corruption and selfishness, though, Garwood is actually more human — more ethical, even — than most, if not all of the more sophisticated individuals he encounters. In short, Bobby Garwood is a real-life Forrest Gump — an apt comparison, I think, since Winston Groom wrote the novel by that name three years after the publication of *Conversations with the Enemy*.

Let's retrace for a moment the two narrative lines I've followed so far. Garwood's "guilt" surfaced in debriefings and classified reports, and became public knowledge through books and articles drawing heavily on interviews with POWs who knew him in captivity. When he reappeared in 1979, these POWs were reunited with him at his court martial, and they testified so compellingly that he was convicted. Though their stories were biased — polished to reflect the tellers' sense of their own lives — these POWs essentially agreed with each other, thus confirming our notions of how group oral history grants us both diversity and a sense of shared experience.

As the defendant in a legal proceeding, however, Garwood had the right to see things differently. He could not be required to incriminate himself, and presenting a narrative of his life that supports his claims of innocence was not just a legitimate, but an expected courtroom practice. Written with professional help, *Conversations with the Enemy* then carried his defense beyond the courtroom. This rationale for personal revelation would pervade Gar-

wood's activities for the next fifteen years. As long as he felt under legal
attack, he understandably left out self-incriminating evidence.[7] As new stories appeared, he revised his own story to accommodate or refute them. (The
post-Watergate publishing career of Richard Nixon comes to mind.) But
another factor was at work as well. By 1984, Garwood's financial and legal
troubles were moving him toward that "collision point" between biography
and conspiracy. Though *Conversations with the Enemy* was in print, there's
no evidence that it made enough money to compensate for his loss of back
pay. Since he had appealed his conviction, he had not been officially debriefed
either. (Not surprisingly, he insisted on immunity from further prosecution
before he would answer questions.) Garwood therefore was broke, with his
military pay and benefits probably tied up in court for years.

At this point, he changed his story.

CONSUMED IN CONSPIRACY:
GARWOOD AS EMPTY CENTER

By the end of 1983, Garwood's accusers had spoken, his judges had convicted him, and with the help of Winston Groom, he had defended himself in
print. From that moment in 1979 when Garwood smuggled out his wish to
come home, however, his story had been tied to another history. Over the
years, and often with Garwood's assistance, his personal experience had been
absorbed into a narrative that represented him as a witness, a scapegoat, a
martyred hero, and ultimately a key for unlocking an American conspiracy in
Southeast Asia that stretched even beyond the POW/MIA issue.

In a December 1984 *Wall Street Journal* interview, Robert Garwood ful-
filled the POW/MIA community's wildest dreams by announcing that he
had seen scores of American captives in Vietnam *after* Operation Homecoming — twenty in mid-1973, thirty to forty in 1977, and as many as sixty in
1978. Interviewer Bill Paul noted that Garwood had not testified during his
court martial, and had not mentioned these sightings to the government or to
his authorized biographer. Why, then, was he speaking now? To "clear his
conscience" (1). Even before his release, Garwood knew that news about
other POWs would be the most valuable thing he could bring home. When he
first managed to contact a Finnish national who was visiting Hanoi, the man
immediately asked, "How many others are there, like you too?" "Fifteen
others" was the reply, although Groom immediately adds that Garwood
hoped "this lie would be believed, would make it more than just a single man's
message on a torn bit of paper" (301). In 1984, however, Garwood announced that the lie was a lie, and while this might seem to have been a way to
shift attention from whether he collaborated to whether he had seen live

American POWs, for the POW/MIA activist community these two issues are inseparable. For *if* the government had conspired to keep Americans from learning about live POWs still in Vietnam, and *if* Bobby Garwood, by playing chameleon, had survived his captivity with honor, *then* his 1979 return would have exposed the government's plot, *unless* he could be branded a traitor, and therefore not a returning POW at all. And that's *just* what happened![8]

The report on Robert Garwood that was prepared for the Assistant Secretary of Defense for Command, Control, Communication and Intelligence (ASD/C3I) in 1993 maps out how Bobby's 1984 claims paralleled his continued refusal to be debriefed by the Defense Intelligence Agency (DIA). Apart from those short, subject-restricted interviews held immediately after his return, Garwood was not officially debriefed for over six years. He first requested immunity from prosecution for his conduct in Vietnam, and later requested an overturning of his conviction. The government refused, so he stayed away. When the *Wall Street Journal* interview appeared, then, even though the DIA suspected that loss of back pay might have led Garwood to "exploit the news value of his information and thus avail himself of commercial opportunities," the agency could not ask him for more details about locations (*Case* IV). By 1985, this pattern was set. Garwood was talking to the media, to paying audiences, and even to legislative sub-committees about live sightings, but turning down government agency requests for a formal debriefing. No amnesty, no details.

Only after all his appeals had failed and he had left the military did Garwood finally talk to the DIA — though still with some restrictions. The session could last no longer than four hours. All questions had to be in writing; there would be no follow-up questioning. When, however, the DIA produced thirty-two pages of questions at the February 26, 1986 meeting, further sessions seemed necessary. At this point Garwood became personally unavailable until September 1987. A June 1987 memo suggests that some people at the DIA found this turn of events frustrating: " 'We are not interested in speaking with his attorney, his various go-betweens, his friends or in reading his newspaper clippings. We want to interview him.' " In the interval, Garwood was independently debriefed by Lieutenant General Eugene Tighe, USAF (Ret), a former DIA Director who had resigned over what he felt was the government's lack of interest in live POWs. He and a polygraph test administrator " 'felt that Garwood was truthful' " (*Case* V).[9] Meanwhile, both Ross Perot and Congressman Bob Smith continued to mediate between Garwood and the DIA. Formal debriefing sessions, with Smith in attendance, finally took place September 17–20, 1987, and February 20–27, 1988.

Though Garwood was debriefed for over one hundred hours, the DIA did not feel the results were worth the wait or the time expended. He displayed "extreme difficulty in remembering the information." His narrative shifted, contradicted itself, and petered out, which he attributed to three causes: "1) he had undergone brain washing by machine in Vietnam; 2) he suffers from survivor's guilt and post traumatic stress; and 3) dredging up the material from memory leads him into fugues, thus necessitating long breaks between sessions" (*Case* V).[10] The DIA met with Garwood one last time in November 1990 to go over again his live-sightings claims. In 1991, the Assistant Secretary of Defense for Command, Communication, and Intelligence commissioned a separate investigation, which included a May 1992 fact-finding trip to Hanoi. The fullest government account of the Garwood case to date, this ASD/C3I report, appeared in June of 1993.

Long before then, however, Garwood's story had spun out into a myriad of conflicting revisions. Although POW/MIA activists had always considered him a key figure, the book that placed him in the forefront of the movement was *Kiss the Boys Goodbye: How the United States Betrayed Its Own POWs in Vietnam (1990)*. Considered the " 'Bible' of the POW/MIA issue" by some, and "nonsense" by others,[11] this book was co-written by Monika Jensen-Stevenson and her husband William Stevenson, best known as the author *of A Man Called Intrepid* and *Ninety Minutes at Entebbe*.[12] Its 492 pages gather together the stories of prominent conspiracy theory activists — Scott Barnes, Bo Gritz, Ross Perot, and ex-POW Eugene "Red" McDaniel to name a few. The impetus for Monika Jensen-Stevenson's quest to learn the sordid truths about the POW/MIA issue, however, was Bobby Garwood. She met him in 1985, at a press conference where he reaffirmed his *Wall Street Journal* claims about live POWs. A producer for *60 Minutes* at the time, she thought he was a promising subject. Her summary of his fortunes to this point stressed how ruthlessly the Marine prosecutors pursued him at his court martial, and how he had "seemed to be in a daze, totally under the control of his lawyers." Though the POW issue never came up in court, Jensen-Stevenson also notes that Garwood's "conviction certainly made it easier to brand him a liar when he claimed he had seen large numbers of American prisoners still alive" (21, 22). As she encountered the activists, and became convinced of a government conspiracy, Bobby remained Jensen-Stevenson's focal point — the constant victim, the constant scapegoat. "The truth about Garwood was simple and clear," she declares:

> There was nothing faintly evil in his background. But his own side had created myths that fed their own suspicions. He had come back from the dead, a challenge to the policy that — for whatever reasons of political expediency, bureaucratic mindset, well-meaning efforts to preserve the morale of the armed forces, commercial gain, or inverted intelligence logic — required that none survive. (386)

Given this atmosphere, Garwood's efforts to tell Americans about live POWs were heroic, and his willingness to appear before a closed session of the House Subcommittee on Asian and Pacific Affairs in March 1985, and to be privately debriefed by General Tighe in April 1987, were the mark of a patriot.[13]

As the first major trade publication claiming that Garwood's court martial and conviction were directly related to his claims about live POWs, *Kiss the Boys Goodbye* is a landmark in POW/MIA conspiracy literature. Its authority rests on Jensen-Stevenson's claims of access. She interviewed Garwood extensively, and she also drew on transcripts of General Tighe's debriefing, as well as notes from interviews with other sources. This cache became her weapon for attacking the public records—government documents, court martial testimony, the accounts of other POWs—as flawed, evasive, or false. The book's narrative strategy is also highly significant. As Jensen-Stevenson tells the story of her journey into the realm of conspiracy, apparently offhand information, gleaned through rumor or hurried interview, returns ominously pages later as fact confirmed by further research or interviews. Stray comments, dark personal revelations, or unpublished manuscripts in her files thus become the spur for extensive sleuthing, detailed source documentation, and seemingly encyclopedic erudition. As the story of Garwood's captivity becomes indistinguishable from the live POW issue, this mystery or detective-story quality becomes increasingly common in Vietnam conspiracy literature. There's a plot afoot, and Bobby Garwood is the key to finding the villains.

ANTI-CONSPIRATORS AND NEW CONSPIRACIES

It was perhaps inevitable that the POW/MIA activists would themselves be accused of conspiracy. The most famous attack is H. Bruce Franklin's *M.I.A. or Mythmaking in America* (1992), a study of how America's obsession with MIAs and POWs has been exploited by the media, the entertainment industries, and the government, which for more than twenty years has poured its resources into preserving the MIA issue as the lynch pin of its Vietnam foreign policy. Garwood is not a major figure in *M.I.A.*, but his presence is important. Not only does Franklin report that many post-1973 live POW sightings were actually of Garwood, but also that Bobby, a man "convicted of collaborating with the enemy," is famous for telling people "whatever they wanted to hear" (24, 116). *M.I.A.*'s conclusion is succinct and damning: "Those who offer Robert Garwood's stories as proof that Vietnam has been keeping American POWs actually demonstrate the opposite" (116–17).

Though less well known outside of the conspiracy community, Susan

Katz Keating's *Prisoners of Hope: Exploiting the POW/MIA Myth in America* (1994) has actually been far more contentious. In structure and tone, this book is quite similar to *Kiss the Boys Goodbye*. Keating also came to the MIA story in 1985, when stories she wrote as a reporter for the *Washington Times* made her "certain that live American POWs remained against their will in Vietnam." Truly "obsessed," through her articles Keating became a major advocate for government accountability and response. As she learned more about the POW/MIA movement, however, a "curious phenomenon" about its layered, contradictory, and ultimately "deceptive" conspiracy narrative became impossible to ignore: "once you scratch the surface, you are convinced that POWs exist; but after you really dig, you discover the truth as put forth in this book" (vii).

Telling her truth leads Keating to dismiss the movement's most famous witness curtly. The "most notorious defector of the Vietnam War," Bobby Garwood was captured in 1965 and "released from captivity in 1967." But he "decided to join his captors," and fought alongside them. Keating suggests that he returned from Vietnam because it "was about to go to war with China, and he didn't want to fight." After being convicted for assault and collaboration, Garwood has spent years trying "to clear his name through various projects designed to show him in a sympathetic light." Since he is "a genuine defector who knowingly harmed his fellow Americans," however, any of his claims about live POWs "must be viewed in light of his campaign to rehabilitate himself" (70–71). Keating's Bobby Garwood is therefore Jensen-Stevenson's in reverse. Each detail is offered to destroy his credibility. Marines who knew him before he disappeared said he was " 'a liar, a thief, and totally untrustworthy' " — " 'a pretty sleazy character,' " in short — who was more than likely captured while on unauthorized leave with a Vietnamese girl-friend. Keating describes a 1968 battle encounter, when Garwood supposedly fired on American servicemen. She also reports that the other POWs called him " 'the Traitor' or 'the Snake' or 'the Son of a Bitch' " (74, 76).

Garwood's court martial, according to Keating, ironically granted him "an expected bonus, a public relations benefit so lucrative he abandoned the mental illness claim and instead took up the mantle of a mysterious, all-knowing intelligence operative." The reason for this change should by now be familiar:

> The key to Garwood's new persona was the rapidly spreading POW/MIA movement. The activists were enamored of Garwood. They saw in him living proof that the United States had lied when it said that no Americans had remained in Vietnam after Operation Homecoming. If Garwood had been kept behind, the activists reasoned, so, too, had other Americans. The activists threw in a conspiracy angle to explain why the Marine Corps had

> prosecuted Garwood so vigorously. The activists said that Garwood had in-
> conveniently returned from the dead, thus proving the government's duplic-
> ity. (78–79)

This scenario produced "a perfect partnership." In return for financial support, Garwood "gave the MIA issue a whole new urgency." All he had to
do "was continue to maintain his innocence — and talk about POWs" (79).
Keating's status as a defector from the POW/MIA movement often leads her
to make claims as overblown as the conspiracy narratives she is undermining. Her charge that pure expediency explains Garwood's prominence within
the movement is nevertheless important, as it comes from someone who
formally helped to publicize the conspiracy version of his story.

But even as commentators denied Garwood's story, its contours were
changing. Formerly minor or unmentioned details in his narrative surged into
prominence as the POW/MIA debate shifted, or expanded in response to new
preoccupations. Garwood, for instance, became a link between the live POW
issue and Middle East terrorism. Jensen-Stevenson had been surprised when
Bobby "spoke Arabic" to a Moroccan waiter in 1985. He had learned it in
Vietnam in 1976, he said, from members of the Palestinian Liberation Organization (41–42). This detail dovetails with his *Wall Street Journal* claim that
the Vietnamese had kept POWs to use in audiovisual aids for training ter-
rorists — " 'to show that Americans are only human, that we do suffer duress
and stress' " (22). In 1991, Nigel Cawthorne claimed that Garwood had met
Mohammed "Abu" Abbas, the person held responsible for the *Achille Lauro*
hijacking. Poor Leon Klinghoffer, the wheelchair-bound Jewish American
passenger thrown overboard, was therefore "another victim of the murky
political underworld that seems to surround the American POWs still missing
in South-East Asia" (221). And in 1997, Jensen-Stevenson goes further, reporting that "Abu" told Garwood in Vietnam to keep his mouth shut about
meeting Palestinians. "There were over two hundred members of the PLO
living in the Indianapolis area," Abu said, and Bobby's family would pay for
any slip (*Spite House* 253).

These revelations appear in *Spite House: The Last Secret of the War in
Vietnam* (1997), Jensen-Stevenson's second book on Bobby Garwood. In
Kiss the Boys Goodbye (1990), she accused the government of knowing far
more than it pretended to about live American POWs. Garwood was again
her source. Officials involved in the General Tighe debriefing told him that
the military had enjoyed "precise intelligence" about "every camp and prisoner": "They showed me photographs of myself in some of the camps. They
told me things even I didn't know, about men like my black-market boss.
They said if I told this publicly, they'd deny it" (382). Now in *Spite House*,

she announces that Bobby Garwood was the intended victim of an elaborate covert operation, revealed only now because one of the agents wanted to clear *his* conscience. The goal had been Garwood's assassination, a charge which in itself was nothing new. In 1991, Nigel Cawthorne had quoted "Former Special Forces Officer Liam Atkins" as saying "that his Intelligence group were given a 'kill' order on Garwood" (152). *Spite House* is doubly revisionist, however, because it argues that an operative who believed the government and the military version now realized that Garwood was no traitor, but one of the few heroes of the Vietnam War.

Jensen-Stevenson's fame as the author of the *Kiss the Boys Goodbye* made *Spite House* possible. "I am Colonel Tom C. McKenney," a man says to her after she had spoken at a 1991 Vietnam Veterans Coalition meeting, "You must know how to reach Bobby Garwood. I directed an official mission to assassinate him behind enemy lines, because I believed what they told me. Would you tell him that I will crawl on my hands and knees to beg his forgiveness?" (5). Supposedly linked to U.S. teams that killed VC officials and other subversive elements, and to a "turncoat elimination program" that targeted roughly one hundred deserters deeply involved in the drug trade (55–56), McKenney's hunter–killer operation to kill Garwood, the infamous White Cong, "was so highly classified it was never put on paper" (42). McKenney himself was willing. A soldier of unmatched integrity, nothing revolted him more than this "Marine who turned on his own" (41). But the mission was never accomplished, and as McKenney became disillusioned with his government over the years, he realized with horror that he had misjudged Garwood. Once again, a reassessment of Garwood leads to the conclusion that the United States had abandoned POWs. According to McKenney, the military so hated deserters that it was killing Americans who collaborated. In Bobby Garwood's case, though, the "deserter" was actually still a prisoner! This conclusion turns McKenney's opinion on its head. Bobby is now "the only American who had beaten their system. Throughout his fourteen years as a prisoner Garwood had remained a good Marine in a way only real jarheads could understand" (359).

In keeping with this version, Jensen-Stevenson retells Garwood's story with all traces of guilt or weakness removed. A disciplinary action against a "simple private who was being punished for doing his job too well" delayed his arrival in Vietnam (23). He "went overboard on required assignments," she writes, actually referring to his "Forrest-Gump style" (19). Though she accuses Dermot Foley and Winston Groom of keeping the lid on Garwood's story because they wanted to control it themselves (290–91), she echoes Groom's explanations for Garwood's supposedly traitorous acts, and also accuses the POWs who claimed he had collaborated with doing the same thing (94). But Jensen-Stevenson separates herself from other accounts when live POWs are the issue. In *Kiss the Boys Goodbye,* the returning Garwood learns from the first officer he talks to that information about Americans still in captivity would not be welcome: "You want to get *killed*?" (41). In *Spite House,* however, the fact of live POWs is the necessary catalyst for McKenney's conversion, and Garwood's redemption.

BACKLASH AND THE NET

In 1997, Garwood's court martial was fifteen years in the past, and conspiracy-driven narratives took for granted that accounts by his fellow POWs, the government, the military, and critics of Garwood, including his authorized biographer, were all false, malicious, and driven by furtive agendas. Though Franklin and Keating both attacked these assumptions, even more publications and the emergence of the Internet raised the dispute to a whole new level. Take, for example, *Why Didn't You Get Me Out? Betrayal in the Viet Cong Death Camps — The Truth about Heroes, Traitors, and Those Left Behind* (1997). POW Frank Anton had told his story during his debriefings, in Zalin Grant's *Survivors,* and at Garwood's court martial. As his book's title suggests, however, Anton now joins many conspiracy writers in claiming that U.S. authorities had known where he was, but left him there to die. And yet, this belief has no effect on his certainty that he suffered more as a POW from being haunted by the "specter of betrayal," in the person of Bobby Garwood, "an American crossover" who proved "so dispiriting," and who so "disgusted and angered" Anton that his own physical deterioration accelerated (x). As an "interpreter, spy, guard, and informant," Garwood was guilty of a "barbarity" that was "a form of torture all by itself" (44, 46). He hit one POW, denounced another until his spirit broke, and showed a third the bullhorn he used to exhort U.S. soldiers to put down their weapons. So intense was the POWs' hatred that one man's dying words were " 'Make sure you get Garwood' " (102). Anton talked at length about Bobby during his debriefing, and agreed to testify against him should he ever reappear (153). Anton did not consider Garwood a traitor — someone who "sells out his country" because he believes in the other side's cause — but rather a "crossover, someone who sells out his fellow prisoners" (174). Three points, however, are for Anton unquestionable. First, Garwood behaved dishonorably as a captive. Second, what he did was markedly different from the other POWs. And third, his claims about live POWs should be examined under the light shed by his fellow captives. Just as "Much of what Garwood said while I knew him in the jungle was not true," his revelations about Americans left behind, while they "should not be summarily dismissed," are probably not "the most reliable indicator of what the truth may be" (188).

Though new books have continued to appear, the Garwood debate rages most heatedly these days on the Internet, where the most active critics and proponents of conspiracy narratives tend to thrive. The chief debunker is retired Army Colonel Joe Schlatter, whose *MIA Facts Site* is the switching station for a massive, expanding, and continually updated library of web-sites. His credentials are listed up front. A career military man and a Viet-nam veteran, he served in the Defense Intelligence Agency Special Office for POW-MIA Affairs—as head of the Analysis Branch, then as Chief of the Office—from February 1986 to July 1990, and also as the Deputy Director, Defense POW-MIA Office from July 1993 to April of 1995. An amateur radio operator, participant in a volunteer Christian ministry in Appalachia, and "Yellow-dog" Democrat, Schlatter finds conspiracy theory interesting in itself as a social phenomenon. He maintains a link site for what he calls *Wackiness on the Web,* and another one for hate groups as well (Dad's Home Page). As a link within the Vietnam Veterans Webring, his site can also serve as a point of departure for visiting virtually everyone in the POW/MIA debate, including those who denounce Schlatter as a traitor, and for finding additional evidence of a government conspiracy.

Schlatter states his beliefs about the POW/MIA activists bluntly. Although conspiracy advocates have constructed a "vast mythology," built on "mis-information," "pseudo-history," and "deliberate fabrication" about "2,583 Americans" who did not return from Vietnam, Schlatter begs to differ:

> ×All U.S. POWs captured during the Vietnam War were released, either at Operation Homecoming (spring, 1973) or earlier.
> ×No U.S. prisoners of war have been abandoned by the U.S. government.
> ×No U.S POWs remained in captivity after the conclusion of Operation Homecoming.
> ×There is no conspiracy within the U.S. government to conceal the abandon-ment of prisoners of war (who were not abandoned in the first place).
> ×No U.S. POWs from Indochina were taken to the Soviet Union, China, or any other third country [*sic*]. (*MIA Facts*)

Given these principles, it is not surprising that materials about Bobby Gar-wood make up a sizable portion of Schlatter's archive. His six-part reproduc-tion of the June 1993 ASDC3I report, including his own clearly marked running commentary, prints up to sixty-five single-spaced pages (*Case*), and new Garwood claims result in new Web pages or updates.

Schlatter pays close attention to the actions of government officials and lobbyists, and to the gatherings and publications of POW/MIA activists.

Like Keating and Franklin, he notes how legislators and ex-legislators who have claimed the POW/MIA issue as their personal cause often use Garwood to stir things up. The massive MIA recovery programs, and Select Committee after Select Committee established to review once more the many claims concerning live POWs, are some of their most impressive results. Though these activities, and the documentation they generate, are almost too extensive to describe succinctly, it can be said that Bobby Garwood's fortunes have been closely linked to such government players and lobbyists as Billy Hendon, Bob Smith, and Ross Perot, to mention only the most notable. Schlatter has little respect for Garwood, but he has even less for these figures. (A sample Web page title: *Former Congressman Billy Hendon: Mendacity Without Shame*.) In fact, Schlatter argues that Garwood is largely the lobbyists' creation. The Web page *The Hendon Connection: My Very Own Conspiracy Theory* links changes in Garwood's claims about live POWs to his contacts with Billy Hendon, and then-Congressman Bob Smith. As time passes, Garwood's memories increasingly conform to live POW stories that were circulating before his release. Schlatter's conclusion? "Frankly, I suspect that Hendon coached Garwood and it was Hendon who led Garwood to fabricate his bogus claims of having seen US POWs in Vietnam after 1973." Schlatter is also scathing about Garwood's return to Vietnam in 1993 — yes, he went back. In the company of Senator Smith and an ABC *20/20* crew, Garwood identified some buildings as the "island fortress" where he had supposedly seen a score of live American POWs in 1977. Unfortunately, 1977 satellite imagery reveals that these structures had not been erected yet. And in any case, Hendon had apparently been there several days before, scouting out locations (*The "Island Fortress"*).

"So, What's Wrong With All This?" Schlatter asks. He replies that Hendon's morally "bankrupt" activities must be exposed because (1) he has perpetuated the fiction that DIA analysts only want to debunk sources; (2) he has given phony information to families, thus sustaining impossible hopes; and (3) he has been behind Senator Bob Smith's efforts to keep the government forever entangled in POW/MIA conspiracies (*Former*). Though Schlatter has "no illusions" that his own "proposal will be adopted in part or in whole," and he also knows that it "will upset many and positively anger some, including old friends," his own suggestions are brief but sweeping:

No More Inquiries[14]
[Stop all official and unofficial investigations.]
Get Real With the Numbers
[List the MIA counts in ways reflecting the real chances that men have
     survived.]
State that They Are All Dead

Stop the Extraordinary Observances
[Flags, POW Recognition Day, and so on.]
Publicize What Is Being Done
[Tell Americans what recovery teams are actually doing.]
Terminate "COIN ASSIST"
[End a government program that provides free travel and support for
    Vietnam MIA families to attend annual briefings.]
Take a Bold Step
[Do everything recommended above.]

These guidelines would allow the repatriation of remains to continue, but
would prevent them from being continually turned into "objects of myth-
makers and charlatans" (*A Proposal*).

Adopting such recommendations would, of course, also make it official
U.S. policy to ignore Bobby Garwood. Schlatter's response to *Spite House*
can stand as representative of his extensive and detailed remarks on Garwood, because it brings together almost the entire cast for my discussion of
how Bobby's history has emerged. On a 1998 Web page called *Attack of the
Primitives,* Schlatter warns about a major attempt to overturn Garwood's
conviction, and to discredit those POWs who testified against him or condemned him in print. Familiar names pepper Schlatter's account:

Ross Perot has hired an individual to "look into" Garwood's conviction. My
concern — and this should be the concern of every other veteran who served
honorably in Vietnam — is that with Perot's money and connections, with
Senator Bob Smith's position, and with former Congressman Billy Hendon's
scheming, enough noise will be made to generate sympathy for Garwood and
possibly have his case re-opened.

Jensen-Stevenson's *Spite House* is also seen as a major source of disinfor-
mation:

At no time in preparing the book did [she] interview other Americans who
were POWs and observed Garwood's collaboration. There is no indication
that she ever attempted to obtain the trial transcripts; never interviewed any
of the Marine prosecutors; never did anything but take Garwood and McKenney at their word.

Schlatter is especially annoyed that this camp is targeting POW Dr. F. Harold
Kushner, who testified against Garwood, and who replied to *Spite House*'s
portrait of him as an unethical collaborator with a lawsuit. After recom-
mending Grant's *Survivors* "for the facts about life in the camps where Garwood was collaborating," Schlatter suggests that Kushner should be believed
precisely because he "has not been one of those professional veterans or
professional victims that we are plagued with." Kushner "has not made
speeches or written a book about his experiences," but has instead "quietly

served in the Army, left the service, and has maintained a private practice, continuing the healing arts."

Then, in a move only possible on the Net, Schlatter posts an intercepted e-mail to a variety of POW/MIA people from Tom McKenney, who claims that Kushner's lawsuit has actually been orchestrated by the "Govt power structure (John McCain, John Kerry, Kissinger & Co—I name these, although the real power people are much bigger than these 3), to kill and discredit the truth told in 'Spite House.'" The fortunes of books and movies here become indistinguishable from the conspiracy movement. McKenney declares that this same power structure "murdered 'Kiss the Boys Goodbye,'" "killed the hardback" of *Spite House*, and "are now after the paperback," because "there is a major movie being made about Bobby and me," and "if they can discredit the book, it could kill the movie and keep this truth from the general public." (I suspect that this "major movie" is Oliver Stone's project, which I'll mention below.) What to do? "We need ammo," McKenney announces, and he asks his readers for "any ugly truth about Kushner and his numerous failures to live up to a soldier's code as a POW." Predictably, Schlatter's response is scathing:

> So there you have it folks. The heroes — Frank Anton, Hal Kushner — are now to be made the villains. McKenney's message is such crap. . . . Lies will become truth and these men, who wanted only to get on with their lives — and did [a] fine job of it — will be vilified, all in an attempt to wash clean Garwood's crimes against his country.

Jensen-Stevenson and the whole *Spite House* controversy were defused in late 1999, Schlatter later reports, when as part of a settlement with Dr. Harold Kushner, she and her publishers were forced to pay a cash settlement, and publicly admit that "Garwood was her sole source for the statements about Kushner and that those statements were false" (*Author Admits*). Despite this exposure, various media sources were reporting as late as mid-2001 that Oliver Stone was planning on making a movie out of *Spite House* ("Oliver Stone").

Schlatter has his own critics on the Net—notably Mark Smith, an ex-POW held from April 1972 until Operation Homecoming. Favorable accounts of his many POW/MIA activities appear in Cawthorne and Jensen-Stevenson. Keating is far less flattering; Smith in reply calls her one of the "Stupid writers of books" (*Historians Again*).[15] Smith declares that Bobby Garwood "has been maligned, verbally and mentally tortured by our Government. He has nothing. No medical care. No back pay. No Purple Heart for acknowledged wounds" (*Code*). Drawing on the entire Vietnam POW bibliography for support, as I have personal reason to know, Smith also attacks

POWs who have spoken or written negatively about Garwood: "Should one care to take the time and ignore 'pie in the sky' stereotypes of POWs, bounce off what Frank Anton says in his book against what he and others say in 'Voices of the Vietnam POWs.' (Craig Howes, Oxford University Press)" (*A Few Thoughts*). Their sites mutually linked, Schlatter and Smith joust away in cyberspace. In *MAJ Mark Smith's Claims,* Schlatter claims that reading Smith's e-mail and web postings led to "a lot of time ROTFLMAO (that stands for '*Rolling On The Floor Laughing My Ass Off*')." As for Smith, Schlatter's claim that no one was left behind leads to the remark that the "Colonel is either being less than truthful or he is incredibly gullible and stupid. I regret to say the former appears to be true" (*Critique*). But given Smith's reasons for believing that there could still be POWs in Vietnam, the latter seems to be true as well: "They were not about to beat to death all the POWs. THEY WERE TOO VALUABLE TO THEM!!!!! Anyone who didn't understand that, regardless of threats made by the enemy, was STUPID, STUPID, STUPID!!!" (*A Few Thoughts*). Most interesting for my purposes, however, are Smith's comments on the current POW debate. "So called 'historians' now ply their trade on the Internet," he writes online, crying out that "The historians and 'computer Rambos' be damned!" (*Historians Again*).

As more stories emerge about America's involvement in the Vietnam War, it is certain that the Garwood story will resurface with them. When CNN in mid-1998 reported, then swiftly retracted, that undercover units during the Vietnam War had used nerve gas to kill U.S. deserters in Laos, activists like Mark Smith immediately put two and two together: "Why can people find the use of gas and the killing of defectors, [*sic*] so believable and still cannot accept the allegations in 'Spite House' about Garwood being targeted?" (*Government*). And ever outward the Garwood story expands, merging with theories and agendas beyond any imagination but a conspiratorial one. Clustered with comments on Leonard Peltier, Waco, Ruby Ridge, Jewish Racism, and White Cowardice, a summary of *Spite House* at redmonkee.com stresses how "white blue collar workers" hounded Garwood's sister, "a small white girl," out of her job, but that Jensen-Stevenson, a "Canadian white girl," had told this story to the world (*Story*). In a guest book posting to Joe Schlatter's home page, Jason A. Kaatz completes the symmetry of the story by reporting that Garwood "is alleged to have eaten in a Washington Restaurant were [*sic*] he had contact with a waiter who just may have been in North Vietnam with him." Calling Bobby "a case for the Counterintelligence guys," Kaatz believes "that at some future date they will bag his b——t and put him in jail for espionage." After twenty years of people insisting that Garwood never crossed over, it seems only fitting that someone would finally suggest that he never crossed back. A Canadian POW/MIA Information Center website called *Bobby Garwood,* however, contains perhaps the most inaccurate statement about his story ever. After asking "Were the other American POWs he saw executed in Hanoi?" the posting ends by declaring that "Nobody's talking!"

What are the implications of the thirty-year Garwood phenomenon for our understanding of how we might know, and will know, one of the most charged legacies of the Vietnam War?

I. PROXIMITY TO THE STORY IS A MIXED BLESSING

A basic premise of conspiratorial reading is that the people who participated in the events at issue will generate the most calculated, deceptive, and fantastic versions. Applying this premise, however, is necessarily a highly selective process. In the Garwood instance, his fellow POWs and his debriefers are the most untrustworthy sources for conspiracy activists, while for the debunkers the trickster figure is Bobby himself. So established, complex, and pervasive are the ideological filters for processing the Vietnam War's narratives that a source's direct involvement in the events can be the strongest or most damning support for his credibility.

II. NO VERSION OF THE STORY CAN EVER BE REFUTED OR REPLACED

This is a corollary of the first remark. If each individual history's relation to events is radically unstable, thanks to a heavily deterministic, conspiracy-tinged theory of knowledge, then no one can be trumped or exposed by anyone, including himself. The Garwood story can now only be endless talk, quotation, and testimony because the incredible outpouring of papers, reports, court martial transcripts, Web pages and the like make it impossible for any story to emerge other than as a pattern shaped by the felt contemporary needs of the investigators.

It is important to recognize, however, that holding onto exploded or denied stories is not simply delusional. Another legacy of the Vietnam era is the need to remember when a society has been tricked. "All previous statements are inoperative," Ron Nessen's notorious announcement about the Nixon White House's earlier public responses to Watergate, is famous precisely because it turned people's attention back to those statements as now-acknowledged lies told to the American people. Or to put this another way, after Nessen had spoken, we knew that even if the details never emerged, there had certainly been a conspiracy. Similarly, everything Bobby Garwood has said, or anything that anyone has ever said about him, lies in wait, always available to recalibrate or injure the newest story, regardless of what anyone, including Garwood, might say tomorrow.

III. TO TELL THE STORY IS TO BECOME THE STORY

An atmosphere of danger, high stakes, and uncertainty not only envelops Garwood, but also all who relate any portion of his story. As someone who has written about the Vietnam POWs, and Garwood in particular, my own relatively innocuous encounters with the conspiracy movement have at times been less than comfortable. When I first read *Kiss the Boys Goodbye,* I felt that Monika Jensen-Stevenson's accounts of being followed, of odd phone calls, of uneasiness at being home alone, were all rather melodramatic. In 1992, though, a friend's innocent remark to his cousin that I was writing a book about the POWs led to a rambling phone call that alluded to many of the conspiracy narratives I've mentioned. The anecdotes escalated in violence, ending with the news that the producer of "The Last POW? The Bobby Garwood Story," a forthcoming made-for-TV movie starring Ralph "Karate Kid" Macchio, eventually shown in 1993, had just been murdered gangland execution style with his son. (Around the same time, one of Susan Keating's sources sent her "a news clipping of the incident, across which he had scrawled 'Got his karma' " [71n.].) My call finished with a request for a copy of my manuscript, which would be passed on to unnamed others. After I hung up, I confess I did feel very much alone with my young son — ironically enough, my wife was in Vietnam excavating MIAs at the time.[16] The story has a sequel. Some weeks later, the caller came down the hallway of the English Department at my university and tried to give me a baggie containing what he claimed were MIA remains. I still receive from time to time long faxes, thick letters, and e-mails — some very welcome, some not — from players major and minor in the POW/MIA debate. Almost always, Bobby Garwood crops up somewhere.[17]

IV. THE STORY DOES NOT EXIST

Here is what I wrote sometime in 1992, at the end of the Garwood section in *Voices of the Vietnam POWs:* "Regardless of what may be discovered, though, I suspect Robert Garwood will have the last word" (230). I can't refute or replace the statement, so I will make another one. Regardless of what may be discovered, there will be no last word on Robert Garwood. The historian, the teller, can only listen — and then decide which voice, for the moment, must have it.[18]

NOTES

1. Garwood 71.

   2. Quoted in Keener 304.

   3. An interview with Garwood conducted and edited by Winston Groom appeared in *Playboy* in July 1981. Drawn from the same taped sessions that would

produce the eventual biography, this interview reveals that both the details and the organization were in place immediately after the court martial. In keeping with general practice, I will refer to the biography as Groom.

4. For a detailed account of the evidence against Garwood, including a reproduced copy of his release order, which he carried for the duration of his captivity, see "Prisoners of War, and Others," Chapter Ten of Solis, and in particular, the section called "White VC? Robert R. Garwood," 223–30. For a recent overview of his captivity, see Rochester and Kiley.

5. The cited source is a government document that Schlatter has posted with some comments of his own. Unless otherwise indicated, I am always quoting directly from the ASD/C3I report itself, which I will identify as *Case,* followed by a roman numeral for the section given by Schlatter.

6. The next few paragraphs draw on my discussion of Garwood in *Voices* 220–30. The quoted phrases in this passage are from Groom 65 and 67.

7. But see Scott Barnes's claim that in 1986 Garwood "admitted that he had collaborated": " 'I am not trying to make excuses for what I did,' he told me, 'but I was only a nineteen-year-old kid, tortured and starved, wanting to come home' " (211). Barnes's own value as a source is the subject of much debate. See Keating 150–54.

8. Here is how a U.S. Senate Committee on Foreign Relations Minority Staff Report put the same argument in 1991. Note how live sighting reports get woven into the fabric: "Garwood was a battle casualty taken into custody by the North Vietnamese under fire. However, his court martial as a collaborator and deserter solved two problems for DOD: By bringing up the charges DOD sought to redefine his case as a voluntary expatriate and therefore not technically a prisoner — and it enabled DOD evaluators to dismiss fully two hundred of the live-sighting reports" (U.S. Senate II).

9. The preceding quotations come from a variety of sources referred to in the June 1993 ASD/C3I Report. The quotation suggesting frustration is from the DIA Memo from Chief, Special Office for POW/MIAs, June 15, 1987. The quotation about Tighe and the polygraph expert comes from a DIA Memorandum for the Record of 16 April 1987.

10. The quotation comes from a DIA Memo for Chief, Special Office for POW/MIAs, August 1, 1988.

11. In his review of *Kiss* on the newsgroup alt.war.vietnam, Bob Destatte attributes the "Bible" reference to "another contributor." The word "nonsense" appears on Joe Schlatter's Web page *Kiss the Truth Good-bye,* which contains Destatte's review, and a critical note by Owen Lock, an editor at Ballantine Books, about the Stevensons.

12. Since William Stevenson's role seems to have been to provide Monika with moral support and suggestions for further research, and since *Spite House* is solely hers, I will follow the practice common in the POW/MIA community, and refer to *Kiss* as her book.

13. Given his refusal to cooperate with the DIA, this sub-committee appearance may seem odd. But the nature of the proceedings insured that the questions would be restricted to his claims about live sightings.

14. The numbered recommendations are Schlatter's; the square bracket explanations are mine.

15. Smith is mentioned throughout Cawthorne, and in both Jensen-Stevenson books. For Keating, see especially 158–75.

16. In the interests of full disclosure, I should indicate that my wife, Sara Collins, worked as a civilian scientist from 1987 to 1992 at the Central Identification Laboratory — Hawaii. Those familiar with POW/MIA conspiracy literature know that for at least some readers, I have just destroyed what little credibility I may have had, and made the motives for writing my book and this essay transparently clear.

17. My favorite correspondent was someone who suggested that the absence of my book from his local bookstore was probably the result of a plot to keep it out of the hands of the American people. This is the only claim emerging from the POW/MIA movement that I uncritically accept as true.

18. I wrote this last sentence on August 3, 1999. Earlier that morning, I checked Joe Schlatter's *MIA Facts* Site, and found a new Web page, posted on July 30, which responds to rumors that he is still on the Department of Defense payroll, and that his website is being ghost written by the Pentagon (*A Word*). And so it goes.

WORKS CITED

Anton, Frank, with Tommy Denton. *Why Didn't You Get Me Out? Betrayal in the Viet Cong Death Camps*. Arlington, Va: Summit Publishing Group, 1997.

Barnes, Scott, with Melva Libb. *Bohica*. Canton, Ohio: Bohica Corporation, 1987.

Bobby Garwood. Canadian POW/MIA Information Center. http://www.ipsystems.com/powmia/documents/Garwood.html (accessed September 21, 2003).

Cawthorne, Nigel. *The Bamboo Cage: The Full Story of the American Servicemen Still Held Hostage in South-East Asia*. London: Leo Cooper, 1991.

Daly, James A., and Lee Bergman. *A Hero's Welcome: The Conscience of Sergeant James Daly versus the United States Army*. Indianapolis: Bobbs-Merrill, 1975.

Franklin, H. Bruce. *M.I.A. or Mythmaking in America*. Expanded and Updated Edition. New Brunswick, N.J.: Rutgers University Press, 1993.

Garwood, Robert, and Winston Groom. "Playboy Interview: Robert Garwood." *Playboy*, July 1981.

Grant, Zalin. *Survivors*. New York: Norton, 1975.

Groom, Winston, and Duncan Spencer. *Conversations with the Enemy: The Story of PFC Robert Garwood*. New York: G. P. Putnam's Sons, 1983.

Hofstadter, Richard. *The Paranoid Style in American Politics and Other Essays*. New York: Knopf, 1965.

Howes, Craig. *Voices of the Vietnam POWs: Witnesses to Their Fight*. New York: Oxford University Press, 1993.

Hubbell, John G. *P.O.W.: A Definitive History of the American Prisoner-of-War Experience in Vietnam, 1964–1973*. New York: Reader's Digest Press, 1976.

Jensen-Stevenson, Monika, and William Stevenson. *Kiss the Boys Goodbye: How the United States Betrayed Its Own POWs in Vietnam*. Toronto: McClelland & Stewart, 1990.

———. *Spite House: The Last Secret of the War in Vietnam*. New York: Norton, 1997.

Keating, Susan Katz. *Prisoners of Hope: Exploiting the POW/MIA Myth in America*. New York: Random House, 1994.

Keener, John F. "Biography, Conspiracy, and the Oswald Enigma." *Biography: An Interdisciplinary Quarterly* 20 (1997): 302–30.

"Oliver Stone Enters *Spite House.*" Film Force. IGN.com. May 19, 2001. http://film force.ign.com/articles/200/200265p1.html (accessed September 21, 2003).

Paul, Bill. "Robert Garwood Says Vietnam Didn't Return Some American POWs." *Wall Street Journal.* December 12, 1984: 1, 22.

Pinsker, Sanford. "America's Conspiratorial Imagination." *Virginia Quarterly Review* 68 (1992): 605–25.

Robert Garwood, POWs and the USG. Posting from the witnesses' testimony at Garwood's court martial. Four sections. http://www.aiipowmia.com/sea/grwd1.html (accessed September 21, 2003). Sections 2–4 are grwd2.html, etc.

Rochester, Stuart I., and Frederick Kiley. *Honor Bound: The History of American Prisoners of War in Southeast Asia, 1961–1973.* Washington, D.C.: Historical Office: Office of the Secretary of Defense, 1998.

Schlatter, Joe. *Rewriting History: The Plan to Clear Garwood: An Assault on Those Who Served Honorably.* Sept. 21, 2003.http://www.miafacts.org/grwd_rehab.htm.

———. *Author Admits Garwood Was Sole Source of Stories. http://www.miafacts .org/author_statement.htm (accessed September 21, 2003).*

———. *The Case of Robert Garwood PFC, USMC.* Posting of the Assistant Secretary of Defense for Command, Control, Communication and Intelligence (ASD/C3I) report on Robert Garwood, published in June 1993. Six sections. http://www.miafacts.org/grwd_1.htm (accessed September 21, 2003). Sections II–VI are grwd_2.htm, etc.

———. *Former Congressman Billy Hendon: Mendacity Without Shame.* http://mia facts.org/hendon.htm (accessed September 21, 2003).

———. Hate group link page. http://www.schlatter.org/spotlight.htm (accessed August 1, 1999).

———. *The Hendon Connection: My Conspiracy Theory.* http://www.miafacts.org/ hendcnct.htm (accessed September 21, 2003).

———. Dad's Home Page. http://www.schlatter.org/Dad/dadshome.htm (accessed September 21, 2003).

———. *The "Island Fortress:" or, The Senator, The Collaborator, and Mendacity.* http://www.miafacts.org/islefort.htm (accessed September 21, 2003).

———. *Kiss the Truth Good-bye.* http://www.miafacts.org/bobkiss.html (accessed September 21, 2003).

———. *MIA Facts Site.* http://www.miafacts.org/ (accessed September 21, 2003).

———. *MAJ Mark Smith's Claims: Fairy Tales.* http://miafacts.org/mrksmith.htm (accessed September 21, 2003).

———. *A Proposal.* http://www.miafacts.org/propose.htm (accessed September 21, 2003).

———. *Wackiness on the Web.* 1 Aug. 1999. http://www.schlatter.org/news_ from_the_weird.htm (accessed August 1, 1999).

———. *A Word About Sources for the MIA Facts Site.* http://www.miafacts.org/ sources.htm (accessed September 21, 2003).

Schwinn, Monika, and Bernhard Diehl. *We Came To Help.* Trans. Jan van Heurck. New York: Harcourt Brace Jovanovich, 1976.

Smith, Mark A. *The Code and Bobby Garwood.* http://www.rossie.com/garwood .htm (accessed September 21, 2003).

————. *A Critique of Colonel Joe Schlatter's "MIA Facts Page."* http://www.ros
sie.com/schlatter.htm (accessed September 21, 2003).

————. *A Few Thoughts on Anton vs Garwood.* http://www.rossie.com/antonvs.htm
(accessed September 21, 2003).

————. *The Government Can't Find the Records?* http://www.rossie.com/records
.htm (accessed September 21, 2003).

————. *Historians Again.* http://www.rossie.com/historians.htm (accessed September 21, 2003).

————. *Zippo's Corner.* http://www.rossie.com/zips.htm (accessed September 21, 2003).

Solis, Colonel Gary D. *Marines and Military Law in Vietnam: Trial By Fire.* Washington: D.C.: History and Museums Division Headquarters, U.S. Marine Corps, 1989.

The Story of Marine Pvt Bobby Garwood . . . http://www.redmonkee.com/garwood
.html (accessed September 21, 2003).

U.S. Senate Committee on Foreign Relations Minority Staff. *An Examination of U.S. Policy toward POW/MIAs.* Thursday, May 23, 1991. Posted on the National Alliance of Families for the Return of America's Missing Servicemen. Many sections as posted. http://www.nationalalliance.org/ovrvw09.htm (accessed September 21, 2003).

6. Resolutely Other

The Vietnam War, Oral History, and the Subject of Revolutionary Socialism

THOMAS CARMICHAEL

In *A Bright Shining Lie: John Paul Vann and America in Vietnam*, Neil Sheehan quotes at length from a May 1965 letter written by John Vann to General Robert York, then commander of the 82nd Airborne Division at Fort Bragg.[1] Reflecting upon the political logic of the intensifying war and American involvement in it, Vann writes, "the principles, goals, and desires of the *other* side are much closer to what Americans believe in than those of the GVN [Government of Vietnam]" (Vann quoted in Sheehan 524). Vann then continues, "I am convinced that, even though the National Liberation Front is Communist-dominated, that [sic] the great majority of the people supporting it are doing so because it is their only hope to change and improve their living conditions . . . " (Vann quoted in Sheehan 524). The imperative of history is clear, as Vann puts it, "If I were a lad of eighteen faced with the same choice — whether to support the GVN or the NLF — and a member of a rural community, I would surely choose the NLF" (Vann quoted in Sheehan 524). Vann's remarks say much about the misdirection of American policy in Vietnam and about Vann himself, the themes of Neil Sheehan's great history, even though, as Sheehan points out, Vann's principled uneasiness never challenged his faith in the dominant Cold War logic that structured American commitment to the war (Sheehan 8, 43). Still, as John Vann admits, were he a rural Vietnamese "lad of eighteen," the choice would be clear, and that decision can be framed, as Vann insists, in terms of what "Americans believe" (Vann quoted in Sheehan 524). Not surprisingly, perhaps, what Vann does not consider is the possibility that the subject of the Vietnamese opposition is simply the subject of a vastly separate historical logic, constructed out of the modern Asian experience of anti-colonial struggle and nationalism, inflected by a Marxist understanding of class struggle and history — a subject for whom "what most Americans believe" might be simply irrelevant.[2] In not taking up this consideration, Vann's remarks are in one sense merely symptomatic of a specific historical moment; but they also represent and even anticipate the course of a cultural logic that will characterize most American and Western representations of the Vietnamese subject in opposition in what will come to be known as the literature of the Vietnam War.

In the United States and throughout much of the West, the literature of the Vietnam War has been, as one might expect, largely the record of an American war, in which the Vietnamese are figured inevitably as an other projection.[3] This is true of much popular historical discourse, for example, which has typically taken the form of personal accounts or oral histories that represent the private experiences of American combat personnel, engaged in complex negotiation of memory and trauma for an implied American audience.[4] And while more recent fiction, memoirs, and critical writing about the discourse on the war have encouraged Americans and those in the West to consider other perspectives (the success of Le Ly Hayslip's *When Heaven and Earth Changed Places* is perhaps the most conspicuous example), the interest in Vietnamese exile memoirs or exile fiction about the war has not typically extended to the subject of the now almost eclipsed world of revolutionary socialism.[5] But without a full accounting of that subject in opposition, discourse in the West about the war, particularly in English, must inevitably be haunted at some level by a phantasmagoric projection that in the last instance obscures historic actuality.[6] Moreover, this absence of the subject of revolutionary socialism from the Western discourse about the war also signals something about the contemporary cultural significance of the war itself, particularly if we understand that this absence is actively sustained and even encouraged, if only indirectly, by the transformations in the world system in the last three decades of the twentieth century. It is with this latter assertion that the present argument properly begins.

We should not fail to observe at the outset that the official end of American involvement in the Second Indochina War — marked by the signing of the Paris peace accords on January 27, 1973, and by the deactivation of MACV (Military Assistance Command Vietnam) on March 29, with the symbolic withdrawal of the last plane load of American troops the same day — occurs at the moment of a vast transformation in the economic and superstructural organization of the world system, or what we commonly know as the arrival of the global system of late capital and the cultural conditions of postmodernity.[7] As Fredric Jameson succinctly terms it:

> it is my sense that both levels in question, infrastructure and superstruc-
> tures — the economic system and the cultural 'structure of feeling' — somehow
> crystallized the great shock of the crises of 1973 (the oil crisis, the end of the
> international gold standard, for all intents and purposes the end of the great
> wave of 'wars of national liberation' and the beginning of the end of tradi-
> tional communism). (Jameson, *Postmodernism* xx)

It may seem odd that despite this assertion of a moment of rupture in 1973,
Jameson will argue specifically that Vietnam is to be read as "the first terrible
postmodernist war" and that Michael Herr's *Dispatches* in particular is to be
understood as a striking representation of the war's conspicuous and frenetic
postmodernity, one that will come to be seen as more widely proleptic in its
vivid accounts of the American subject's lived experience of the furiously
heightened "new machine" of an emergent social totality (Jameson, *Postmodernism* 44–45).[8] However, I believe that Jameson is right on both counts
here, and that the historical ironies that arise out of the coincidence of "the
end of the great wave of 'wars of national liberation' " with "the first terrible
postmodernist war" should not be lost on us, particularly as it shapes the
subsequent course of cultural representations of that war.

After all, it is surely one of contemporary history's more cunning ruses
that transforms an independent socialist Vietnam, seemingly from the moment of its triumph, into a struggling member of a shadow system that will
not survive the arrival of the very different world system of late capital in
the advanced industrial economies of Western Europe, North America, and
Japan.[9] But if we are to retrieve the Vietnamese subject in opposition from
behind this moment of transformation, we need also to recover something of
the systemic logic of that all-but-eclipsed form of social organization. Again,
a remark by Fredric Jameson might point us in the appropriate direction.
Taking his cue from the work of Immanuel Wallerstein, Jameson has observed with respect to the socialist economies of Eastern Europe and the
former Soviet Union that

> actually existing socialism was not and could never have been an alternative
> system, when at any given moment only one world system can hold sway;
> the various socialisms, rather, were antisystemic movements within the force
> field, of a capitalist world system itself; geared for one form of capitalism,
> they were largely undone by its unexpected mutation into a different moment,
> what we now call late capitalism, whose new laws and intensities peremp-
> torily disrupted structures built only to withstand the more primitive pressure
> of the older moment. (Jameson, *Seeds* 76)

In a specifically Asian context, Arif Dirlik, the American historian of Chinese
communism, makes much the same point when he observes that "socialist
societies as we have know them appear to have corresponded to one phase

within the history of capitalism" and that it is "probably not fortuitous that the emergence of socialism as an alternative to capitalism and the political establishment of socialist societies coincides with the second phase of capitalism, while the phase of flexible production has brought about their demise" (Dirlik 39, 41).

Rather than discounting the significance of Cold War conflicts, this nuanced reading of the dynamic of oppositionality in the world system after World War II allows for a more complex understanding of anti-systemic forces. Socialist economies were anti-systemic movements formed out of and in resistance to a dominant capitalist world system, and these anti-systemic movements took several forms, as Fredric Jameson himself insisted in the Preface to his volume, *Marxism and Form* (1971): "it is perfectly consistent with the spirit of Marxism . . . that there should exist several different Marxisms in the world of today, each answering the specific needs and problems of its own socio-economic system" (xviii). Jameson then went on to enumerate them: "one corresponds to the postrevolutionary industrial countries of the socialist bloc, another — a kind of peasant Marxism — to China and Cuba and the countries of the Third World, while yet another tries to deal theoretically with the unique questions raised by monopoly capitalism in the West" (Jameson, *Marxism* xviii). While Vietnamese socialism, according to Jameson's categories, would necessarily be understood as another instance of "peasant Marxism," what Jameson has observed more recently with respect to the subject of Second World culture in the former Eastern bloc is equally suggestive for the Vietnamese subject in opposition. In a published lecture that dates from 1991, Jameson speculates that now, when the Soviet institutions of the East have been dismantled, we might uncover even to our surprise "the existence of something like a genuine socialist culture, a socialist literature based on a socialist characterological and pedagogical formation" (*Seeds* 73–74). And if, as Jameson cautions, "we resist the temptation . . . to attribute such differences to the old stereotypes of nationalism and ethnic peculiarity," we might then awaken to the simpler but less mystifying notion "that people formed in a nonmarket non-consumer-consumptive society do not think like we do" (*Seeds* 74). In its ability to represent "what a life world without advertising might look like" or to present narratives structured for "the lives of people empty of the foreign bodies of business and profit," Second World culture, as Jameson wants to argue, might even in the last instance be anticipatory in figuring forth elements that could only arise on the far side of what we currently know in North America as the iron logic of consumer capitalism (*Seeds* 74, 78).

The point of the present discussion is not to insist that the subject of revolutionary Vietnamese socialism was somehow anticipatory; however, the observations that inform Jameson's reading of socialist culture are certainly germane. What the present argument urges is that Jameson's insistence upon a separate characterological formation in the anti-systemic cultures of the former Second World should be extended to the productive organization of "peasant Marxism" and must inform a reading of discourses by and about the Vietnamese subject in opposition. Moreover, this informed reading must embrace as part of its project a refutation of a dominant popular historical tendency to reduce the terms of the war's opposition to a stereotyped partisanship, or to something akin to a fatal "lifestyle" choice, beneath which the revolutionary socialist subject is effectively buried by some now dominant form of personal or national resentment.[10]

One way to orient this reading of the Vietnamese subject in opposition is to conceive of the subject and the subject's relation to the social totality in broadly Althusserian terms. "Ideology," in Althusser's often repeated formula, "represents the imaginary relationship of individuals to their real conditions of existence," and like the dynamic structure of the social totality, the form or structuring logic of ideology is "eternal" in that there is no subject position outside it ("Ideology," 36). In terms of the revolutionary subject of Vietnamese socialism, perhaps the most conspicuous way in which this ideological structuring announces itself is in the representation of the subject's relation to the collective. We might further conceive of this relationship in rhetorical or narratological terms and suggest that the relation to the collective is fundamental to the construction of proto-narrative and narrative representations by and about Vietnamese subjects in opposition. As Frances Fitzgerald observed so long ago, " 'Socialism'—xa hoi, as the Viet Minh and the NLF translated it—indicated to the Vietnamese peasantry that the revolution would entail no traumatic break with the past, no abandonment of the village earth and the ancestors" (145). In Fitzgerald's reading of Vietnamese socialism, a reading that owes much, as she acknowledges, to the work of John T. McAlister and Paul Mus, the Viet Minh (see McAlister), and later the NLF, were engaged in a revolution directed in large part against "the disintegration of village society," a disintegration that had become already acute in the French colonial period (178–79). What the socialist project offered to the Vietnamese peasantry, as Fitzgerald points out, was that "Instead of a leap into the terrifying unknown, it [the revolution] would be a fulfillment of the local village traditions that the foreigners had attempted to destroy" (145). But the success of this appeal was also in large part owing to the affinities between revolutionary socialism and traditional rural Vietnamese existence. Again, as Fitzgerald argues, "The traditional Vietnamese village was in a special sense a collective enterprise," in which "villagers identified themselves not as individual 'souls' but as members and dependents of the collectivity"

(178–79). This intersection of the collectivity of traditional Vietnamese culture with the class-based collectives specific to peasant Marxism is also mirrored on another level in the conjunction of nationalism and socialism in the singular program of Vietnamese communism. As Huynh Kim Khanh points out in his history of Vietnamese communism, "The most outstanding feature in the growth of Vietnamese communism has been its internal fusion of two separate movements: an anti-imperialist movement integral with Vietnamese patriotic traditions, and a Communist movement affiliated with, and deeply affected by developments in the international Communist movement" (20). It is, in fact, the emphasis on the former that specifically marks Vietnamese communism, and its successful popular front coalition movements, the Viet Minh and the National Liberation Front (Huynh 333–38).

But Vietnamese communism did not pursue merely a repetition of traditional Vietnamese culture; instead, it attempted to effect a sympathetic reconfiguration and redirection of its basic structural impulses. As Frances Fitzgerald observed of the NLF and its political work in the villages, "the Front was not merely trying to restore the old villages. It was attempting to create a community of individuals rather than of families. In the Liberation Associations men, women, and children had to work with their peers" (Fitzgerald 189). The point of this, as Fitzgerald argues, is to encourage villagers to step outside the traditional familial productive organization and to enter into a reconfigured national sense of a collective through "the capacity to work with strangers," a collective characterized by a "basic and revolutionary notion of human equality" (Fitzgerald 189). In practical terms, this reorientation is apparent even in the organization and recruitment of Viet Cong fighters. As military analyst William Henderson, for example, observes in his study of motivation within the Viet Cong, "the PLA understood that a soldier's strong attachment to his family and village made it difficult to organize main force units capable of operating anywhere in South Vietnam" (55). The PLA's "ingenious" solution to this dilemma, in Henderson's description, "demonstrated its success in harnessing the power of the group over the individual": "the PLA first inducted him [the recruit] into a local guerrilla force, assigning him to his home area and allowing him to live with his family when possible. Next, the soldier was encouraged to develop loyalty toward a new group. At this point the soldier, along with his group, was ready for transfer to a main force unit" (55).

In terms of the narrative and proto-narrative representation of the Vietnamese in opposition, this negotiation of an identification with a nationalist collective, often based on the experience of rural Vietnamese village tradition and a specifically socialist collective, typically forms a structural horizon that shapes the rhetoric, thematics, and narrative organization of individual texts and utterances. Perhaps one of the best self-conscious representations of this structural logic is to be found in French journalist Jacques Doyon's *Les Viet Cong*, published in 1968, in which Doyon records his extensive meetings and interviews during the pre-Tet '68 period with members of local and regional Viet Cong units, both in the Delta and in the area around Ban Me Thuot in the Central Highlands. In recounting his conversation with a northern veteran of the trek down the Ho Chi Minh trail, an officer in a Viet Cong unit positioned south of Ban Me Thuot, Doyon recalls that "Le jeune officier de Nam Dinh," as he terms him, emphasized the national collective nature of this conflict (Doyon 122).[11] The officer from Nam Dinh explains: "C'est une guerre d'indépendance et de libération que le peuple vietnamien, tout entier, du Nord au Sud, est en train de soutenir contre les Américains, dit-il. Les soldats de la République Démocratique ont l'obligation de venir libérer le Sud envahi par les force américaines" (Doyon 123). Moreover, the officer insists that "Nord ou Sud-Vietnam sont des mots vides de sens, . . . nous sommes un seul peuple qui se bat pour sa liberté," but that project of national emancipation is also caught up in the officer's mind with the project of social transformation, or as he puts it, "Les inégalités sociales du Sud-Vietnam sont trop grandes actuellement et la paysannerie est malheureuse. Il faute refaire le régime" (Doyon 124,125). These themes are repeated in Doyon's extended conversation with one of the officer's senior colleagues, a soldier named Tri, who identifies himself to Doyon as "un cadre politique et militaire élevé dans la hiérarchie du Front" (131). While he echoes the officer from Nam Dinh's insistence that this is a war about the reuniting of a single people, Tri, a trained political officer, is more explicit about the war's socialist logic. When asked, for example, if he has ever met Nguyen Huu Tho, the nominal leader of the NLF, Tri replies, "Non, je ne l'ai jamais vu . . . il est le président du Front, c'est entendu, mais notre combat est collectif . . . lui ou un autre homme, cela n'a pas tellement d'importance par rapport à notre lutte, tous ensemble, la lutte de peuple" (Doyon 142). In order to temper Doyon's fascination with individual opposition leaders, Tri then similarly remarks of the cadre named Ama Phim, the NLF shadow province chief in Dar Lac, " . . . il n'est que Ama Phim, un individu, et nous sommes, tous ensemble, une unité collective" (Doyon 142). As in his conversation with the officer from Nam Dinh, Doyon learns from Tri that the war for liberation and independence is simply the first step in a larger struggle that will lead to the construction of "une nouvelle société," which Tri envisions as "Une société socialiste et agraire. Son modèle sera le système économique de la République Démocratique. Une société semblable est la mieux adaptée à la paysannerie vietnamienne" (Doyon 141).

While the theme of the collective, specifically the socialist collective fitted to the needs and traditions of Vietnamese peasant life, resonates throughout the conversations that Doyon has with members of the NLF and the Viet Cong, it resonates no less in oral histories from disaffected Viet Cong prisoners and defectors, and in the exile narrative of Le Ly Hayslip. A good example of the former is to be found in Susan Sheehan's 1967 book *Ten Vietnamese,* in which she profiles a Viet Cong defector, Huynh Van Kim.[12] Sheehan first encounters Huynh Van Kim in the closing weeks of 1965, when he is in a political re-education program at the government Open Arms center in Saigon, and in the course of their conversations he tells of his life history in the Viet Cong and the reasons for his defection. Huynh Van Kim tells Sheehan that he joined the Viet Cong for many reasons, including admiration for the Viet Minh and fear that he would be forced to join in any event. He also acknowledges that, in Sheehan's words, he was "favorably impressed by the VC indoctrination lectures," and that as middle child in a large poor family the Viet Cong presented the only appealing alternative to a life of physical toil in his grandfather's rice fields (Sheehan, *Ten* 151). What is of particular interest in this account of his motives is the ways in which the familial/village collective becomes woven into the collective fabric of the national struggle. Huynh Van Kim tells Sheehan that he also joined the Viet Cong and its struggle for national reunification because many of his cousins had fought for the Viet Minh and had rallied to the North in 1954. These cousins were greatly missed by Huynh Van Kim and by their families and national reunification presented the only real possibility for seeing them again (Sheehan, *Ten* 150).[13] In a similar vein, Sheehan reports that "The VC . . . promised Kim he could stay near his village if he joined them," and so he enlisted in the Viet Cong, fearing that "if he was drafted into the government Army, he would be sent far from home" (Sheehan, *Ten* 151). In fact, it is Huynh Van Kim's inability to give himself over to what Frances Fitzgerald describes as the Viet Cong's "community of individuals rather than of families" that occasions his disaffection and ultimate defection (189).

Huynh Van Kim enlists in the Viet Cong in January of 1958; during the first two years, as Sheehan reports, "Kim saw his family only infrequently, at night, when he was on his way to a recruiting mission near his home" (Sheehan, *Ten* 153). Though "happy with his work," Huynh Van Kim discovers that life in the Viet Cong becomes more violent and more dangerous after the end of 1960, when he is assigned to a military section that carries out assassinations of local government officials and their village supporters, and clashes with government troops in nearby outposts and on patrol; but what distresses Huynh Van Kim most is the subsequent breakdown of his family. In 1962, his wife returns to her father's house, leaving their son with Huynh Van Kim's mother, and then in 1963 Huynh Van Kim is promoted to the main force Viet Cong and assigned to a unit based seventy-five miles away in Tay Ninh province. In retrospect, according to Sheehan, Huynh Van Kim "had wanted to leave the Viet Cong ever since his transfer to the main forces in early 1963," but it was a tearful visit to Tay Ninh in 1964 by his mother that pushed him to act: "I probably would never have gotten started on the road to defection if my mother hadn't come to see me in Tay Ninh. I didn't like to see her weeping" (Sheehan, *Ten* 161). Huynh Van Kim actually defects a year later in August 1965, and though by then he is alarmed at the war's escalation and despairs at the prospect of a protracted struggle with no end in sight, his aspiration in leaving is to be reunited with his family.[14] Still, Huynh Van Kim, the Viet Cong defector, remains an admirer of the "spirit of democracy" and the freedom to criticize in the Viet Cong, and he remains convinced of the justness of its cause: "The VC are right in saying that there are no real opportunities for poor people in this country" (Fitzgerald 189).

In one sense, Huynh Van Kim's journey through the Viet Cong might simply be read as an example of failed interpellation; however, I believe that we might come closer to apprehending the truth of the record of lived experience he offers to Susan Sheehan if we read it as an exemplary instance of the logic of overdetermination at work in the ideological subject of revolutionary Vietnamese socialism. Huynh Van Kim's experience is the record of the clash of levels and instances within, to borrow Althusser's formulation, a dynamic "structure articulated in dominance," which in this specific historical situation is the totality of the national war and social revolution (manifested in military conflict and class struggle) between the forces of the Democratic Republic of Vietnam and the NLF on the one side and, on the other, those of American imperial power and its client regime in Saigon (Althusser, "Materialist" 202). Within this horizon of possibility, the local conflicts of Huynh Van Kim's experience in the struggle come to know a larger resonance in relation to a conflict articulated as a collective struggle, from which, like ideology itself in Althusser's famous assertion, there is no escape. Shaped by his memory of the French army's burning of his father's house and of his older brothers killed fighting for the French against the Viet Minh; inspired by the knowledge of his cousins who rallied to the North; tormented by the presence of his weeping mother in Tay Ninh, the loss of his wife, and the separation of his family; still impressed by the justice of the Viet Cong cause by his own former conviction with which he assuages any guilt for killing, by his own count, fifteen people; and, at the same time, dispirited by the grinding hardship, disappointment, and terror of a seemingly endless guerrilla war, and his flight from it, Huynh Van Kim finds it almost impossible to reconcile the historical conflicts and contradictions of his own lived experience. The weight of this personal struggle is particularly apparent at the end of his profile when Huynh Van Kim muses, "I wonder if I'll ever find anything to believe in again," which then leads him to conclude that he has been consumed by his time in the jungle, and that what he can look forward to most is his own death (Sheehan, *Ten* 165, 166).

Something similar can be found in the collective-inflected journey of lived experience and speculation that shapes Le Ly Hayslip's celebrated memoir of exile, *When Heaven and Earth Changed Places*. As in the experience of Huynh Van Kim, Le Ly Hayslip's early understanding of the political struggle is fully incorporated into the life of her village, then called Ky La, near Da Nang. As she points out, "Everything I know about the war I learned as a teenaged girl form the North Vietnamese cadre leaders in the swamps outside Ky La. During these midnight meetings, we peasants assumed everything we heard was true because what the Viet Cong said matched, in one way or another, the beliefs we already had" (Hayslip x). Moreover, as Hayslip points out, these northern cadres "had all been born on the Central Coast. They did not insult us for our manners and speech because they had been raised exactly like us" (xiii). In contrast to her experience of the Republican officials and military, the Viet Cong, as Hayslip insists, worked tirelessly to ensure and often to coerce the loyalty of the peasantry: "Even when things were at their worst — when the allied forces devastated the countryside and the Viet Cong themselves resorted to terror to make us act the way they wanted — the villagers clung to the vision the Communists had drummed into us" (xii). To the extent that this vision extended to political analysis, it included, as Hayslip recalls, a crude caricature of Republican and American motives; however, as Hayslip also insists, this vision included an education in the political power of the traditional collective of the peasantry. Hayslip explains, "as peasant, we defined 'politics' as something other people did someplace else, it had no relevance to our daily lives," and so "we overlooked the power that lay in our hands: our power to achieve virtually anything we wanted if only we acted together" (xiii). Significantly, Hayslip adds, "The Viet Cong and the North, on the other hand, always recognized and respected this strength" (xiii).

As in the case of Huynh Van Kim, Le Ly Hayslip's family is divided by the conflict. Two brothers are fighting in the Viet Cong and the NVA respectively, and an uncle is a southern policeman. However, Le Ly Hayslip is drawn to the Viet Cong, for which she works and is imprisoned briefly and interrogated when still a young girl. In Hayslip's narrative, though, the escalation of the war with the arrival of Americans in force transforms the relationship between the village and the Viet Cong. After a battle, staged in and around her village, between the Viet Cong and American and South Vietnamese troops, two-thirds of the civilian population is removed for interrogation by Government forces. Though the reduced population renders the village an insignificant source of support and assistance for the opposition, the local Viet Cong, almost perversely Le Ly Hayslip suggests, then begins to take much stronger steps to control the loyalty of the villagers. For example, they hold public trials and executions of villagers suspected of spying, and later executions for real and imagined minor offences against the revolution. This violence extends to a near-execution of Hayslip's mother, and ultimately, to her own death sentence, which is only averted when her two Viet Cong executioners rape and then release her (Hayslip 88–97). As Le Ly Hayslip recounts in her memoir, it is this brutality that transforms forever her relationship to the struggle and to the wildly escalating, and increasingly senseless, violence and suffering around her: "Both sides in this terrible, endless, *stupid* war had finally found the perfect enemy: a terrified peasant girl who would endlessly and stupidly consent to be their victim — as all Vietnam's peasants had consented to be victims, from creation to the end of time!" (97). After this, she recalls promising to herself, "I would only flow with the strongest current and drift with the steadiest wind — and not resist. To resist, you have to believe in something" (97).

More than twenty years later, however, when she returns to Vietnam in 1986 after surviving the rest of the American war as a desperate single mother, who suffers repeated abusive encounters with American soldiers, and after the experience of exile and long residence in the United States, Hayslip finds herself in her niece's house, where she notices a map of Vietnam on the wall, "showing no North and no South, but a continuous patchwork of provinces" (207). At that moment, she confesses, the fact of reunification "hits me like a truck as I sit with them toasting our family with tea. That single, simple map was what the war — our decades of suffering — was all about: one people, one family" (207). Hayslip's quick association of national and familial identities, and her qualified reconciliation to "our decades of suffering" as a road that leads to national and now familial reunification, is greatly tempered throughout by her uneasiness at the harshness of life in post-1975 Vietnam, and by her recognition that her own family continues to be shaped by personal and national trauma, including her own. But as in the case of Huynh Van Kim, and as in Jacques Doyon's conversations with the officer from Nam Dinh and with Tri, the Viet Cong political officer and senior cadre, Le Ly Hayslip's memoir presents a subject who is interpellated under the structuring logic of the collective.

But if the determining instance of the collective provides one of the major structural and figural elements in narratives by and about the Vietnamese subject in opposition, the other major structural feature of these texts is the pressure of the utopian impulse that shapes and directs the affective dynamic and narrative logic of their representations. One way to think about this utopian imperative is to situate it as a particular instance of the utopian impulse that may be said to reside in every cultural artifact. As Fredric Jameson argues in *The Political Unconscious,* if there is no escape from ideology, then every cultural artifact is at once a representation of class interest and at the same time, to the extent that it is socially conditioned, a representation of some collective imagining. Moreover, Jameson persuasively maintains, to the extent that every artifact is the representation of a collective interest or fantasy, it is in its expression of that collective desire a form of utopian imagining, if we understand, as Jameson insists, that "The achieved collectivity or organic group of whatever kind — oppressor fully as much as oppressed — is Utopian not in itself, but only insofar as all such collectivities are themselves *figures* for the ultimate concrete collective life of an achieved Utopian or classless society" (*Political,* 291). In literature by and about the Vietnamese subject in opposition, utopian imagining lies at the heart of discursive representations of the revolutionary struggle and its aftermath, so that even the rhetorical tone of the discourse is inflected by its pressure. A good example of the practical implications of this imagining is found in David Chanoff and Doan Van Toai's *Portrait of the Enemy,* a collection of narratives and narrative fragments by and about former members of the North Vietnamese Army, the Viet Cong, and the National Liberation Front. In their Introduction to the 1986 collection, Chanoff and Toai explain that they had assembled the volume over the previous two years, but that they had deliberately chosen not to go to Vietnam to gather narrative accounts because they suspected that the developed state security and surveillance apparatus would prevent them from obtaining the frank stories that they hoped to acquire. Still, a small part of their published collection is made up of short accounts translated from *Nhan Dan* (*The Party Daily*), and the arguments that Chanoff and Toai set out for their inclusion are of particular interest. Chanoff and Toai caution that all accounts are biased, and these selections from *Nhan Dan* are no exception, in that they reflect "the officially inspired (and enforced) requirement that the nation's war experience be portrayed in the colors of epic poetry" (xvii). Still, Chanoff and Toai explain that they have taken a few selections from *Nhan Dan* in part because of the events they describe, but also because they provide "a small taste of the heroic style that is common among Vietnamese revolutionaries when they are addressing their own" (xx). Chanoff and Toai continue, "To the Western ear, some of this may sound turgid and stylized, but the fact is that Vietnamese often do view themselves as heroic people. . . . Westerners, used to self-doubt and introspection, may not find this Vietnamese trait endearing, or even particularly hu-

man. But it is no less real for that" (xx). What is of particular interest in
Chanoff and Toai's remarks is their uneasiness at the tone of these accounts,
and their evident embarrassment and impatience at their idealizations, even
as they characterize this discursive style ("heroic style") as belonging somehow to a national collective ("Vietnamese trait") and to a collective socialist
project ("Vietnamese revolutionaries"). But what seems so alien and recalci-
trant to Chanoff and Toai is precisely what is so central to the representation
of the Vietnamese revolutionary subject; what they describe as "heroic style"
can from another perspective be understood as a conspicuous sign of the
pressures of the utopian impulse, which both characterizes and unites the
collective idealizations in the accounts from the official party daily with the
very different accounts elsewhere in Chanoff and Toai's collection and in the
wider field of exile narrative.

In contrast to Chanoff and Toai's suspicions, what confounds the utopian
impulse most frequently in literature by and about the Vietnamese subject in
opposition is simply the counterweight of wartime suffering and postwar
disillusionment. Chanoff and Toai's own collection presents a number of
vivid accounts of the lived experience of the stress and misery of prolonged
murderous struggle, and often the logic of initiation plays into these accounts
as though to emphasize the distance between expectations and reality or
between the hopeful aspirations and motivations that occasion participation
and the actual horror of the struggle. A particularly effective, brief account is
that of Nguyen Trong Nghi, a former NVA political cadre, who recounts the
experience of marching south on the Ho Chi Minh trail:

> On our way to the South we often met groups of wounded who were going
> North. Some had lost their arms or legs, some had been burned by napalm.
> Some had malaria. They all looked like skeletons. Every day we would meet
> them walking or riding the opposite direction, groups of two or six or ten of
> them. We told each other that some day we would be like that. We began to
> feel the war.
>   . . . No one argued with the cadres. But everyone was frightened, espe-
> cially when we met those men for the first time. It was horrifying. It was like
> looking at our future selves. (Chanoff and Toai 68)[15]

Though a description of the first confrontation with the visceral horror of
war is a common feature of combat narratives, Nguyen Trong Nghi's brief
description is nonetheless marked by the logic of collective utopian imagining that is so typical of the discourse of the revolutionary Vietnamese subject.
Rhetorically, of course, one might point to the conspicuous use of the first-
person plural pronoun, but more important perhaps is Nghi's observation
that these frightening encounters do not motivate his companions to take
issue with the arguments or exhortations of the political cadres. Even though

what is most acute in Nghi's description is the anticipation of suffering, his brief narrative situates the felt reality of individual fear and suffering into the collective project, and it is the combination and struggle of these informing pressures that typifies narratives by and about the Vietnamese subject in opposition.

More recently, feminist scholars have emphasized the specifically gendered nature of these experiences, arising out of the traditional Vietnamese construction of the womanly ideal in terms of a figure who embodies martial prowess along with maternal devotion and acceptance.[16] During the war, Madame Nguyen Thi Dinh, the Deputy Commander of the South Vietnamese Liberation Armed Forces (the Viet Cong), became an official model of this patriarchal version of ideal womanhood. Her official biography, published in Hanoi in 1968, "depicts a superwoman who manages to make tough decisions, all the while remaining modest and feminine," but in the actual accounts of women who fought in the war, the overwhelming impression is of unremitting suffering, and of a suffering apprehended through the structural logic of a gendered reading of a collective utopian project (Turner and Hao 99). For example, Turner and Hao recount their conversation with the Vietnamese writer Le Minh Khue, who worked as an engineer and road builder on the Ho Chi Minh trail from 1965 to 1975. Le Minh Khue recalls:

> One night I went to bathe in a stream. It was dark, and something bumped into me. It was a dead body, floating there. What I feared the most was dying naked, while bathing, or having my clothes blown off by the bomb pressure. It happened to a lot of the girls. It was terrible, but we were young and we made jokes. Sometimes we even got in the coffins to play, or to sleep in them. We had no idea when we signed on how life would be. We had to encourage each other. Sometimes we would be so tired we would fall asleep on the march, or not be able to get out of our hammocks. Sometimes as we walked we would come upon a skeleton, someone at the rear of a column who had died alone, of malaria or some other disease. (Turner and Hao 99)

As in Nguyen Trong Nghi's brief account of marching south, Le Minh Khue's narrative turns on the thematics of fear and the collective. It is not insignificant that Le Minh Khue's fearful encounters with death are also characterized by individual isolation: first, the single body floating in the dark, and then, at the end of her narrative, even more tellingly, the skeleton of the comrade who becomes separated or who is left behind and dies alone.

But it is not only suffering that exerts pressure on the collective utopian imagining in these accounts; it is also the historical experience of disappointment and the lived experience of an historical promise left unfulfilled. An anticipation of this postwar disappointment is succinctly presented at the end of a lengthy autobiographical account given to Chanoff and Toai by the celebrated Vietnamese writer, Xuan Vu. Originally from a village near My Tho, Xuan Vu was a revolutionary combat reporter with the Viet Minh, who rallied to the North in 1954 and then as the American war intensified returned south to join the propaganda arm of the mainline units in Ben Tre province. In many respects, Xuan Vu's account of his final decision to leave the Viet Cong recalls that of Huynh Van Kim, in that he is disheartened by the increased hardship and dangers of the American war. After two years in Ben Tre, he recalls, "It took every ounce of energy I had just to stay alive" (Chanoff and Toai 186). In the difficult and demoralized situation after Tet 1968, Xuan Vu and other cultural cadres are sent back to Cambodia for safety, and on the journey there Xuan Vu takes advantage of a pass to walk away from the Viet Cong. But Xuan Vu's lived experience of disappointment and disillusionment in the American war takes the form of an attack on what he considers to be a corrupt and cynical leadership in the North, with whose bureaucracy the writer Xuan Vu had a difficult relationship like many other Viet Minh fighters and supporters, in 1954. As Xuan Vu explains to Chanoff and Toai:

> The whole thing was a hoax. Our Southern people had been at war for thirty years and they hadn't gotten anyplace. I started realizing what they had done to us, what they were doing to us. The Northern leaders were sending their sons to Russia and Eastern Europe while our poets and composers were getting killed off wholesale. I thought, What kind of communism is that? What kind of equality is that? I hadn't liked the Northern leaders when I lived there, and I didn't like them now. (Chanoff and Toai 187)

As in the case of Huynh Van Kim, Xuan Vu's disaffection is not a repudiation of the collective struggle but rather a confirmation of its value, symbolized by a refusal to sacrifice himself for a once noble but now hopelessly corrupted and compromised cause. Xuan Vu's position is further complicated by his investment in a determinedly non-Marxist view of the place of literature and culture, but his early disappointment and disillusionment are emblematic of the thematic logic of much literature by and about the Vietnamese subject in opposition.[17]

A woman who worked on a volunteer road building crew on the Ho Chi Minh trail recalls for Karen Turner, for example, that she suffered so acutely from malaria that she could neither speak nor hear; consequently, she was returned to the rear, where she found her boyfriend married to someone else and her family reluctant to take her, so "I went for awhile to live in an all-women's collective farm with other women who had no place to go" (Turner and Hao 77). The woman who recounts this story to Turner in 1996, whom Turner calls Teacher Mau, is the unofficial secretary for the surviving veterans of her volunteer troop, whose reunions occasion a conversation that

dwells upon past suffering, inadequate postwar medical care, general government neglect, and present poverty (Turner and Hao 77–78). On the one
hand, as Turner points out, these former volunteers "revere the memory of
Ho Chi Minh and expressed no doubt about their decision to respond to his
plea for help" (Turner and Hao 81). The volunteers assert, "The work we did
in the past was worth it, and we are proud" (Turner and Hao 81). On the
other hand, they admit that "Yes, our lives are hard now" and that "sometimes we think they haven't treated us properly" (Turner and Hao 81). As in
the case of Le Ly Hayslip who can only conceive the possibility of redeeming
the trauma and suffering of the war by emphasizing national and familial
reunification, the survivors of volunteer troop C814 can only formally or
symbolically resolve the contradictions of their lived experience and the fate
of the national collective struggle by recasting it as a familial narrative. As
they maintain to Turner, "We are like the children of poor parents. Well,
sometimes we think they haven't treated us properly, but then we see or read
about other people and we know that we have better lives than theirs. So we
wish the government would help them first, before it is too late" (Turner and
Hao 81).

What structures the discursive organization and logic of the literature of
the Vietnamese subject in opposition — the subject's relation to the collective
and the vicissitudes of the weight of the historical struggle against a collective
utopian imagination — is also and perhaps not surprisingly reproduced in
dissident fiction from a reunified Vietnam. Though these highly crafted narratives do not belong to the same discursive field as oral narratives, interviews, and even exile memoirs, their narrative organization and structural
logic recalls much that is characteristic of the oppositional subject's discourse
about the war. Duong Thu Huong's *Novel Without a Name* is a particularly
rich example of this, one that is also important in terms of the present discussion because of Duong Thu Huong's conspicuous profile in the United States.
In *Novel Without a Name*, the protagonist, Quan, a twenty-eight-year-old
NVA company commander, is torn between a collective of his family and
village and that of the army and the national political struggle. Early in the
novel, for example, Quan, whose mother died when he was eight, recalls
marching off to war from his village as an eighteen-year-old recruit and
ignoring the other village mothers weeping for their children, his comrades:
"Vietnam had been chosen by History: After the war, our country would
become humanity's paradise. . . . We believed this, so we turned away from
those tears of weakness" (Duong 31). Ten years later, in 1975, when an
extraordinary leave enables him to pay a brief visit to his family and village,
Quan finds his father living alone and in misery, routinely failing to provide
adequately for himself on "the meager pension allocated to cadres who had

taken part in the anti-French resistance" (Duong 118). Moreover, during this visit, Quan learns that his younger brother has been killed at the front, which subsequently occasions him to reflect that the struggle and the Party have destroyed his family forever: "His [Quan's brother's] fate had been sealed the second my father raised his hand at that Party cell meeting: 'I promise to convince my boys to enlist'. The whole family thrown into the game of war! From the depths of his ignorance, my father's ambition had overcome him" (Duong 124).

Although at one point Quan closes a reflection on his ten years in combat with the observation that "I had never really committed myself to war," his disaffection, typical of the literature of the Vietnamese revolutionary subject in opposition, never extends to the national struggle for reunification or to the project of social reformation itself, but rather focuses upon a persistent official failure to accept the weight of suffering that is the lived experience of being engaged in this utopian collective project, and upon the corruption and cynicism of the Party functionaries. Quan recalls, for example, reading in *Nhan Dan,* the Communist party daily, of "the glorious victories on the B3 front during the Tet offensive" in 1968, about which Quan remembers only that "We had been there. I had with own hands countless numbers of my companions," including a very young soldier named Hoang, about whom he reports, "All he had left was one arm, one leg, and a diary filled with gilded dreams" (Duong 83). Later, on a train in North Vietnam, Quan observes and overhears the conversation of two well-fed party ideologues who are now utterly self-interested and cynical about their own revolutionary pasts. Recalling their own youthful ardor and the songs they sang as they made their way from "one battle to the next," one observes, "Now they're starting to fade. That's the universal law. Revolution, like love, blooms and then withers. . . . The less it's true, the more we need to believe in it. That's the art of governing. Spreading the word, now that's you intellectuals' job. We pay you for it" (Duong 161). Quan's disaffection is well underway at this point, and so the conversation he overhears only confirms his indignation at the immense sacrifice being made on behalf of an ideal that was doomed to betrayal. At the end of the novel, he finds himself in 1975 sweeping toward Saigon and the end of the war: "Our vehicles advanced along a road littered with boots, shoes, uniforms, berets, sacks, and packages, sparkling cartridges, broken toothbrushes, bras, smashed sandwiches, headless dolls. . . . The enemy's demise had just begun" (Duong 280). Quan's own soldiers are enthusiastic: "They were bursting with energy. They could have kept on shouting forever"; however, Quan's own reaction is very different: "We would win. The triumphal arch flickered on the horizon. My heart brimmed over with a poignant, painful joy. At the same time, my mind was etched with a chilling image"

(Duong 281, 281–82). Just as in the oral history by and about the Vietnamese subject in opposition, Duong Thu Huong's dissident fiction thematically structures the narrativization of Quan's lived experience in familiar categories. Huong's novel traces the relationship of the subject to the village/familial collective and to the socialist collective of the national liberation struggle, and the subject's attempt to reconcile the weight of hardship and suffering with a utopian collective imagining.

Much the same is true of Bao Ninh's 1991 novel, *The Sorrow of War: A Novel of North Vietnam*. Kien, the novel's protagonist, a former officer in a North Vietnamese army scout-platoon, recalls the war as an unremitting experience of violence, horror, and sudden death for almost everyone around him, but one that held out a utopian promise that the present cannot accommodate. Bao Ninh's novel is full of disillusion: as one character observes to Kien, ". . . Look at the chaotic postwar situation in the cities, with their black markets. Life is so frustrating, for all of us. And look at the bodies and the graves of our comrades! The ones who brought the peace. Shameful, my friend, shameful" (Bao 42). For Bao Ninh, as for Duong Thu Huong, this disillusionment proceeds in part from official corruption and cynicism. In *The Sorrow of War*, for example, Kien and his scout team pay a wartime visit to a coffee plantation in the Central Highlands, a well-managed refuge from the war that surrounds it. Driving away from the plantation in their jeep, Van, one of the scout team and a former "university student in economics and planning," observes, "What a peaceful, happy oasis. My lecturers with all their Marxist theories will pour in and ruin all this if we win. I'm horrified to think of what will happen to that couple. They'll soon learn what the new political order means" (Bao 199). Much earlier in the novel, Kien contrasts his postwar existence with his life before the military; "The future lied to us, there long ago in the past. There is no new life, no new era, nor is it hope for a beautiful future that now drives me on, but rather the opposite. The hope is contained in the beautiful prewar past" (Bao 47). Much of that hope is caught up in Kien's memory of his relationship with Phuong, his equally brutalized beloved, but the utopian impulse in Kien's account belongs specifically to his experience of wartime struggle. He recalls, for example, that in 1974, he was offered the opportunity to return to Hanoi for advanced officer training: he was reluctant, preferring to remain and to die with "the regular troops . . . who had created an almost invincible fighting force because of their peasant nature, by volunteering to sacrifice their lives. They have simple, gentle, ethical outlooks on life," and although relentlessly subject to the "catastrophic consequences of the war, . . . they never had a say in deciding the course of the war" (Bao 18). Similarly, at the end of the novel, the editor who prepares Kien's abandoned manuscript realizes that he knew Kien in the war, or at least that "both he and I, like the other ordinary soldiers of the war, shared one fate," ultimately a crushing fate but one that cannot overshadow the experience of a collective utopian project. As the unnamed editor observes in the novel, "I envied his inspiration, his optimism in focusing back on the painful but glorious days. They were caring days, when we knew what we were living and fighting for and why we needed to suffer and sacrifice" (Bao 233). He then concludes, "Those were the days when all of us were young, very pure, and very sincere" (Bao 233).

In this respect, whatever the official Vietnamese government reaction to their work, Duong Thu Huong's *Novel Without A Name* and Bao Ninh's *The Sorrow of War* must be read as acts of recovery, narratives that, like the often fragmented oral historical accounts available to English readers from the Vietnamese subject in opposition, aspire to reach back before the moment of historical eclipse and to retrieve something of what it felt like to be interpellated as an historical agent within an active peasant Marxism and, perhaps more specifically in the Vietnamese context, to have lived out the conflicts, contradictions, and aspirations of the last great wave of anti-systemic collective struggle. As the literature by and about the Vietnamese subject in opposition so forcefully demonstrates, no canon of oral history about the war can claim to be representative or to be in any way complete without a full accounting of the revolutionary subject who inhabited those great collectives that struggled successfully for more than thirty years, from the founding of the Viet Minh, to the defeat of the French, the American war, and the fall of Saigon.

NOTES

1. In 1965, Vann was Hau Nghia province representative for USOM (United States Operating Mission—later AID or Agency for International Development), but his relationship with York began in Vietnam in 1963 when York had been the only American general to inspect personally the site of the disastrous attack at Ap Bac by the South Vietnamese 7th Infantry Division, for which Vann was then the often frustrated and, on that day, infuriated chief U.S. military advisor (Sheehan, *Bright* 272–76).

2. The same might be said of another mode of Western identification with the Vietnamese revolution, one at least implicit in Vann's remarks, that has its origins in popular constructions of the American citizen subject and in the legitimate forms of masculinist revolt granted to the subject of Cold War liberalism. Vann's "lad of eighteen" who chooses to support the NLF is constructed as an American *I* consonant with the figures who make up the citizen militias and imagined fraternities of the popular American historical imagination. Moreover, that this "lad of eighteen" might

become a Viet Cong guerrilla fighter connects the Vietnamese resistance with the romantic construction of the masculinist guerrilla fighter, whose putative qualities of non-conformist self-reliance, fraternal solidarity, and high-minded purpose resonated with culturally accepted forms of Cold War masculinist revolt. In this context, John Vann's observations on the situation in Vietnam in the spring of 1965 are not far removed from C. Wright Mills's reported guerrilla challenge to a 1960 class at Columbia, "I don't know what you guys are waiting for. . . . You've got a beautiful set of mountains in those Rockies. I'll show you how to use those pistols. Why don't you get going?" (quoted in Gosse 182). For an invaluable account of the American Cold War masculinist romance with the figure of the guerrilla, see Van Gosse's superb *Where the Boys Are: Cuba, Cold War America and the Making of a New Left.*

3. By "literature of the Vietnam War" here I mean fiction, popular memoirs, and oral history collections, or what has come to be recognized as the canon of Vietnam War literature. There is, of course, another large body of scholarly literature in English about the Vietnamese and about the American war that presents a sophisticated and complex understanding of the Vietnamese and of modern Vietnam. John T. McAlister's *Vietnam: The Origins of Revolution* (1969), Alexander Woodside's *Community and Revolution in Modern Vietnam* (1976), the journalist Frances Fitzgerald's earlier *Fire in the Lake* (1972), Huynh Kim Khanh's *Vietnamese Communism, 1925–1945* (1982), and, more recently, Gareth Porter's *Vietnam: The Politics of Bureaucratic Socialism* (1993) are only a few examples of this rich scholarly tradition. In terms of the public cultural imaginary in North America, however, it is the body of Vietnam War literature that has had the widest impact, and it is largely with the representational field of this popular cultural imaginary that the present discussion is concerned.

4. On the combat memoir and its work in privatizing and psychologizing historical events and experiences, and for the history of the representation of Asians in American culture, see Renny Christopher.

5. Truong Nhu Tang's *A Vietcong Memoir* is perhaps the exception that proves the rule. Though a founding member of the NLF and later Minister of Justice in the Provisional Revolutionary Government, Truong Nhu Tang, as he repeatedly insists, was simply a southern nationalist. As he remarks, for example, of the communist presence in the united opposition to Diem in the late 1950s, "I was not overly concerned at that point about potential conflicts between the Southern nationalists and the ideologues. We were allies in the fight, or so I believed. . . . I was not alone in drawing this conclusion. And I was not the only one whom time would disabuse" (Truong 69). Truong had expected that after victory against the Americans and its client regime, South Vietnam would be regarded "as 'a separate case' whose economy and government would have the opportunity to evolve independently, prior to negotiating a union with the DRV [Democratic Republic of Vietnam]" (Truong 269). Embittered and disenchanted with the way in which the PRG [Provisional Revolutionary Government] had been swept aside after the 1975 victory, Truong fled Vietnam in 1978. His "Vietcong memoir" might thus more accurately be understood as an exile account of his relationship with the Vietcong and with the Communist leadership in the North, with whom he worked, but whose goals and politics he did not share.

6. This is not to suggest that a "phantasmagoric projection" does not accurately describe the reality of the experience. Much American discourse about the war, par-

ticularly that which is found in personal accounts, places great emphasis upon how little most American participants knew about Vietnam, its history, culture, or language, and upon how elusive the enemy was, even when engaged in combat.

7. These dates are confirmed in the Chronology in *Reporting Vietnam: Part Two* (794–95). This volume also contains a report by Flora Lewis on the signing of the Paris peace accord, "Vietnam Peace Pacts Signed: America's Longest War Halts" (420–24), which originally appeared in *The New York Times* the day after the signing, and an account by H. D. S. Greenway of the end of MACV and the symbolic last plane load of American troops to leave Vietnam some two months later, "Last GIs Leave South Vietnam" (464–69), which originally appeared in *The Washington Post* on March 30, 1973, the day after the events it describes.

8. For a scathing attack on *Dispatches* and on the positive academic reception of the text, including my own, which nonetheless manages to exculpate Jameson's enthusiasm, see Neilson 135–64.

9. We cannot overlook the details of this historical experience. In the years immediately after 1975, Vietnam was greatly challenged economically and socially by the wartime destruction of its agricultural economy, by the withdrawal of U.S. aid from the South, and by a rigorous U.S. embargo. Moreover, economic renewal was inhibited by the Vietnamese government's pursuit of industrial modernization and delinking at the expense of other national investments, and by Vietnam's military conflicts with Cambodia and China, which arose out of an effort to negotiate a balanced relation with the USSR and with a Maoist China, the latter regarded with suspicion by the Vietnamese leadership. In addition, throughout this period the Vietnamese leadership persisted in the notion that Vietnam was the center of a worldwide struggle against imperialism, and officially espoused the view that the capitalist world was in crisis and would be overtaken by the socialist states in a matter of years (Porter 189). This view was only officially revised in the 1980s, as first indicated by General Secretary Le Duan's 1984 declaration that there was only one world market with interdependent socialist and capitalist economies (Porter 190). For a detailed summary discussion of the social and economic conditions of Vietnam in the fifteen years after 1975, see Gareth Porter's *Vietnam: The Politics of Bureaucratic Socialism,* especially Chapters 2, 3, 5, and 7.

10. This is not to suggest that any representation of the war is not caught up in personal suffering and misery. The February 1999 protest by hundreds of Vietnamese exiles against a Vietnamese exile who hung a poster of Ho Chi Minh in the window of his video store in a strip mall in Westminster, California, is perhaps an object lesson of the presence of suffering and the continuing effects of personal trauma in the Vietnamese exile community (Terry 1–2).

11. In Doyon's own words, "Il est originaire de Nam Dinh, petite ville du delta tonkinois, qui a été rasée par les bombardements américains" (123).

12. Sheehan's book attempts to present a representative survey of ordinary Vietnamese at the height of the American war. As Sheehan puts it, "It was these Vietnamese — the people I've heard called 'the ninety-five per cent that don't count' — who interested me, for the war is being fought over them and they are its chief participants and chief victims" (Sheehan, *Ten* xii).

13. As with many Vietnamese, Huynh Van Kim's relation to the two sides in this conflict is complex. As Sheehan notes, "The fact that two of Kim's older brothers had been killed by the Viet Minh while serving with the French Army left him with no ill

feelings toward the Viet Minh" (Sheehan, *Ten* 150). Sheehan then explains, "He thought his brothers would never have joined the French Army if they had seen French soldiers burn down their own parents' home, as Kim had" (Sheehan, *Ten* 151).

14. Sheehan reports that Huynh Van Kim has been promised by the Army officials who interrogated him in Bien Hoa that they will assist him to find a job there. Although his wife has remarried, he hopes to be reunited there with his mother and his son (Sheehan, *Ten* 165).

15. The reader should keep in mind that this account may not be quite what it seems. One of the sources for the accounts in Chanoff and Toai's collection is the repository of military interrogation reports from the war, housed in the Indochina Archives at the University of California, Berkeley, which is the specific source for Nguyen Trong Nghi's brief description. As Chanoff and Toai explain in the Introduction, these reports are records of responses to series of questions, which, although often wide ranging, result in "a disconnected and difficult-to-read report whose awkwardness has likely been compounded by the unidiomatic English of the original Vietnamese translator" (xx). Moreover, as Chanoff and Toai freely admit, "In such cases, we have drawn together stories that have been fragmented, and edited the language into conversational English" (xx). While there is no reason to think that Chanoff and Toai have misrepresented Nghi's remarks, one should keep in mind that we are at several removes from Nghi's own words.

16. In addition to the text by Turner and Hao that I draw upon in my discussion, see also Sandra Taylor's *Vietnamese Women at War: Fighting for Ho Chi Minh and the Revolution.*

17. In the case of Xuan Vu, the ironies that surround his relationship to literature and politics are complex. In 1952 he won the revolution's Cuu Long Prize Literature for his story and poetry celebrating the Viet Minh resistance against the French (Chanoff and Toai 10). When he returned to the American war in Ben Tre, his personal task, in addition to working as part of a propaganda team preparing the population for a general uprising, was to write a novel or a series of stories about the resistance in Ben Tre. The hardships of the war, however, left him no time to write, and it was not until after he defected from the Viet Cong and settled in Saigon that he was able to write. What he wrote, however, was a book about the Ho Chi Minh Trail, entitled *The Endless Road,* which won South Vietnam's National Prize for Literature and Arts in 1972 (Chanoff and Toai 187). But when Chanoff and Toai met Xuan Vu in exile in the United States in the mid-1980s, Vu's circumstances were not free of difficulties, although of a somewhat different order. Chanoff remarks, "he came to meet me at my hotel in the red pickup truck he uses in the painting business that keeps him alive while he writes for half a dozen Vietnamese-language magazines. The move to the United States hasn't been kind to him. You sense the pain that leaving Vietnam has caused. He is a wordsmith deprived of his audience" (Chanoff and Toai 44).

WORKS CITED

Althusser, Louis. "Ideology and Ideological State Apparatuses (Notes toward an Investigation)." *Essays on Ideology.* London: Verso, 1984. 1–60.

———. "On the Materialist Dialectic." *For Marx.* Trans. Ben Brewster. London: Verso, 1996. 163–218.

————, and Étienne Balibar. *Reading Capital.* Trans. Ben Brewster. London: New Left Books, 1997.

Bao Ninh, *The Sorrow of War: A Novel of North Vietnam.* Trans. Phan Thanh Hao. Ed. Frank Palmos. New York: Riverhead Books, 1996.

Chanoff, David, and Doan Van Toai. *Portrait of the Enemy.* New York: Random House, 1986.

Christopher, Renny. *The Viet Nam War: The American War.* Amherst: University of Massachusetts Press, 1995.

Dirlik, Arif. *After the Revolution: Waking to Global Capitalism.* Hanover, N.H.: Wesleyan University Press, 1994.

Doyon, Jacques. *Les Viet Cong.* Paris: Éditions Denoël, 1968.

Duong Thu Huong. *Novel Without a Name.* Trans. Nina McPherson and Phan Huy Duong, 1996.

Fitzgerald, Frances. *Fire in the Lake: The Vietnamese and the Americans in Vietnam.* Boston: Little, Brown, 1972.

Gosse, Van. *Where the Boys Are: Cuba, Cold War America and the Making of a New Left.* London: Verso, 1993.

Hayslip, Le Ly, with Jay Wurts. *When Heaven and Earth Changed Places: A Vietnamese Woman's Journey from War to Peace.* New York: Doubleday, 1989.

Henderson, William Darryl. *Why the Vietcong Fought: A Study of Motivation and Control in a Modern Army in Combat.* Westport, Conn.: Greenwood Press, 1979.

Herr, Michael. *Dispatches.* New York: Knopf, 1977.

Huynh Kim Khanh. *Vietnamese Communism: 1925–1945.* Ithaca, N.Y.: Cornell University Press, 1982.

Jameson, Fredric. *Marxism and Form.* Princeton, N.J.: Princeton University Press, 1971.

————. *The Political Unconscious: Narrative as a Socially Symbolic Act.* Ithaca, N.Y.: Cornell University Press, 1981.

————. *Postmodernism; or, The Cultural Logic of Late Capitalism.* Durham, N.C.: Duke University Press, 1991.

————. *The Seeds of Time.* The Welleck Library Lectures at the University of California, Irvine. New York: Columbia University Press, 1991.

McAlister, John T., and Paul Mus. *The Vietnamese and Their Revolution.* New York: Harper and Row, 1970.

Neilson, Jim. *Warring Fictions: American Literary Culture and the Vietnam War Narrative.* Jackson: University Press of Mississippi, 1998.

Porter, Gareth. *Vietnam: The Politics of Bureaucratic Socialism.* Ithaca, N.Y.: Cornell University Press, 1993.

Reporting Vietnam. Vol. 1: *American Journalism 1959–1969.* Library of America 104. New York: Library of America, 1998.

Reporting Vietnam. Vol. 2: *American Journalism 1969–1975.* Library of America 105. New York: Library of America, 1998.

Sheehan, Neil. *A Bright Shining Lie: John Paul Vann and America in Vietnam.* New York: Vintage, 1989.

Sheehan, Susan. *Ten Vietnamese.* New York: Knopf, 1967.

Taylor, Sandra. *Vietnamese Women at War: Fighting for Ho Chi Minh and the Revolution.* Lawrence: University Press of Kansas, 1999.

Terry, Don. "Vietnamese Immigrants Protest Hanging of Ho Chi Minh Poster." *New York Times on the Web*. 16 February 1999.

Truong Nhu Tang, with David Chanoff and Doan Van Toai. *A Vietcong Memoir*. New York: Harcourt Brace, 1985.

Turner, Karen Gottschang, with Phan Thanh Hao. *Even the Women Must Fight: Memories of War from North Vietnam*. New York: John Wiley, 1998.

Woodside, Alexander. *Community and Revolution in Modern Vietnam*. Boston: Houghton Mifflin, 1976.

7. Oral History and Popular Memory in the Historiography of the Vietnam War

VAN NGUYEN-MARSHALL

There was excitement in my household when the movie *The Deer Hunter* opened in 1978. My parents and several of my older siblings trudged off one cold winter evening to see their first movie in Canada, a movie about the Vietnam War. They came home that night, disappointed and frustrated. Very little was said to the younger family members, who could not attend, except that the movie was all about Americans. This was my first insight into the complexities of narrating the Vietnam War.

Nearly three decades have passed since the end of the Vietnam War, and yet emotions still run high and divisions deep in the interpretations of this war. Inside and outside Vietnam, the need still exists for those who suffered through the war to revisit its spectre and tell their stories. From the American and Vietnamese foot soldiers to the generals and top government officials, stories about the war continue to be published, and yet there seems to be no end to the controversies, no consensus on how the history of the war should be understood.

As a historian by trade, I find the task of grappling with the history of the war enormously difficult. Thus I have purposely steered away from the subject of the Vietnam War, burying myself instead in the history of the French colonial period. I cannot, however, seem to escape the later period. One of the difficulties for me is to relate my own experience and the stories I have heard from families and other overseas Vietnamese to the larger history of the war. Both my parents were originally from North Vietnam. As landowners and Roman Catholics, both sets of my grandparents threw in their lot with the French and later with the non-communist South Vietnamese. In 1954, my grandparents and their children migrated south and resettled in Saigon. My father went to the military academy and became an officer in the South Vietnamese Army. In 1975, just before North Vietnam entered Saigon, I fled with my family by jumping on a U.S. barge leaving Vietnam. I was eight years old that year. In all probability my family's background and the stories I grew up with make me hypersensitive to the lack of space given in the English-language historiography to personal and collective experiences of the non-communist Vietnamese who fought and suffered in the war.

Alessandro Portelli writes that war is the "space where the individual narrative of biography meets the collective narrative of history" (Portelli 161). Moreover, war is "the most tangible claim for having been in history" (7). Portelli goes on to explain that "oral history expresses the awareness of the historicity of personal experience and of the individual's role in the history of society and in public events" (6). In other words, oral history can act as a bridge between personal and collective memories. With regard to the Vietnam War, however, this task of bridging is complicated in that there is no one orthodox narrative, or officially sanctioned written history, but many contesting versions.

Unlike other major wars, such as World War II, in which there were only two sides — the Allies and the Axis — in the Vietnam War there were actually three sides: The United States, North Vietnam, and South Vietnam.[1] On each side were significant divergences and divisions, though we were not privy to details about the ruptures in North Vietnam until recently. In 2002, Robert McMahon, historian of American foreign relations during the Vietnam War, stated that "[no] other event in U.S. history since the Civil War has been quite so vigorously contested as the Vietnam War" (McMahon 159). He quoted another writer who explored the Vietnam War, Marilyn Young, in referring to the war as a "zone of contested meaning." The struggle over the meanings of the Vietnam War continues to take place both in the United States and in Vietnam.

This chapter will identify and provide brief summaries of the various "zones of contested meaning" among three groups: American scholars, Vietnamese citizens living in Vietnam, and Vietnamese living abroad. I will also touch briefly on features that oral history contributes to each zone. I suggest that in order to navigate and make sense of an overwhelming amount of scholarly, literary, polemical, and personal narratives on the war, one must see them as part of a contest in shaping not only the written accounts of professional historians, but also the collective or public memory of the war.[2]

Before I venture into the three contested zones, I should say a few words about my understanding of the relationship between oral history, written history, and popular memory.

ORAL HISTORY, WRITTEN HISTORY, AND POPULAR MEMORY

Oral history became a genre in the discipline of history in the 1960s and 1970s as a project to allow ordinary people to tell "how it really was" (Thomson 33). By the 1980s, the practitioners were interested in exploring how people remember as well as what they remember. As Alistair Thomson, a leading oral historian in Britain, comments: "We seek to explore the relationships between individual and collective remembering, between memory and identity, or between the interviewer and interviewee" (34).

According to Michael Frisch, two extreme positions can be taken in the practice of oral history (9). On one end of the spectrum oral history is seen as a subversion of the document-dependent history written by historians. He calls this approach "no history," meaning that practitioners of this approach believe they are bypassing the professional historian to allow ordinary people to relate their experiences directly. On the other end of the spectrum oral history is a way to fill in the gaps that conventional history misses. He calls this approach "more history," for which oral narratives are seen as an additional type of historical source. With regard to the Vietnam War, both views of oral sources can be detected, with more recent publications adopting oral history as a means to examine how people remember and how their private memories relate to the larger collective memory (Turner).

Collective, social, or popular memory "is a body of beliefs and ideas about the past that helps a public or society understand both its past, present, and by implication, its future" (McMahon 162). Oral history is considered a constituent of collective memory (Thomson 39). While there is a tendency to regard public memory as more democratic and authentic than written history, public memory is not forged without a contest, without an attempt to foreclose other possibilities (Tai, "Introduction" 7). Portelli reminds readers that collective memory is "mediated by ideologies, languages, common sense, and institutions" (158). As Hue-Tam Ho Tai points out, the state is interested in "shaping not only written history but popular memory as well" and that official "history and public memory thus are as likely to coexist in symbiotic fashion as to be in tension with each other" (7). With regard to the Vietnam War, history and social memory are in flux and are being challenged in both the United States and Vietnam.

AMERICAN SCHOLARSHIP AND THE ROLE OF THE
UNITED STATES IN THE VIETNAM WAR

As divisive as the writings on the Vietnam War are in the United States, they generally share one focus: to explain the role of the United States in the war while assessing the legitimacy of U.S. intervention and its conduct in the conflict. There is increasingly additional primary material available for research purposes, and more nuance in the interpretations of the war. Recently declassified material from American and British archives has allowed for more detailed studies of the policy and decision-making process at the highest government levels (Herring, "History" 28–29). At the same time, a growing number of scholarly works, based on archival material from Vietnam, China, and Russia, examine the communist side.[3] The bulk of American writing on the war still focuses on evaluating U.S. involvement. However, the interpretations can be roughly divided into three camps: those who argue that American involvement was immoral, those who argue that Americans intervened with honorable intentions, but bad judgment, and those who argue that the United States could have won the war.

THE IMMORAL WAR

According to George Herring, the dominant interpretation of the Vietnam War among U.S. scholars is one that is highly critical of U.S. involvement in Vietnam (Herring, "History" 24). This position, which Herring refers to as the "orthodox" view, originated during the war as part of the anti-war movement, and has since been refined and modified. In essence, however, this position still maintains that U.S. intervention was morally wrong.

Among the most vocal and convincing writers of this group was the late George Kahin, whose first book (co-authored with John Lewis), *The United States in Vietnam* (1967), was the "bible for opponents of the war in the 1970s" (Herring, "Review" 354). Kahin's second book on the Vietnam War, *Intervention: How America Became Involved in Vietnam,* maintains the conviction of his earlier work that U.S. involvement in Vietnam had no legitimate basis and that consequently the U.S. government deliberately deceived its people in order to wage war against the Vietnamese communists. Kahin based his argument on a rich source of official documents obtained through the Freedom of Information Act, and on interviews with American and Vietnamese leaders. Among the Vietnamese Kahin interviewed were prominent Buddhist monks, leaders of the National Liberation Front (NLF — derisively known by the Saigon government as the *Viet Cong,* which means "Vietnamese communist"), as well as government officials and supporters from Saigon.

Unlike his earlier book, *Intervention* does not claim that the NLF was a completely autonomous organization (Herring, "Review" 354). Despite the NLF's ambiguous relationship with North Vietnam, Kahin maintains that U.S. actions in Vietnam were not justifiable. Kahin's detailed description of the successive South Vietnamese governments provides evidence for the argument that U.S. involvement in Vietnam had little to do with cultivating democracy and everything to do with rendering the Saigon government "into an instrument supportive both of U.S. strategic and geopolitical objectives"(ix).[4]

HONORABLE INTENTIONS

In contrast to the focus on the immorality of the war, the other important interpretation in American Vietnam War literature focuses on U.S. military strategies and perceptions of the war. At the heart of the issue for these writers is to explain why the United States lost, and not to debate the morality of its involvement. Larry Cable's book, *Unholy Grail*, for example, points to the fundamental flaws in U.S. military strategies and America's failure to understand the nature of the war as reasons for the communist victory in Vietnam.[5] Cable's book is solidly based on U.S. archival documents that include combat action reports, CIA studies, and the minutes and memoranda of U.S. government officialdom. *Unholy Grail* shows that the U.S. government and its military leaders had misunderstood the nature of the war and had few clear ideas about their goals.

According to Cable, U.S. military decisions were based on assumptions that had little relevance to the war. For example, political and military leaders were working with the notions that victory could be achieved if the enemy were destroyed by firepower, and that the Vietnamese communists could be defeated through the employment of American military and technological strength. According to Cable, no one other than Undersecretary of State George Ball "questioned the relevance of either goal or method to the realities as they had developed on the ground in South Vietnam"(5). Cable goes on to explain that the U.S. civilian and military leaders all shared a "common intellectual heritage," cultivated by shared experience within a Cold War discourse. As a result, the leaders saw "the hidden hand of the Kremlin behind all political violence directed against the status quo" and had limitless faith in U.S. military capabilities (6). Imbued with this Cold War paranoia, the U.S. government and its military mistakenly thought the war was being impelled by Moscow, Beijing, and Hanoi as opposed to revolutionary forces indigenous to Vietnam itself. In other words, "the basic error had been that of seeing the emerging war in South Vietnam as being of the partisan [Cold War] sort" (236).

Cable thus concurs with anti-war writer George Kahin in seeing the war as an "armed expression of organic political disaffection" throughout Vietnam and the "Viet Cong" (or the NLF) as an insurgent force (236). But Cable does not share Kahin's negative judgment of the U.S. administration. Cable takes seriously the Administration's intellectual heritage and its Cold War concern for containment. While focusing on the "intellectual failure" of U.S. war policies, Cable does not question the morality of the U.S. endeavor to attain a position of global hegemony while violating the sovereignty of other nations. He concludes by absolving President Lyndon Johnson of any sin: "[Johnson] had been *misled* by the calculus of rational reward and *misdirected* by the theories of victory employed by the military commanders. He had been seduced by the shared intellectual heritage" (emphases added 241).

Cable's argument is reinforced in a recently published book, *Prelude to Tragedy: Vietnam 1960–1965*. Editors Harvey Neese and John O'Donnell bring together eight accounts, five from Americans and three from Vietnamese who had been participants in counterinsurgent activities during the war. While *Prelude to Tragedy* was not an oral history project, it nonetheless provided an opportunity for relatively unknown actors to tell their stories. The contributors felt compelled to present their personal narratives as a corrective to written accounts and popular memories of the Vietnam War. The editors state that they and the contributors were reacting especially against Robert McNamara's book, *In Retrospect,* which argues that the U.S. government lacked expert advisors during the early phases of the Vietnam War. State Neese and O'Donnell:

> [the] sad truth is that in the initial stages of U.S. involvement in South Vietnam in the early 1960s, there were many individuals with experience in Asia and in dealing with communist revolutionary warfare who were not consulted or whose advice was ignored or dismissed. (1)

This collection of essays argues that in the early 1960s the Strategic Hamlet Program (in which the peasantry was herded into fenced-in camps), along with the U.S. Office of Rural Affairs, was making progress in securing the countryside from communist infiltration. The authors contend that rather than continuing to focus on protecting the civilian population, and improving their lives, American decision makers redirected energy toward reorganizing the South Vietnamese army into a conventional military force, sent in American soldiers, and pursued search-and-destroy operations that antagonized the people. The book's contributors charged that arrogant American and Vietnamese leaders, including McNamara himself, did not listen to the experts who had field experience, and who were calling for a political war in order to win the hearts and minds of the people.

The contributors to this book rely on their own experience in the field, as civilian and military officials connected with the rural program, to give authority to their accounts. They were thus assessing their own performance, just as McNamara was evaluating his own part in the tragedy of Vietnam. A truth revealed in this book is the great amount of frustration felt by mid-level U.S. and Vietnamese officials in their attempts to change the overall war strategy. What is also clear is that there were many divergent views within the American side over how to wage the war.

"WE COULD HAVE WON"

Gary Hess mentions Harry Summers (*On Strategy,* 1982), Bruce Palmer (*The 25-Year War,* 1984), and Phillip Davidson (*Vietnam at War,* 1990), as a few examples of writers who argue that

> [had] Washington recognized Vietnam as a war of aggression from the North and not as an insurgency supported by the North, had U.S. power been used fully against the North, and had Johnson enlisted popular support and a national commitment, the war could have been won quickly and decisively. (242)

Far from losing ground, this "revisionist" interpretation continues to surface in a number of recent publications. In the foreword of Mark Woodruff's *Unheralded Victory,* General James Jones commends Woodruff for arguing that the United States fought the war with "a high degree of professionalism and competence, and the outcome of the war was in great doubt until the U.S. decided to withdraw from the battlefield" (ix). Using mainly English-language secondary materials, Woodruff (who served in the Vietnam War) argues that the United States actually "won" the Vietnam War. Limiting himself to narrating various battles and military operations, Woodruff measures victory in strictly military terms, emphasizing the number of enemy killed. Woodruff praises American conduct in the war, while at the same time criticizing the U.S. press and the anti-war movement for distorting American military "victory" in Vietnam. In focusing only on the military side of the war, Woodruff re-enacts the division that existed on the U.S. side about how the war should have been conducted. As other authors, such as Cable, Neese, and O'Donnell argue, the United States lost the war because it did not pay attention to political and social issues. Thus while Woodruff praises General Westmoreland's search-and-destroy strategy for allowing the South Vietnamese Army to pursue pacification, Neese and O'Donnell in particular point to this approach as the cause of the failure of their counterinsurgency activities.

Woodruff's and other revisionists' interpretations, while not current or even considered credible among academics, remain influential, for such works bolster the official memory of the Vietnam War. Echoing the sentiments of the writers noted above, Ronald Reagan insisted at a press conference in 1985 that the United States did not really lose the war: "We continue to talk about losing that war. . . . We didn't lose that war. We won virtually every engagement" (qtd. in McMahon 168–69). According to McMahon, there has been a concerted effort by successive U.S. administrations since the end of the war to "forge a positive societal memory of both the Vietnam War and the soldiers who served there, while ignoring the more problematic legacies of the conflict" (169). When Jimmy Carter became president, for example, he retreated from his previous stance critical of U.S. involvement in Vietnam, and began to celebrate American heroism instead. Carter not only publicly reinstated the Vietnam veterans as heroes who deserved extra praise since American society was so divided by the war, but also chose to "endorse without equivocation the cause for which they fought as well" (167).

ORAL HISTORY AND THE AMERICAN EXPERIENCE

It is clear that there has yet to be a consensus in American society over the memory and meaning of the Vietnam War. American public memory and historiography of the war continue to be contested domains. While political leaders try to ascribe a positive meaning to the war, anti-war academics continue to counter this effort with detailed accounts of the immoral premise of American intervention. Other writers, many with actual military or political participation, point to the mistakes, missed opportunities, and misunderstandings that led the United States to wage the "wrong" type of war. In this adversarial atmosphere, oral history, personal narratives, and memoirs flourish. Oral histories and personal narratives of the war should therefore be read in the context of these competing interpretations of the Vietnam War.

Two recent publications on the history of the Vietnam War are especially notable for their incorporation of oral history. In *A Grand Delusion: America's Descent into Vietnam,* Robert Mann masterfully weaves oral sources with traditional written records to produce a massively detailed political history of the United States during the Vietnam War. Focusing on five U.S. presidents (from Truman to Nixon), their advisors, U.S. congressmen, and senators, Mann's book examines how these key figures led their nation into the "quagmire" of Vietnam. Mann argues that the United States became involved in Vietnam because American leaders were deluded by the myth of an international communist threat and by miscalculations about the nature of the war. While he focuses on these mistakes, Mann does not argue that

U.S. foreign intervention in Vietnam was, as Larry Cable and others have contended, a result of good intentions gone astray. On the contrary, Mann suggests that fear of the domestic political consequences of losing Southeast Asia to communism motivated many administrations to increase U.S. involvement in Vietnam. In other words, bringing democracy to the Vietnamese people and fighting global communism were not the only factors shaping U.S. foreign policies in Vietnam:

> The [Vietnam] war dispelled the widespread and erroneous belief that, in its foreign and military policies, the United States had always exhibited the purest of motives and actions. . . . From Truman to Nixon, the decisions about Vietnam were almost always made by presidents and other political leaders seeking to preserve or enhance their domestic or international political standings. (731)

To this end, successive presidents, such as Johnson and Nixon, and their advisors misinformed and lied to Congress and the American public about the situation in Vietnam. Mann also faults members of Congress for "abdicating their constitutional responsibilities" (729) in their uncritical and ill-informed stance regarding the war. This belief puts Mann squarely in the orthodox camp, which argues that there was no moral basis for U.S. intervention in Vietnam, and that the war was waged with much duplicity and abuse of power on the U.S. government's part.

In giving perspective to archival documents, government publications, and memoirs, Mann makes effective use of approximately 170 oral interviews with prominent U.S. figures. With the exception of the several dozen interviews Mann personally conducted, the majority of the interviews cited in his book had already been collected in the late 1960s and early 1970s by various oral history projects. These interviews, in combination with other sources, allow Mann to give life to his narrative. In the discussion of the Gulf of Tonkin incidents of 1964, for example, oral evidence is used to dramatize vividly how deceitful the White House was to members of its government. Quoted below is the secretary of defense, Robert McNamara, upon being questioned during a joint session of the Armed Services and Foreign Relations Committees about the relationship between the provocative raids being conducted against North Vietnam along the Gulf of Tonkin coast and the U.S. ships that were on patrol on the night of the alleged second attack by the North:

> When his time to question the witnesses arrived, [Wayne] Morse was blunt. "I am unalterably opposed to this course of action which, in my judgment, is an aggressive course of action on the part of the United States. I think we are kidding the world," he told McNamara, "if you try to give the impression that when the South Vietnamese naval boats bombarded two islands a short distance off the coast of North Vietnam, we were not implicated."

In response, McNamara, with convincing deceit, unequivocally denied Morse's charges. "Our Navy played absolutely no part in, was not associated with, was not aware of, any South Vietnamese actions, if there were any," he said. "I want to make that very clear to you. The *Maddox* was operating in international waters, was carrying out a routine patrol of the type we carry out all over the world at all times." Despite the fact that little of what he had just said was true, McNamara insisted that "I think it is extremely important that you understand this. If there is any misunderstanding on that we should discuss the point at some length" (359–60).

In Mann's book, oral history is used to augment traditional written sources — to produce "more history" as opposed to "no history" (Frisch 9). Yet Mann's use of oral history does not give voice to the previously unheard; rather, the influential politicians, officials, and their close advisors are the ones who are highlighted. Since the views and interpretations of historical events of influential policy makers are readily available and heavily documented, the use of oral evidence in this case might provide a new interpretation, but not a new perspective. Thus while Mann's use of oral history is effective in shoring up his argument, the use of oral evidence itself makes less of an impact on readers than when unknown players are brought to the fore.

A more compelling impact is achieved with the use of oral history in Christian Appy's *The Working-Class War*. Appy's book explores the "war-related experience and attitudes of the 2.5 million young American enlisted men who served in Vietnam" (6) in an attempt to provide a deeper social context for the Vietnam War. Appy's focus is the enlisted men, the young, low-ranking, non-career (mainly combat) soldiers, non-commissioned officers, and Marines, who comprised the great bulk of the American military in Vietnam (324n). The premise of *The Working-Class War* is that the working class and the poor carried the burden of fighting the Vietnam War. Not only did the working-class bear the brunt of the war, but it also bore (and still bears) the guilt of fighting a war that, according to Appy, was clearly unjust. Appy believes the reason why many Vietnam War veterans find it difficult to readjust to civilian life is that they, and more importantly, U.S. society at large, have not fully confronted the "social and moral cruelty of the Vietnam War" (321). This failure leaves veterans feeling more alienated from postwar society:

> Thus the veterans have had to confront the war in social and moral isolation, an isolation exacerbated by the class inequalities of the war. The working class not only shouldered a disproportionate share of the war's fighting but a disproportionate share of its moral turmoil. (321)

Without a doubt, Appy is of the opinion that the United States was wrong to intervene in Vietnam. The belief is essential to the book's argument that U.S.

society as well as its veterans still need to deal with the moral legacy of
the war.

The Working-Class War is a highly provocative and readable account of
the Vietnam War, from the perspective of American soldiers. Appy uses oral
sources effectively to provide readers with vivid details of basic training,
soldiers' first impressions of Vietnam, their grueling experience on the front-
lines, and their difficult re-entry into American society. Appy provides a
compelling description of soldiers' typical experiences in combat that, contrary to popular images of intense fighting, consisted of endless and seemingly purposeless marches through jungles or paddy fields. Here Appy allows
a soldier to describe his experience:

> The average operation lasted 30 days or so. And during that time we did
> nothing but walk. We would just walk — no rhyme, no reason — from the
> crack of dawn until dusk. (180)

The same soldier goes on to describe the sheer physical difficulty of marching
in the heat:

> I never fully understood the value of water until I got to 'Nam. . . . There were
> times when I seriously considered drinking my own urine. If we did manage to
> run across some water, we were supposed to fill our canteens, then add two
> purification tablets, shake well, and wait 5 or 10 minutes. What we actually
> did was, fill our canteens, grit our teeth together (to filter out bugs and what-
> ever) and drink, and drink and drink some more. Around the third canteen I
> would start thinking about the bugs that slipped by my teeth and stop. And
> then I would add the purification tablets. (180)

Appy mentions in his acknowledgments that in-depth interviews with
Vietnam veterans, and the weekly Vietnam vet rap sessions he attended from
1981 to 1988, were crucial to this book (ix). Nevertheless, with the exception
of Chapter 2 (on the prewar lives of the veterans), the book relies heavily on
previously published oral history collections such as Mark Baker's *Nam,* and
fictional treatments of the war such as Tim O'Brien's *Going After Cacciato.*
More importantly, Appy does not discuss the methodology he applied to the
interviews he conducted. It would have been helpful had Appy shared his
experience of interviewing the veterans. Since, as Appy himself states, there
was a high level of distrust among Vietnam veterans, it would have been
illuminating to know how he was able to gain their confidence.

In a book review of four publications based on oral accounts of U.S. veterans, Ralph Mavis states that there is a tendency to use veterans' oral narratives to illustrate "moral judgment," and to paint the war as either evil or
noble (Mavis 105). Mavis thus suggests that oral histories of the Vietnam
War should be judged "on how well they avoid the pitfalls of either of these

positions and how much they increase our understanding of the war and the soldiers who fought it" (Mavis 106). Considering the intensity of the polemics still animating the historiography of the Vietnam War, this search for cool objectivity may involve a tall order. Since historians using conventional sources can and have used their evidence to argue that the war was either right or wrong, asking oral historians to do differently is unrealistic in the present atmosphere. What readers should ask of oral historians, however, is to treat their oral sources as rigorously as they do their documented sources — to discuss openly the difficulties and limitations of the sources and to acknowledge the selectivity of any account, written or oral. For while no one historical treatment can claim to deal with all perspectives, being explicit about one's choice of focus and acknowledging the inevitable silences and absences would be a step toward reaching some consensus about the history and meaning of the Vietnam War.

ALTERNATE VIEWS EMERGING IN VIETNAM

The interpretation of the Vietnam War in Vietnam itself has been, until recently, dominated by the state's version. The Vietnamese state casts the war as a struggle against foreign aggression, a revolutionary movement that had its roots in the fight for independence from French colonialism. The orthodox Vietnamese version, both in written history and in popular memory, therefore views the Vietnamese communist state "as the legitimate inheritor of the Vietnamese patriotic tradition and the dominant force in the recent history of the country" (Tai, "Introduction" 3).

From the mid-1980s on, a few political exposés were published that revealed the tensions and discontent felt by a number of important players on the communist side. Of works such Bui Tin's *Following Ho Chi Minh: Memoirs of a North Vietnamese Colonel* and Truong Nhu Tang's *Journal of a Vietcong,* Greg Lockhart notes "exile is more or less a precondition" (321). While these memoirs, like all political memoirs, should be read cautiously since self-justification and the author's own personal motives inevitably skew the narrative, they represent a prelude to the challenges that the official history of the war has begun to encounter.

In 1986, Vietnam began on a new economic and political path called *Doi Moi* (Renovation). While international events such as Mikhail Gorbachev's *Perestroika* and *Glasnost* had an impact on Vietnam's decision to move away from a state-controlled economy and toward more political openness, domestic challenges coming from peasants played an important role in pushing for change. In the atmosphere of openness during this period, intellectual and artistic discourses illustrated that the public memory of the Vietnam War is as contested a field in Vietnam as it is in the United States, albeit in less overt forms.

In the realm of literature, the state's sanctioned history of the war is being directly challenged. In the late 1980s, a body of work known as "literature of dissent" (*van chuong phan khang*) emerged following the pronouncement of the then Secretary-General of the Communist Party, Nguyen Van Linh: "Whatever happens, never curb your pen" (quoted by Tai, "Duong Thu Huong" 82). Fiction writers such as Bao Ninh, Nguyen Huy Thiep, Le Minh Khue, and Duong Thu Huong took up this task.[6] Bao Ninh's and Duong Thu Huong's novels, in particular, question the cost of waging the war, and both novels conclude that the cost was too high. Internationally recognized Duong Thu Huong's *Novel Without a Name* and Bao Ninh's *The Sorrow of War*, both of which have been compared to Erich Maria Remarque's classic *All Quiet on the Western Front*, highlight the human cost, the myth of heroism, and the hollowness of war propaganda.

Duong Thu Huong was born in 1947 in a northern province of Thai Binh. In 1967, at the age of twenty, and already a member of the Communist Party, Duong Thu Huong volunteered for the army and was sent to the Central Highlands, near the border between the North and South (Tai, "Duong Thu Huong" 83). Her Youth Brigade was in charge of entertaining troops and raising their morale. But of the forty members of her troupe, only three survived the war. In 1979, four years after the war ended, Duong Thu Huong was the first female volunteer for the border war with China. Her impressive record of military and political commitment makes her rebellion all the more formidable.

Duong Thu Huong began writing fiction in the mid-1970s, but it was not until 1988 with the publication of *Paradise of the Blind* that she began to voice her dissent and challenge the orthodox history of the war and the Communist Revolution. This novel sold 40,000 copies before the authorities banned it. Duong Thu Huong's next novel, *Novel Without a Name,* which was published abroad, was also banned. As a result of her writing, Duong Thu Huong was expelled from the Communist Party, and in 1991 she was arrested on false charges. She still lives in Hanoi and maintains a tense relationship with the government.

Novel Without a Name is about the horrors of war, mass killing, and the destruction of the spirit and humanity of the survivors. The main character is Quan, the chief of a battalion. Though Quan is only twenty-eight years old, he has already spent ten years fighting in the jungle. Contrary to the heroic image of the Northern fighter who is totally committed to the revolutionary cause, Duong Thu Huong's characters lack the enthusiasm and ideals they had at the start of the war. The soldiers' main preoccupation is to fulfill the basic physical needs of hunger, thirst, and sexual desire. Worse still, the soldiers have grown indifferent to violence after ten long years of war. Quan narrates this change:

> I had watched all of this while we young recruits, drunk on our youth, envisioned ourselves marching toward a glorious future; we were the elect in a grandiose mission.
>
> This war was not simply another war against foreign aggression; it was also our chance for a resurrection. Vietnam had been chosen by History: After the war, our country would become humanity's paradise. Our people would hold a rank apart. At last we would be respected, honored, revered. We believed this, so we turned away from those tears of weakness.
>
> Ten years had passed. None of us spoke about this anymore. But none of us had forgotten. The deeper we plunged into the war, the more the memory of that first day haunted us. The more we were tortured by the consciousness of our appalling indifference, the more searing the memory of our mothers' tears. We had renounced everything for glory. It was this guilt that bound us to one another as tightly as the memory of our days tending water buffalo together. (31–32)

Like Duong Thu Huong, Bao Ninh served in the Youth Brigade and was one of the ten survivors of the original five hundred members of the unit (Kleinen 411–28). *The Sorrow of War* is about the brutal war experience and also the disenchantments of the postwar period. The novel alternates between the protagonist Kien's nightmarish memories of the war and his present attempt to cope with his new, postwar life. In a conversation with another soldier after the war, Kien struggles with questions about the higher moral cause of the war, as well as his own personal loss:

> "But isn't peace better than war?"
>
> The driver seemed astonished. "This kind of peace? In this kind of peace it seems people have unmasked themselves and revealed their true, horrible selves. So much blood, so many lives were sacrificed for what?"
>
> "Damn it, what are you trying to say?" Kien asked.
>
> "I'm not trying to say anything. I'm simply a soldier like you who'll now have to live with broken dreams and with pain. But, my friend, our era is finished. After this hard-won victory fighters like you, Kien, will never be normal again. You won't even speak with your normal voice, in the normal way again." (38)

What both *Novel Without a Name* and *The Sorrow of War* highlight is the personal loss that people experienced during and after the war. The focus on loss is a counterpoint to the state's heavy emphasis on collective victories. Wayne Karlin notes that the tendency to focus on private loss also appears in non-dissident writers' works (Karlin 1). He mentions, for example, the literature of "establishment" writers such as Vu Bao, Ho Anh Thai, and Le Luu. Karlin gives us an English translation of Vu Bao's short story, "The Man Who

Stained His Soul," a satire about a coward who is made into a celebrated hero. The charade is continued even when the authorities realize they have made a mistake. Ho Anh Thai's novella, *The Women on the Island,* examines the lives of a group of female veterans who, because of years spent fighting in the war, lost the opportunity to get married and bear children. This anamoly in a society that values family above all is depicted as a truly significant sacrifice made for the war effort. Another non-dissident writer, Le Luu, shows in his novel that people's levels of commitment to the war effort varied. In *A Time Far Past,* the main character's reason for enlisting was not so much political conviction or moral belief in the cause, but an opportunity to separate from his estranged wife.

The subdued debate on the legacy of the war in Vietnam shows that, as in the United States, the social memory of the Vietnam War is being contested and challenged. Far from being forgotten or relegated to tempered academic analysis, the history of the war is being claimed by individuals and groups who vie for their right to shape the discourse. Personal narratives, in the form of prose fiction, are produced to counter the officially sanctioned written and popular memory of the war. Whereas officially sanctioned history portrays the war as heroic, and holds as redemptive its mass death and colossal destruction, personal accounts continually emphasize the enduring, traumatic effects of individual loss and sacrifice. The Vietnamese soldiers in Duong Thu Huong's and Bao Ninh's novels resemble the American "grunts" of Christian Appy's *The Working-Class War.* The foot soldiers on both sides seem to lack political fervour and the faith that the war was worth the sacrifice. The North Vietnamese novelists' judgments of the war, however, were formed in the context of postwar corruption and betrayal. Much of the evaluation of the war is influenced by the soldiers' and civilians' feelings of betrayal by the communist state after 1975. The blatant corruption of the high-level officials and the continued deprivation in the 1970s and 1980s shaped how these fictional accounts depict the war. These narratives, therefore, should be read not only as a protest against the war but also as a protest against postwar corruption, and as a challenge to the Communist Party's claim to power.

The importance of postwar disenchantment in shaping people's memories is illustrated in Karen Turner's oral history records of North Vietnamese female veterans. *Even the Women Must Fight,* based mainly on interviews with female veterans of the Volunteer Youth Team C814, shows the complicated relationship between personal memories and collective history. While this book was a joint effort with Pham Thanh Hao, Turner retains the narrative authority, framing the oral testimonies within her own narration. The active participation of the interviewees is evident, and one gets a vivid sense of the female veterans as subjects who drive and divert Turner's narrative. A stated purpose of the book is to examine how the women veterans placed their personal experience within the larger national narrative. Turner discovers that the Vietnamese government's constructions of the ideal Vietnamese woman during and after the war were fraught with ambiguities and did not speak to the experiences that the women themselves remembered. While the state's wartime feminine model was a warrior-mother who was a hard fighter at the same time as she was gentle and womanly in her familial role (35–38), the oral interviews stress the hardship, male biases, and fear they endured. One of the veterans Turner interviewed, a Mrs. Hoa, recounts her trek to the front as part of a road-building brigade:

> It took twenty-one days to reach our destination in Quang Binh Province. Our feet were torn, infected, and bleeding. We couldn't put our feet directly into our rubber sandals; it was too painful. So we had to cover our feet with towels, pieces of cloth from our blouses, anything we could find. And we cried. We were so frightened by the bombs, constantly falling down on us, everywhere.
>
> We came upon a woman about to give birth. We were all young girls, and we knew nothing about it. There was no one else to help her. When the baby came out the cord was wrapped around its neck. We cut it, and the woman stood up, bleeding. The American flares helped us see. We don't know what happened to her or her baby. As we got closer to the battlefields, sometimes we came upon dead women, still holding on to dead babies. (94–95)

Mrs. Hoa's oral account expresses feelings of personal hardship, fear, and loss that could easily have been overlooked in document-based histories focusing on the "bigger picture" — on the major battles, or on prominent decision makers. Another veteran, a Mrs. Linh, relates in detail what daily survival in the jungle was like:

> I tried to keep myself clean, to maintain some feeling of order and routine in these conditions, which were terrible, especially for women. There were no sanitary supplies, but women's menstrual periods often stopped anyway because of bad diet and stress.
>
> I lived this way from the age of eighteen to twenty-four. The men did the harder physical work and they got sick more easily than women. We made our own clothes and helped them with their sewing. Some people couldn't live in this way, and some went mad. Women seemed better able to endure. We gave the men our best rations, because we felt sorry for them. The most terrible time came when two of my male comrades-in-arms starved to death. We couldn't take time out to cook rice because the smoke would attract the planes. Their diet of freshly picked grass wasn't enough to keep them alive. (122)

Mrs. Linh's account also touches upon the sexual roles and stereotypes that persisted even as men and women fought together. Throughout the book there is a revealing tension between Turner's own Western feminist beliefs and the traditional ideas of the female veterans. While Turner seeks a feminist dimension to the women's combatant efforts, there is a tendency among the Vietnamese veterans to view their contribution as part of the traditional women's role. In other words, rather than challenging gender relations, women's wartime service reflected the traditional female role within Vietnamese society, one that idealizes women's capacity to sacrifice themselves for the good of the collective. Turner's reflexive struggle with her own views and those of the veterans is both instructive and important as a starting point for further explorations of cultural differences.

Turner, however, reminds readers that the North Vietnamese female veterans' stories, like those apparent in anti-war Vietnamese novels, emerged in a period of growing disenchantment and questioning of postwar social values and morality. The veterans' oral testimonies to their wartime service must be placed within a context of the veterans' postwar criticism of state neglect and the ingratitude of the society at large, within a society that has become more capitalistic and materialistic.

THE OVERSEAS VIETNAMESE

On the rare occasions that American writers venture to examine the "other side" of the war, they usually refer to the communist side. Jayne Werner and Luu Doan Huynh's important collection of essays, for example, titled *The Vietnam War: Vietnamese and American Perspectives,* includes only three Vietnamese contributions (out of eighteen), all representing the communist side. In 1990, George Herring wrote that in the historiography of the Vietnam War "the South Vietnamese are conspicuous by their absence, and virtually nothing has been done on their dealings with the United States" ("Presidential" 1). Little has changed since Herring called attention to this gap. Moreover, with the exception of Charles Callison's book on the land reform policies of the 1970s, little attention has been given to South Vietnamese society. In general, one does not get a sense of South Vietnam as an entity, or society with an intellectual or cultural life. Perhaps this is telling of the lack of coherence in South Vietnam. But the Vietnam War was also a civil war; however fractious, dependent on U.S. aid, and lacking in coherent vision, there *was* a South Vietnam.

Some in South Vietnam supported the Saigon regime, some supported the National Liberation Front (NLF), and some worked for a neutral solution (such as Nguyen Cong Hoan and Tran Ngoc Chau, members of the National Assembly in South Vietnam who opposed the war and tried to work for a negotiated peace with the National Liberation Front). While the supporters of the NLF and neutralists have received some scholarly attention (Chanoff,

Truong Nhu Tang), it is the first group—those who fought for and supported the South—whose voices have been muted in the historiography and the popular memory in both the West and Vietnam. While within the overseas Vietnamese communities in the West strong efforts are made to preserve the popular memory of the heroism and patriotism of the "nationalist" fighters, within the larger, non-Vietnamese society, the non-communists' stories are often neglected. Within Vietnam itself, the supporters of the former Saigon government, routinely referred to as the "puppet regime" in books and government publications, have no claim to a place in national history or popular memory. In sharp contrast to the elaborate commemorative monuments built in honour of Northern soldiers, Southern soldiers' cemeteries were razed after 1975 (Tai, "Faces" 191). Hue-Tam Ho Tai's work on social memory of the war in Vietnam suggests that the politics of forgetting is important for maintaining the outer appearance of peace within Vietnamese society and families (191).

While English-language historiography tends to neglect the viewpoints of those who supported the South Vietnamese regime, sources providing their perspectives do, in fact, exist. John Kleinen and Cao Xuan Tu cite a number of important South Vietnamese writers whose literary works provide insight into the dilemma faced by the non-communist South Vietnamese (415). The stories of Nhat Tien and Thao Truong, for example, deal with the difficulty of choosing sides in a civil war. According to John Kleinen and Cao Xuan Tu, Nhat Tien's and Thao Truong's writings examine the sorrows of a people separated and divided by politics and wars (415). An English translation of a selection of work in Thao Truong's *Trial by Fire* can be found in Neil Jamieson's *Understanding Vietnam* (285–89). In this translated selection, the narrator rages against the artificial border between North and South Vietnam as he stands on a bridge linking both sides. The narrator argues that both North and South are essentially one nation and rejects the imposition of borders and divisions. Another famous South Vietnamese writer, Nha Ca, writes about violence and brutality in the ancient imperial city of Hue during the Tet Offensive (416). This body of literature, produced in Vietnam during the war, can shed light on the intellectual and moral reasoning of the non-communist Vietnamese in their support for an obviously ineffective regime.

Ly Qui Chung's *Between Two Fires* offers a rare glimpse at what some unknown South Vietnamese writers thought during the war. The book is a collection of nine stories that won a contest organized by the newspaper, *Tieng Noi Dan Toc* (The People's Voice). The anti-war sentiments expressed by the daily and by the contest stories eventually led to the closure of the newspaper by the South Vietnamese government. With the exception of Ngoc Ky's "autobiographical account" (75–93), neither the editor nor the writers claim the stories to be anything other than fictional. These accounts, however, all bear high degrees of realism and provide intimate daily details of various aspects of life during the war.

Memoirs and fiction published by overseas Vietnamese also provide an important entrée into the experience and thinking of the non-communist side. Nguyen Ngoc Ngan's *The Will of Heaven*, for example, traces the traumatic refugee experience, opening with a glimpse of life in the South Vietnamese Army toward the end of the war. Both Nguyen Thi Thu-Lam's and Le Ly Hayslip's memoirs recount their experiences in South Vietnam and their association with American G.I.'s. Other works tell of the hardships of the re-education camps in postwar Vietnam (Metzner; Thong).

Notable is Duong Van Mai Elliott's family history in revealing the experience of the upper-middle class South Vietnamese during the war. Elliott's book *The Sacred Willow,* based on archival research as well as oral interviews, extends the timeline back into the French period, presenting the dilemma of a mandarin family trying to choose between supporting the French or the Viet Minh. Elliott shows that her father was torn between sympathy for the communists and repugnance for the violence they advocated (48). In 1954, some members of her immediate and extended family chose to remain in the North while other family members supported the Southern government. In a grounded way, Elliott was able to show how her family's experience, fraught by diverging sympathies, mirrored the general history of Vietnam.

Complementing this body of personal narratives is the fiction produced by overseas Vietnamese writers in both English and Vietnamese. Prevalent in this literature is the sense of personal loss and displacement, as well as an expressed need to reconcile with both the "enemy" and with the new host country (Karlin). Wayne Karlin cites the writings of Vo Phien and Hong Khoi Phong, as well as younger writers of the new generation, who struggle with the question of exile: "What is lost, what is kept and what is gained?" (1).

Personal narratives in the form of prose fiction, memoirs, and family history can thus provide insights into dilemmas faced by the non-communist contingents in South Vietnam. As the most underrepresented in English-language historiography, the non-communist South Vietnamese perspective can benefit enormously from oral history projects. Oral accounts can help illuminate perspectives of the war, and perhaps can explain why the South Vietnamese threw their support behind such a weak and fractious regime. From the perspective of standard North American historiography, it is difficult to see why the Saigon government received support, yet many Vietnamese people did extend exactly such support. In her account of the Vietnam War, Marilyn Young characterizes the anti-communist immigrants who chose to migrate South after the 1954 Geneva Conference as sheep following the dictates of their parish priests. Young cites

> the exodus of almost 1 million Catholics from north to south who were said to have "voted with their feet" for freedom. They did not use their feet, nor was their flight entirely for freedom. Encouraged by Catholic hierarchy and organized by Lansdale [a U.S. Air Force Colonel] and his team, entire parishes were carried South in American ships, following priests who told them Christ had moved south, as well as making promises of land and livelihood. (45)

There is clearly a lack of scholarly research on the population who left the North, of which one-third were not Roman Catholic (Turley 11). Oral narratives could assist in filling the gap but very few have been produced and their quality is uneven. Susan Sheehan's *Ten Vietnamese*, published in 1967, sought to humanize the war by giving voice to the ordinary Vietnamese caught within it. As a journalist for *The New Yorker*, Sheehan conducted interviews with ten Vietnamese through an interpreter, and published their stories in the second person, with herself as the narrator. In an attempt to present a cross-section of South Vietnamese society, Sheehan presents the stories of ten people of diverse backgrounds, ranging from an orphan boy to a South Vietnamese soldier to a Viet Cong. The book provides compelling accounts of how ten supposedly ordinary people viewed the war and coped. What is striking is that the majority of the interviewees were stubbornly apolitical, expressing only a desire to be left in peace. There is, however, little self-reflection on Sheehan's part; she does not tell us why she interviewed the people she did. It is thus difficult to judge how representative these ten Vietnamese are, and despite Sheehan's stated intention of allowing readers access to the ordinary Vietnamese people (xi–xii), her subjects come off stilted and objectified. In other words, her book does not fully allow "the people" to speak directly.

A more illuminating contribution of oral history is Al Santoli's *To Bear Any Burden*, composed of interviews with forty-eight Asians and Westerners. The oral narratives are presented thematically and temporally. Thus in the section titled "April 1975," readers are presented with various memories of this day of liberation or defeat, depending on the subject's point of view. Unlike his earlier oral history project, *Everything We Had*, which focuses on U.S. soldiers, this collection includes non-veterans as well. Some interviewees are famous U.S. and Vietnamese personalities, a few of whom have authored/edited their own books on the war, such as General Edward Lansdale, Col. Harry Summers, Truong Nhu Tang, and Doan Van Toai.

Santoli makes clear that he thinks North Vietnam and the Viet Cong were the wrong side (xxi) and that while U.S. soldiers did their best, there "was no mandate for victory" (xxii). He believes that there is a need to come to terms with "the Vietnam trauma" and hopes that *To Bear Any Burden* speaks to the common humanity of all those involved in the war: "This is a book about values. We who remember invite you to look back with us, behind the veil of myth and rhetoric" (xxiv). Santoli clearly sees his oral history projects as revealing deeper truths that have been missed by conventional historiography; he presents his text as a way of bypassing professional historians, allowing the participants to "tell it like it was" (Frisch 9).

While Santoli does not say exactly what myth and rhetoric he hopes to dismantle, the book provides valuable glimpses of non-communist Vietnamese, Laotians, and Cambodian perspectives that are often not highlighted. Some of the non-communist narratives address the perceptions of and dilemmas faced by this population during the war. Their interviews provide insight into why Vietnamese nationalists would support the Saigon government, considering how discredited it became. The interview with Le Thi Anh, for example, conveys why she joined the French side in the first Indochina War. Le Thi Anh had joined the Viet Minh and fought underground from 1945 until 1952:

> In 1947, I got married to a fighter in my group. And my son was born in the underground. As the war continued to go against us, we finally had to retreat into the Plain of Reeds, a mostly uninhabitable marshy area. Sometimes we didn't have rice or regular meals. And we always dressed in rags.
>
> I stayed in the underground until 1952, a couple of years before Mr. [Ngo Dinh] Diem came home. I left because I saw too many frightening things. The Communists were grabbing all the power by killing off the nationalists.
>
> The Communists had organized in the resistance with us. We fought together and regarded them as comrades in arms. But sometimes in the middle of the night they would tell us, "Hold the area." And they would leave to indicate to the French where our nationalist positions were. The Communists betrayed us all the time. Ho Chi Minh's people began to kill off all of the strong non-Communist leaders and Trotskyite Communists in the resistance. One of my uncles, Le Trong, and friends like Dr. Suong, after collaborating with the Communists were killed by them. Huynh Phu So, the leader of the Hoa Hao Buddhist sect, whom I knew personally, was also killed by Ho's people. (36)

Another interviewee, Ha Thuc Ky, refers as well to the political assassinations and rivalry between the Communist Party and the other nationalist groups, such as the Dai Viet Party, within the Viet Minh front:

> In 1946 I first heard that Ho Chi Minh's agents were killing off rival nationalists . . . When we discovered Ho's Communists were killing non-Communists throughout the country, we realized that our leaders were in danger. I received orders from Truong Tu Anh, the Dai Viet Party leader, to work undercover in Hanoi, to report on both the French and the Communist activities. . . . Our party leader, Truong Tu Anh, had been captured by the Communists while I

was in Hanoi. Around that same time, the Communists killed the great Hoa
Hao resistance leader, Huynh Phu So, who had two million followers in the
Delta. A real hatred developed between the Viet Minh Communists and the
non-Communist nationalist parties. (39)

These oral accounts show that the distrust between communists and non-
communists began very early on during the struggle for independence from
France. Both the communist and non-communist factions of the Vietnamese
nationalist movement competed for political dominance. Their mutual an-
tagonism was therefore as much a political rivalry as it was an ideological
clash. This is an important point for comprehending the civil-war aspect of
the Vietnam War.

These oral narratives, however, provide us with more than the historical
facts often missed in written histories of the war. They also reveal how
individuals make political choices. For both Le Thi Anh and Ha Thuc Ky,
knowing someone who had been assassinated by the communists played a
big role in cementing political loyalty. Despite Marilyn Young's assertion that
North Vietnamese migrants were enticed to the South primarily by their
priests and material promises, these oral accounts suggest that Northern
migrants might have had other reasons for not supporting the communists.

Santoli's work shows how oral histories can illuminate our understanding of the Vietnam War. In its broad coverage, however, *To Bear Any Burden*
provides only a few perspectives from the non-communist side. What is
needed is a project to examine critically and more deeply the perspectives and
experiences of this other population, for it is only when this third side is
acknowledged and written into history that the Vietnam War will be better
understood.

CONCLUSION

Within the three "zones of contested meanings," both the history and social
memory of the Vietnam War remain highly controversial, inconclusive, and
painful subjects. It will be many years before the historiography of the war
reaches a level of completely dispassionate academic analysis, and it will
take even longer, if it ever occurs at all, for the social memory to become
less highly charged. As we have seen with other major historical events, even
ones of our distant pasts such as the "discovery" of the Americas by Co-
lumbus, the social memory of events can periodically be challenged and
contested. This process is necessary, particularly if the challenge brings about
new understandings and unearths the voices and stories that had previously
been buried. As it stands now, the official memories of the war in both the
United States and Vietnam seek to suppress those that do not contribute to

the construction of a positive national image or to national unity. While there was much talk about reconciliation between the U.S. and Vietnam in the early 1990s, reconciliation within each society is also dearly needed. Robert McMahon makes the comparison between the American Civil War and the Vietnam War in terms of their divisive effects on American society. But unlike the open disputes over meanings in the United States, the war's divisiveness in Vietnam has yet to be addressed by the Vietnamese state, which belatedly acknowledged only in 1995 that the Vietnam War was a civil war (Tai, "Faces" 180–81). The lack of a forum in Vietnam for honest and free dialogue about wartime divisions and differences makes the coming to terms with the disruptions of the civil war a difficult task. The neglect of the noncommunist Vietnamese, both in American writings and Hanoi's official narrative of the war, has led to a major gap in scholarship. Filling this gap will be important for a fuller understanding of the history of the war, for the process of collective healing among the overseas Vietnamese population, and for national reconciliation in Vietnam.

NOTES

1. For the sake of brevity, I have chosen to focus on only three perspectives. There are, of course, many others. I am thinking in particular of the Cambodians and Laotians who suffered much violence and disruption during the war. I am also thinking of the many minority ethnic groups in Vietnam who do not see themselves as Vietnamese.

2. Here I am informed by McMahon's essay and the collection on commemoration in Vietnam edited by Hue-Tam Ho Tai, *The Country of Memory*.

3. Chen Jian and Qiang Zhai have published material on China's role in the war; Ronnie Ford has written about the Tet Offensive using North Vietnamese sources; Ilya Gaiduk has described Russia's role in the war; and Ang Cheng Guan deals with "Hanoi's decision-making process" in 1962–1964 (Ang Cheng Guan 601–18).

4. Examples of other writers who share Kahin's evaluation of the war are Gabriel Kolko and Marilyn Young.

5. Others who share Cable's approach are Robert McNamara and Thomas Thayer.

6. In this section I am surveying only the translated literature that is easily accessible for North American readers.

WORKS CITED

Ang, Guan Cheng. "The Vietnam War, 1962–1964: The Vietnamese Communist Perspective." *Journal of Contemporary History* 35.4 (2000): 601–18.

Appy, Christian G. *Working-Class War: American Combat Soldiers and Vietnam.* Chapel Hill: University of North Carolina Press, 1993.

Bao, Ninh. *The Sorrow of War.* London: Secker and Warburg, 1991.

Bui, Tin. *Following Ho Chi Minh: The Memoirs of a North Vietnamese Colonel.* London: Hurst and Company, 1995.

Cable, Larry. *Unholy Grail: The United States and the War in Vietnam.* London: Routledge, 1991.

Callison, Charles. *Land-to-the-Tiller in the Mekong Delta.* Berkeley: University of California, 1983.

Chanoff, David, and Doan Van Toai. *Portrait of the Enemy.* New York: Random House, 1986.

Chung, Ly Qui, ed. *Between Two Fires. The Unheard Voices of Vietnam.* New York: Praeger, 1970.

Duong, Thu Huong. *Novel Without a Name.* New York: William Morrow and Company, 1995.

Elliott, Duong Van Mai. *The Sacred Willow: Four Generations in the Life of a Vietnamese Family.* New York: Oxford University Press, 1999.

Frisch, Michael. *A Shared Authority: Essays on the Craft and Meaning of Oral and Public History.* New York: State University of New York Press, 1990.

Hayslip, Le Ly. *When Heaven and Earth Changed Places.* New York: Penguin, 1989.

Herring, George. "History and Historiography of the Vietnam War." *The Vietnam War: Its History, Literature and Music.* Ed. Kenton Clymer. El Paso: Texas Western Press, 1998, 21–37.

————. "Presidential Address. 'Peoples Quite Apart': Americans, South Vietnamese, and the War in Vietnam." *Diplomatic History* 14.1 (Winter 1990): 1–23.

————. "America and Vietnam: The Debate Continues." *American Historical Review* 92 (April 1987): 350–62.

Hess, Gary. "The Unending Debate: Historians and the Vietnam War." *Diplomatic History* 18.2 (Spring 1994): 239–64.

Ho, Anh Thai. *The Women on the Island.* Seattle: University of Washington Press, 2000.

Jamieson, Neil. *Understanding Vietnam.* Berkeley: University of California Press, 1995.

Kahin, George. *Intervention: How America Became Involved in Vietnam.* New York: Alfred A. Knopf, 1986.

————, and John Lewis. *The United States in Vietnam.* New York: Dial Press, 1967.

Karlin, Wayne. "Hot Damn Vietnam: Twenty-Five Years Later—A Literature of War and Remembrance." *Los Angeles Times* April 23, 2000, Sunday, Home Edition, Book Review, 1.

Kleinen, John, and Cao Xuan Tu. "The Vietnam War through Vietnamese Eyes." *Vietnam Review* 3 (Fall–Winter 1997): 411–28.

Kolko, Gabriel. *Anatomy of a War.* New York: Pantheon Books, 1985.

Le, Luu. *A Time Far Past.* Amherst: University of Massachusetts Press, 1997.

Le, Minh Khue, *The Stars, the Earth, the River: Short Stories by Le Minh Khue.* Willimantic, Conn.: Curbstone Press, 1997.

Lockhart, Greg. "Constructing the Vietnam War: A Review Article." *Contemporary Southeast Asia* 18.3 (December 1996): 320–36.

Mann, Robert. *A Grand Delusion: America's Descent into Vietnam.* New York: Basic Books, 2000.

Mavis, Ralph. " 'Go Tell Americans . . . ': Soldiers' Narratives and Recent Histories of the Vietnam War." *Oral History Review* 22.1 (Summer 1995): 105–13.

McMahon, Robert. "SHAFR Presidential Address: Contested Memory—The Vietnam War and American Society, 1975–2001." *Diplomatic History* 26.2 (Spring 2002): 159–84.

McNamara, Robert. *In Retrospect: The Tragedy and Lessons of Vietnam*. New York: Times Books, 1995.

Metzner, Edward, Huynh Van Chinh, Tran Van Phuc, and Le Nguyen Binh. *Reeducation in Postwar Vietnam: Personal Postscripts to Peace*. Texas: A & M University Press, 2001.

Neese, Harvey and John O'Donnell, eds. *Prelude to Tragedy: Vietnam, 1960–1965*. Annapolis, Md.: Naval Institute Press, 2001.

Nguyen, Huy Thiep, *The General Retires and Other Stories*. Singapore and New York: Oxford University Press, 1992.

Nguyen, Ngoc Ngan. *The Will of Heaven: A Story of One Vietnamese and the End of His World*. New York: E.P. Dutton, 1982.

Nguyen, Thi Thu-Lam. *Fallen Leaves*. New Haven, Conn.: Yale Center for International and Area Studies, Lac Viet Series, 1989.

Nha Ca. *Giai Khan So Cho Hue* [*A Mourning Headband for Hue*]. Saigon: Thuong Yeu, 1969.

——. *Les Canons Tonnent la Nuit*. Arles, France: Philippe Picquier, 1997.

Nhat Tien. *Them Hoang* [*The Abandoned Veranda*]. Westminster, Calif.: Van Nghe, 1989.

Portelli, Alessandro. *The Battle of Valle Giulia: Oral History and the Art of Dialogue*. Madison: University of Wisconsin Press, 1997.

Santoli, Al. *To Bear Any Burden*. Bloomington: Indiana University Press, 1999.

Sheehan, Susan. *Ten Vietnamese*. New York: Alfred A. Knopf, 1967.

Tai, Hue-Tam Ho. "Duong Thu Huong and the Literature of Disenchantment." *Viet Nam Forum* 14 (1993): 82–91.

——. "Faces of Remembrance and Forgetting." *The Country of Memory. Remaking the Past in Late Socialist Vietnam*. Ed. Hue-Tam Ho Tai. Berkeley: University of California Press, 2001, 167–95.

——. "Introduction: Situating Memory." *The Country of Memory: Remaking the Past in Late Socialist Vietnam*. Ed. Hue-Tam Ho Tai. Berkeley: University of California Press, 2001, 1–17.

Thao Truong. *Thu Lua* [*Trial by Fire*]. Saigon: Nam Son, 1962.

Thayer, Thomas. *War Without Fronts: The American Experience in Vietnam*. Boulder: Westview Press, 1985.

Thomson, Alistair, Michael Frisch, and Paula Hamilton. "The Memory and History Debates: Some International Perspectives." *Oral History* 22.2 (Autumn 1994): 33–43.

Thong, Huynh Sanh, ed. *To Be Made Over: Tales of Socialist Reeducation in Vietnam*. New Haven, Conn.: Yale University Council on Southeast Asia Studies, Viet Nam Forum 16, 1997.

Tran Ngoc Chau. "My War Story: From Ho Chi Minh to Ngo Dinh Diem." *Prelude to Tragedy. Vietnam, 1960–1965*. Ed. Harvey Neese and John O'Donnell. Annapolis, Md.: Naval Institute Press, 2001, 180–209.

Truong, Nhu Tang. *A Vietcong Memoir*. San Diego: Harcourt Brace Jovanovich, 1988.

Turley, William. *The Second Indochina War*. Boulder: Westview Press, 1986.

Turner, Karen Gottschangm with Phan Thanh Hao. *Even the Women Must Fight: Memories of War from North Vietnam*. New York: John Wiley and Sons, 1998.

Vu, Bao. "The Man Who Stained His Soul." Trans. Wayne Karlin. *Los Angeles Times* April 23, 2000, Sunday, Home Edition, Book Review, 14.

Werner, Jayne, and Luu Doan Huynh, eds. *The Vietnam War: Vietnamese and American Perspectives*. Armonk, N.Y.: M. E. Sharpe, 1993.

Woodruff, Mark. *Unheralded Victory: Who Won the Vietnam War?* London: Harper Collins Publishers, 1999.

Young, Marilyn. *The Vietnam Wars*. New York: Harper Collins Publishers, 1991.

8. Queering Vietnam
Katherine V. Forrest's Fictional Oral History

PRISCILLA L. WALTON

Given *Soldier Talk*'s explicit focus on oral history and the war in Southeast Asia, this essay may appear rather anomalous. Katherine Forrest's *Liberty Square* is a novel, a form not traditionally associated with "oral" histories. Its genre is also detective fiction (the sixth in the Kate Delafield series, featuring Forrest's ex-Marine-turned-LAPD-cop protagonist), a feature rendering its inclusion even more dubious. Yet while Forrest's *Liberty Square* seems removed from the subject matter of *Soldier Talk,* it creates a critical space from which to complicate the assumptions that underpin conventional constructions of orality and history, and as it digresses from conventional oral histories, it engenders an especially fecund venue for theoretical inquiry.

If oral histories are not usually associated with novels, neither are detective fictions generally linked to war stories. *Liberty Square*'s deviation from its generic locus becomes apparent when one studies readers' responses to the novel's Amazon.com Web page. There, reviewers display uncharacteristic bafflement over how to read or categorize Forrest's text. Puzzled by *Liberty Square*'s focus on Vietnam, an atypical topic for mystery fiction, one reader admits to her surprise at the text's content: "a full 25% of the book is devoted—literally—to Old War Stories. " Another reviewer notes the strange construction of Forrest's work, which is "written like a reunion journal itself—lots of can-you-top-this horror stories about the war to wade through." A third reader suggests that Forrest, a two-time winner of the Lambda Literary Award for Best Mystery, has lost her touch with *Liberty*

Square, since "memories of the war in Vietnam weren't really fleshed out, leaving me with the feeling that Forrest was rushed or over edited," and then refers potential readers to Forrest's earlier novels.

That Forrest would either be rushed or over-edited in *Liberty Square* is highly unlikely, for it is the first time this prominent lesbian novelist and editor of the small press Naiad has written for a mainstream publishing house. Her Kate Delafield series sports one of the only lesbian protagonists to attract attention outside of the women's press community (the second novel in the series, *Murder at the Nightwood Bar,* is presently being turned into a film, already in pre-production with Island Pictures). And Forrest's decision to publish *Liberty Square* with Putnam Press rather than with Naiad was almost certainly calculated and "premeditated." For Forrest, mainstream publication was a literary goal, as she admits in the following interview:

> Initially, most of us [lesbian writers] went to small presses because the major presses simply wouldn't publish us. They had no notion of any sort of audience out there. There just wasn't that much interest in the kind of books we wrote, and so that gave rise to all of these small lesbian and feminist presses, which are still flourishing. . . . To some degree, those of us who are moving from small press to large press are doing it because our dreams have come true. . . .
>
> [In turn, since] review media in this country tend to pay more attention to mainstream books, and I write to be read, it is my hope that more people will be aware that I'm here. (Walton and Jones 107)

Because Forrest has never shied away from political issues (McCarthyism, gay bashing, child abuse, teenage prostitution), her decision to focus on gays in the military in her mainstream debut speaks volumes, since the plight of gay men and women is clearly significant to the author, who opts to "queer" Vietnam in her first mass-market novel.

I would suggest that the confusion generated by *Liberty Square* has to do with the ways in which the novel crosses borders. On one level, it crosses the boundary from small press to mainstream mystery house, a venue where lesbians are still few and far between, having made their initial appearance there only in 1993.[1] Heretofore, Forrest's open treatment of gay issues had been too hot for the mass-market to handle. The novel's centralization of Vietnam (within it, Kate, who has buried her ordeals as a Marine in Southeast Asia, must confront her situation at a reunion party in Washington, D.C.), is unquestionably a political statement, and while *Liberty Square* is not an oral history per se, its publication raises integral questions about the very nature of oral history, questions that deserve to be critiqued and examined.

While oral histories appear to be simple emotive and transparent accounts, it is important to remember that these "simple" accounts are always already mediated: be it through print publication, a television camera, a tape recorder, or by other means. They are not, thus, simple transmissions at all, although their seeming simplicity invites readers or listeners to acquiesce to their deceptive "directness." In that *Liberty Square* concerns a fictional character's ordeals in Vietnam, it is doubly mediated — it is a fiction, and its character speaks her history within a novel; but it is no less mediated than a soldier's recitation of his or her memoirs to an historian, who then interprets (since she or he cannot help but interpret) and publishes or broadcasts the account. Appearances to the contrary, "orality" is no more immediate than writing, as Jacques Derrida noted in 1967, making his first impact on the intellectual community. He suggested then that the historical primacy granted speech over writing had not been problematized sufficiently, and proceeded to outline traditional philosophical thought, which argued:

> the voice is closest to the signified, whether it is determined strictly as sense (thought or lived) or more loosely as thing. All signifiers, and first and foremost the written signifier, are derivative with regard to what would wed the voice indissolubly to the mind or to the thought of the signified sense, indeed to the thing itself. . . . The written signifier is always technical and representative. (11)

Derrida takes issue with this position, a position that goes back to classical Greek philosophy, and begins to complicate its tenets. Refusing to accept the trivialization of writing to speech, he goes on to offer his own initial and highly controversial position that writing is the primary means of transmission. He contests how

> within this epoch, reading and writing, the production or interpretation of signs, the text in general as fabric of signs, allow themselves to be confined within secondariness. . . . We are disturbed by that which, in the concept of the sign — which has never existed or functioned outside the history of (the) philosophy (of presence) — remains systematically and genealogically determined by that history . . . [simply put] there is no linguistic sign before writing. (14)

If the philosophical tradition that posits speech before writing is open to question, and Derrida has spent his career questioning it, then his premises challenge and work to negate the idea that speech is more immediate than writing. In turn, when the oral or written account is read or interpreted, the presence of the listener/translator who constructs the rememberer's story in another medium (be it storytelling or written narrative), adds a further dimension of distance. These contentions suggest that the oral is no more transparent than any other form of storytelling. Hence, while *Liberty Square* raises the question of just what constitutes oral history, it also implicitly suggests that one must be able to narrate one's story before it can be historicized. This novel, as a result, serves as a textual springboard from which to examine the ways in which desire shapes different narratives, just as different narratives shape desire.

"OURS ARE THE ONLY UNTOLD STORIES"

Superficially, the construction of oral history appears to be a simple rendering of particular events. Yet the very act of telling is underpinned by various assumptions. Certain questions haunt the act of narrating, and disturb the ostensible simplicity of narrating a story: Is there an audience for the tale? Can the story be told? Does anyone want to hear it? Is the teller placing himself or herself in jeopardy by imparting the account? These queries point to the political dimensions of the narrative performance.

As a means of dramatizing the force of such lines of inquiry, I have constructed a fictive scenario. My dramatization begins with a lesbian ex-Marine entering a VFW hall. She walks to the bar, and begins to discuss her war experiences. The audience (largely male, given the late admission of women to the armed forces) is disconcerted by her account, and begins to make snide and derisive comments. The gay, lesbian, and anti-homophobic vets seated in a corner, who do want to hear her story, are afraid to make their presence known because they do not want to become similar targets of derision. The homophobic vets, disturbed by this alternative war narrative, lie in wait for the lesbian teller outside the club. They beat her; and, in so doing, cut short her narrative, which — now, a story left untold — is denied to her prospective audience.

I hope that my overgeneralized example sheds some light on the perils of speaking an unspeakable narrative. Since a story requires both a teller and an audience in order to be told, the listeners I constructed above, who do not want to hear the story, engage in a silencing endeavor and succeed in erasing the story's presence for those interested but fearful that their interest might jeopardize them. Same-sex preference, particularly in relation to the military, remains an extremely contentious issue, and an issue that enforces silence because to "tell" leads to expulsion.

If an oral telling raises these complications, a written fictionalized account then becomes a viable means of telling the untold story. The written narrative overtly distances the teller from a potentially homophobic audience (at least to some extent, for she does not have to face her listeners directly),[2] and allows those who wish to hear the story to consume it in private, without outing themselves in the process, or risking the danger their empathy might induce.

While the written fictive form of *Liberty Square* may therefore at first seem suspect, it allows for a conceptualization of lesbian desire, if in a venue not generally associated with oral history. Stories that arise from a desire largely unrecognized in dominant cultural narratives require alternative forms of postulation. As queer theorists have pointed out, a non-discursive desire must be made discursive before it can be analyzed or discussed. And conventional theorizations of desire have not allowed for the possibility of same-sex orientations. In order to provoke such analyses, Teresa de Lauretis's recent work, *The Practice of Love: Lesbian Sexuality and Perverse Desire*, reevaluates Freud's writings on sexuality, and moves to fashion a space, working through Freud, for the interrogation of lesbian desire. De Lauretis builds upon Freud and Michel Foucault's tenets to suggest that conventional analyses of the fetish might be put to use in queer theory. She argues that the fetish is "peculiarly fitted to make satisfaction possible," for it "stands for what is absent or denied but fantasmatically wished for, and is suitable to signify at once its absence and the subject's desire for it" (307–308).

Marty Roth's work, in "Homosexual Expression and Homophobic Censorship," supports de Lauretis's premises; he contends (relying on the work of Christian Metz) that "homosexuality is both present and absent, and that circumstance makes its condition . . . analogous to that of the fetishistic film signifier . . . dedicated to concealing and revealing the body of desire. Homosexuality is revealed only to be concealed through disavowal and concealed only to be revealed through the mechanism of the symptom" (274). The fetishistic concealing/revealing dynamic that Roth foregrounds serves, for de Lauretis, as a tool for opening psychoanalytic discourse to postulations of lesbian desire. By coupling re-readings of the fetish with Foucault's theory of "reverse discourse," de Lauretis stresses the importance of fantasy in queer narratives, since fantasy engenders "something of the process by which a representation in the external world is subjectively assumed, reworked through fantasy, in the internal world and then returned to the external world resignified, rearticulated discursively and/or performatively in the subject's self-representation — in speech, gesture, costume, body, stance, and so forth" (308).

De Lauretis's stance on the fetish and fantasy provides for a means of analyzing written "oral" testimonials of sexuality and war. Given the "unspeakability" of homosexuality in war, even (or perhaps, especially) in oral histories, some of these testimonials must be articulated fictively, or as de Lauretis has argued, "reworked through fantasy . . . and then returned to the external world resignified," in order to encourage and promote further queering practices.

Popular genre fiction is a venue amenable to the signification and/or resignification of discursive constructions of queerness. That is, it provides a forum for enactments of queer desire and for the performance of queer figurations. Within it, alternative perceptions and constructions can be explored through the practice of reading or writing genre fiction (i.e., fiction for which a formulaic structure is already established and which acknowledges and works to meet readers' expectations). In turn, the mass market of genre fiction allows the teller to reach a much broader audience than she or he would in an oral telling. It is, thus, useful for articulating the "love that dare not speak its name," since it has the ability to assist in the process of altering ideological norms on a broad scale. As John G. Cawelti argued in 1976, formula fiction embodies a "controlled space," through which social concerns and cultural fears can be probed by a wide readership. To support his argument, Cawelti draws attention to the alterations apparent in the genre of the American Western, for it

> has undergone almost a reversal in values over the past fifty years with respect to the representation of Indians and pioneers, but much of the basic structure of the formula and its imaginative vision of the meaning of the West has remained substantially unchanged. By their capacity to assimilate new meanings like this, literary formulas ease the transition between old and new ways of expressing things and thus contribute to cultural continuity. (143)

Consequently, the ways in which questions of sexuality and race have filtered into the mainstream market testify to popular media's potential for offering general readers a space through which to engage with them, and to the market's attempt to incorporate the cultural ramifications of these concerns. Christine Gledhill argues for the importance of disenfranchised or minority groups' depictions in mainstream narratives, which, she points out, play an important role in identity formation:

> We need representations that take account of identities — representations that work with a degree of fluidity and contradiction — and we need to forge different identities — ones that help us make productive use of the contradictions of our lives. This means entering socio-economic, cultural and linguistic struggle to define and establish them in the media, which function as centres for the production and circulation of identity. (72)

Gledhill's observations, here, highlight the representational potential of popular culture, and her work, in general, illustrates how mass market productions comprise a complicated weave of conflicting and even paradoxical components, which confound simplistic binary analyses (72). Her work offers a means of interrogating the significance of popular culture (as well as its complications) for those outside the "norm" of the mainstream.

On a practical level, mystery writers are well aware of the potential impact of their texts. Detective novelist Valerie Wilson Wesley, for example, believes that writing for the mainstream enables her to bring particular concerns to the attention of a large audience:

> Because part of a mystery is escaping anyway, I think that there's a sense of travelling in someone else's shoes. These novels take you into a different world for a while. I like the openness of mystery readers. I'm an African-American woman — or, I should say, I'm a Black woman — because the books have been published in England and Germany, and I understand that they're really catching on in Great Britain. . . . I think that a lot of White women who read them say, "Well you know I get into the character and she's just like me." So I think that these books enable readers to get into different worlds. (Walton 271)

The different world Wilson Wesley opens for her non-African American readers is the world of systemic racism, and through her dramatization, she enables audiences to be alerted to the problematics of cultural positioning. At the same time, Wesley's African-American readers may find an enactment of their particular social locus.

To return to Katherine Forrest, it was readers' demands for lesbian novels that generated Forrest's shift from small press to large publishing house, and she perceives her novels to be "crossover" texts. The author is the first to admit that she writes for a lesbian audience, but she has noticed that a "wider audience has found them. Mystery readers like good mysteries" (Walton and Jones 107). And one of her reasons for shifting from Naiad to Putnam lies in reviewers' tendencies to overlook small press publications; her shift in venue, therefore, means that more people will be aware of her novels. Forrest reiterates Dutton editor Carole DeSanti's observation that "ours are the only untold stories," and she is concerned that these stories be told. Her character, Kate Delafield, "is in a high-visibility, high-profile, very high-pressure job," and her situation enables the author to explore "how that impacted on her as a lesbian and her lesbian identity"; in turn, these elements have become "a crucial dynamic in the series" (Walton and Jones 107).

Liberty Square, Forrest's first mainstream publication, stages an articulation of gay and lesbian war performances. A detective novel about a lesbian ex-Marine, turned LAPD cop, who has buried her ordeals in Vietnam, *Liberty Square* offers a venue ("fictitious," and thus "safe") for speaking the unspeakable. As it recounts the stories of gays, lesbians, and nurses in Vietnam (whose combat records largely have been ignored), the novel explores how untold narratives can be brought to life. Concomitantly, it manifests a vehicle for the examination of gays' and lesbians' combat experiences, experiences that are quite different from those of their heterosexual counterparts. Destabilizing the boundaries between fiction and history, then, *Liberty Square* is itself a testimonial to those whose stories have been written off. By writing those stories back in, the novel offers an important commentary on the erasures of (and in) history, at the same time that it affords a form of fictive catharsis for its readers and subjects.

QUERYING "LIBERTY" THROUGH LIBERTY SQUARE

Liberty Square takes place in Washington D.C., at a twenty-fifth reunion party of Kate's Vietnam troupe. Now working as an LAPD cop, she has avoided contact with her former comrades, but her lover, Aimee, is curious about Kate's war years, and firmly believes that Kate should confront her buried memories. Despite Kate's trepidation at reconnecting with her old friends and confederates, the party goes well — until the body of a reunion attendee, Allan Gerlock, is discovered in his hotel room. Because Kate and the D.C. police believe that the motive for Allan's murder lies in the years Gerlock spent in Vietnam, Kate is compelled to investigate both her own past and that which she shared with her Vietnam "family."

Initially, Kate tries to dissuade the D.C. cops from their effort to involve her in their investigation, partly because she is afraid of her memories. As she admits to herself: "Memory was lawless and illogical. Arbitrary. Capable of bending back on itself like a ribbon" (36). Yet if she is to uncover Gerlock's killer, she *must* remember, and the process begins when she attempts to explain to the D.C. cops (and readers) what it meant to be a Marine. She historicizes the Corps for them as follows: "[O]ther military branches put you through hell to get you in good shape to be a soldier. The Marine Corps orders you to get into top shape before you even report for service. Then they still half-kill you. Ten weeks of boot camp and you're expected to run — not march, but run twelve miles up hills and through streams carrying thirty pounds of gear" (79). Of her own role in the Marines, and the training she received as a woman in the 1960s, she recalls:

> I had eight weeks of OCS — Officer Candidate School. Lots of marching for good posture, lots of classes about how to be feminine and a soldier. Twenty-one weeks of what they called the basic school to learn more fine points about being a proper woman Marine officer. Then a Supply course — school training in my military occupational specialty so I could be a glorified secretary looking after supplies for the troops. We're talking late sixties. . . . Women weren't taken seriously, even by women commanding officers. Precious few of us ever got accepted into the Corps; I'm one of a handful who even got to Vietnam. I happened to be recruited when the Corps was ordered to expand their allotment of females. (79)

Kate was assigned to Supply Duty in Da Nang. Her colleagues, and the group with which *Liberty Square* is concerned, consists of ten characters: Doc and Martin, combat doctors; Bernie and Rachel, nurses; Melanie, an SRAO troupe entertainer (or "doughnut dolly"); Dacey, Gabe, and Woody, combat Marines; in addition are the absent presences who permeate the group's reminiscences: Allan (the murder victim) and Cap (an MIA), both of whom were combat Marines.

After each has been questioned by the police, the former colleagues and now suspects gather in Kate's room. As they drink and smoke their way into the night, they recollect their war years and the resulting casualties. Subjects of the conversation range from the group's present welfare, to incidents that changed their perspective, to topics about which they disagree — such as the issues of gays in the military, the act of war, and the treatment of each other and civilians.

The structure of *Liberty Square* parallels the situations commonly found in oral histories. Aimee, new to the group, is asked to leave because her "outsider" status might impede the flow of reminiscences. In so doing, she is in a position analogous to the reader's, as she listens in on the group through an open window:

> Aimee went into the bedroom and closed the door. . . .
> "Aimee can't hear us in there with the door closed."
> Kate's voice, coming in faintly through the bedroom window. The house-keeper . . . had opened the side louvers of this window and the one in the living room to allow fresh air into the suite.
> Aimee slid over to the side of the bed nearest to the window. Conversation from the suite's other room would be inaudible if Kate or Bernie moved away from the table or if the rain increased, but for now she could hear. (102–103)

The reader, who moves from eavesdropping with Aimee to the room itself, serves, with her, as an unknown audience/recorder. The primary group is left with the (illusory) comfort of "confidentiality," and the novelistic structure provides the requisite elements for the telling of histories.

Woven throughout the group's reminiscences are their present circumstances, and the ways in which their war years had an impact on their lives. Kate has become a detective, she realizes, as an act of self-imposed penance for her not having seen action. Doc, too, is punishing himself for his perceived "perpetration" of the war (through his medical skills, he patched up bodies and sent them back to the front — only for them to be shot at again). Upon returning home, Doc discovers that he can no longer practice medicine:

> I couldn't be a surgeon anymore, and believe me I tried practicing every other kind of medicine, I really tried, but I couldn't do that, either. I was fine for about five or six years after I got back and then suddenly I couldn't pick up a scalpel without having flashbacks. (179–80)

The others are relatively "whole," but they remember their return from the front, and the treatment they received (or that they didn't receive). Rachel recalls her efforts to talk to her family about her state of mind:

> My family didn't have a clue how damaged I was. . . . I was just paralyzed with grief, I desperately needed to talk. But my mother said everybody knew war was horrible. . . . She didn't want to hear about it. (175)

The others recollect the political reception offered to returning vets. Bernie remembers how "Afterward, people I considered good friends cut me down because I served. I never forgave them, ever" (175). Woody, the macho combat Marine, took out his frustration in anger:

> I thought I'd get some respect risking my life in that fucking place. So I come home and some fucking hippie at the airport asks how many people I killed, how it felt to kill people. I told him he was the one I'd enjoy killing. (175)

Ironically, despite the horrors the vets witnessed, many tried to recapture the excitement and intensity of wartime in civilian life. Bernie, who now works in a VA hospital, admits to Kate that she

> Tried like hell to find it again, Katie. . . . Couldn't find anything like it. Job after job, man after man, couldn't find any man that lived up to the boys I knew over there, couldn't find the A-number-one team like we had over there, the way all of us came through hell together. (104–105)

Melanie, too, could never rediscover the excitement and camaraderie she felt in Vietnam, nor the sense of accomplishment she experienced there:

> "I wanted to serve too. . . . I thought all the people criticizing this country were scum. I still do, goddammit. Nobody thought I could go off to war and take on responsibility, but I did. Besides . . . I thought it would be fun. And it was. It—" She coughed. "It was. . . ." Her voice broke. "It was the greatest goddamn year of my goddamn life." (110)

The group both loathed and loved their Vietnam years, and as they grow comfortable with each other again, they begin to revel in old "war stories." Bernie breaks some of the initial tension by recalling a story that leaves everyone gasping in laugher:

> Felicia's this brand-new nurse, okay? Just in-country, just off a C-130 from Tan Son Nhut, she comes in right after we get incoming wounded, bad stuff, a claymore mine, so there's amputations. And here's sweet young Felicia, all enthusiastic to check out her new hospital and meet her new team. So in she bounces, into our operating room, and we're finishing up and there's blood just fucking everywhere, and Martin's tying off this guy—he got choppered in with his arm all but hanging by a thread—and the deal is, I'm helping Martin and rummaging around for a bag—you put amputated limbs in special plastic

bags, they go to Graves Registration for disposal just like bodies do. So anyway, here I am just busy as hell, but I notice Felicia, she's the color of putty from the scene in there but she's being a brave girl, she's gonna meet everybody no matter what. Then somebody says, "This is Bernie O'Rourke," and I turn around and my scrubs are dripping blood, and Felicia reaches out and shakes the one hand in the room that doesn't have a gory glove on it — and the hand's on this guy's arm that I fucking forget I'm holding, I've got it tucked under my arm, it's got tattoos all over it, and the poor bastard's wristwatch is still on it, and poor Felicia faints dead away on the floor. (168–69)

Inevitably, the horrors of combat resurface, and through this discussion, the group turns to an examination of the role of women in war. Woody begins by noting, snidely: " 'Some things even if you were there, you had to do 'em' " (155). This leads to a heated discussion about the roles of women and medics at the front:

"Woody, goddamit, cut the crap," snapped Melanie. "I'm sick of you guys acting like women didn't come close to what you guys went through over there. Like we didn't have our asses on the line every bit as much as you did. . . .
        Listen. . . . Just listen, okay? I was all over the fucking place. I was in combat as much as any of you guys except that they wouldn't let me have a gun so I could shoot back. I was in Cu Chi and Chu Lai, and it was hell. I got shot at I don't know how many times in helicopters. I was in the line of fire." (155–56)

Woody replies: " 'We're not saying you gutsy women did anything but a great job. . . . But it's nothing like a firefight. The noise, the fucking terror —' " (164)

Bernie, however, cuts him off:

"You ever been in an operating room with incoming wounded, Woody? Let me tell you about noise and fucking terror. The wounded packed in so tight there's hardly any space, you can't walk anywhere that you don't leave bloody footprints, the floors so slick after a while you can hardly walk at all, and after you finally sort through the dead and get the wounded taken care of, your scrubs are soaked right through to your skin and you can't even hope to clean those floors any other way but to use a garden hose to sluice out all the gore." (164)

(Later in the text, one of the D.C. cops confirms the importance of the Vietnam women: " 'My cousin Jamille . . . [a] Gulf War veteran, in training now as a fighter pilot. She says the Vietnam women made the big breakthrough, made it all possible' " [239]). The combat vets, however, are unwilling to concede the important role women played in the war. Gabe, the sergeant, tries to pour oil on the waters by admitting: " 'It was real tough on you women, I know that. But we —' " Melanie quickly interrupts him:

"Let me tell you something, Gabe. And you too, Dacey. And Woody. We know how tough it was for you guys, how brutal. All the women in this room, even Aimee, we know your stories from how many newspapers? How many movies? How many books?" She gestured to Rachel and Bernie, to herself. "Nobody knows our stories. One fucking TV series about what we did—" (167)

Melanie gets the last word in this debate, and the text clearly acknowledges the ways in which women's "combat" histories (and I use the term *combat* advisedly) have been either ignored or marginalized. Yet, ironically, the text's recognition of women's war records works to highlight the paucity of information available on gays and lesbians in the military. Melanie's quite legitimate comment that women in Vietnam merited only "one fucking TV series" (i.e., *China Beach*), concomitantly points up how this is still one more series than have the gays and lesbians who served.

The absent presence of gays and lesbians in the war permeates the group's interactions with Kate. These vets, who ate together, slept together, fought together, and mourned together, are cautious in discussing Kate's (now) "out" lesbian status. Aimee notes, in the midst of sharing confidences with Bernie, that she must be careful of how much she reveals about her life with Kate:

But she could not explain all that to this straight woman until she knew from Kate how much she could reveal. What a pain in the ass, always having to decide how much of a lesbian you could be, always having to edit your life for everyone you met. (93)

Editing her words with Bernie and cautious in her questioning of Kate, Aimee's (and the reader's) desire to know and understand is impeded. There is too much that cannot be spoken, as Aimee discovers through her efforts to uncover the past:

Aimee could not ask the question whose complete answer she was most anxious to know: what had it been like for Kate as a lesbian in the elite corps of America's military? She had asked Kate, of course, and Kate had been her usual unforthcoming self: "The men all believed that women had no business whatsoever in the Marine Corps. If we were there it had to be because we were whores or lesbians. I watched out for myself." (97)

It is, in fact, Aimee's interest in Kate's Vietnam experience as a lesbian that had sparked the pair's attendance at the reunion in the first place: "The whole gays-in-the-military debate had set her [Aimee] off, and into the private areas Kate did not want exhumed—What were the gay people like over there? How did you protect yourself? What would you have done if the investigators had come after you?" (56).

Kate had protected herself through silence, a silence that is broken after

Allan's body is discovered, and the D.C. cops question her. She finds herself
in the near impossible position of trying to explain her status to the two
detectives, one of whom airily observes: " 'One day a year the gays go parad-
ing around saying how proud they are, the rest of the time they hide their
heads' " (132). Kate responds, " 'I'm not hiding my head,' " but discovers
that she must admit to more than her own sexual orientation. When Cap's
name surfaces in the investigation, Kate is forced to "out" him:

> She had had to reveal such information about herself, but never had she
> identified anyone as gay to someone outside the circle of the gay people she
> knew, even if a straight person claimed inside knowledge. Still — what differ-
> ence did it make now? Cap was either perfectly hidden, or perfectly dead.
> "Yes, he was gay," she said. (132)

Over the course of the investigation, the D.C. detectives ascertain that
Cap and Kate were engaged. The engagement was, of course, a camouflage,
but in querying it, the detectives compel Kate to reveal some of the history
that Aimee has been intent to uncover. In response to their question: " 'So, if
everybody over there knew he was gay, why wasn't he investigated? Kicked
out?' " (132), Kate attempts to articulate the situation of gays and lesbians
in Vietnam:

> "I can't verify that everybody knew it," Kate said. Although it looked to her
> today as if everyone had. "But I can tell you that the military kicks gays out
> only in peacetime, not wartime." She remembered reading in a magazine
> article that Randy Shilts' book, Conduct Unbecoming, claimed that the ve-
> randa of the officers' club in Da Nang had been prime gay cruising territory —
> a fact not evident to her while she was there. The book also claimed that
> General Westmoreland had been surrounded by a staff of gay men. Maybe so,
> but women were kicked out anytime and all the time. As she discovered when
> she returned to the World and witnessed the military careers of women all
> around her picked off for destruction with the seeming randomness of target
> practice. Her rank and her service in a combat arena had distanced her from
> most other women Marines, had served as a wall of protection — and iso-
> lation . . . [I]n the eyes of all branches of the military, and especially the
> Marine Corps, she would be held in equal contempt with gay men — and
> considered far more expendable, the Marine Corps expelling for sexual orien-
> tation seven times more of its tiny component of women than it did men.
> (132–33)

These reminiscences propel Kate to confront her own past, as she ponders the
engagement and its necessity. Cap, who had just returned from R&R in
Australia, had brought back pictures and mementoes he could not bear to
destroy. A routine search of quarters unearthed the pictures, and Cap was
terrified about the consequences. His brush with military censure led him to
reveal himself to Kate, and the two concocted their engagement as a safety

measure. As Kate informs the detectives: " 'He found out there was speculation over his sexual identity. . . . We got engaged to help each other out, to
keep people off our backs' " (140). The engagement meant that while most
people "knew" about Cap and Kate's sexual orientation, no one "really"
knew, leaving Cap's "reputation" intact for the duration of his stay in Vietnam, and for the twenty-five years he has been missing in action.

When the mystery of Allan's murder is resolved, so is Cap's status, since
the novel reveals that he was killed in Vietnam by homophobic Marines.
Because Allan's knowledge of Cap's sexual orientation would expose to the
group both Cap's murder and his murderer, he is killed in a further effort to
keep the crime secret. This secret, and the secrets resulting from the ruling
against gays in the military, then, continue to engender yet more Vietnam
casualties.

In the novel's conclusion, Doc draws an interesting analogy between
Vietnam vets and gay people. Reflecting on Cap's situation, Doc muses:

> "I thought about Cap during that whole gays-in-the-military fiasco, and this
> year too when the gays marched in New York for the twenty-fifth anniversary
> of that civil rights riot . . . "
>
> "The Stonewall Inn in Greenwich Village," Aimee supplied.
>
> Doc nodded. "Yes. Here all of us were in Vietnam that very same year,
> serving in the name of everything this country stands for — and we come home
> to find out none of it mattered. It didn't matter how heroic our conduct was,
> how many medals anybody won, our country had turned its back on us. So we
> end up keeping that whole part of our life a secret. Just like the gays. It took a
> long time to get together and recognize our right to be angry and bitter as hell
> at our country, just like it did for — " (183–84)

Not all members of the group are comfortable with this comparison, but
Doc's comment provides a parallel that serves to demonstrate how closeting
works on a number of levels, with a different influence on those who must
hide aspects of their identities — be it due to sexual orientation or war conduct. And within the forum of the text, the policy of "don't ask, don't tell"
(232), which has led to Allan's death, is tentatively abandoned, exposing
Cap's fate, and bringing about some form of closure for the reunion group.

The final pages of the novel also offer an interactive resolution to readers.
During the group's culminating visit to the Vietnam memorial, the intensity
of their encounter also becomes the reader's, who is prompted to share their
experience through the second-person omniscient narration that concludes
the text. This monologue invites readers to participate in the trip to the Wall,
and includes them in the telling of yet another oral history. This history
recounts the emotional pull of the Wall and all that it stands for. As a final
recitation of the war and its memory, this powerful commentary ends the

novel, and will also end this essay, for its inclusive construction encourages
readers, critics, and "listeners" to hear all of the untold stories that the Wall
represents, untold stories that this novel has helped to articulate. The monologue begins at the entrance to the memorial:

> The way to do this has to be one step at a time. Enter this place, and look only
> at the first shiny black panel, it has one line and five names etched into it. . . .
> Then to the next shiny black panel, same width, wedged deeper into the earth,
> three lines of five names. The next one, deeper still, more lines of five names.
> You're descending into the earth. . . . The height of the shiny black panels
> waist level, many more lines and many names now on the shiny black panels,
> and the lines and names are shoulder level and you go down and down into
> the earth, each shiny black panel with its lines and lines of five names illumi-
> nated by a small spotlight imbedded in the brick and granite pathway, and the
> shiny black panels are head-high and they hold more names on more and
> more lines, and you're absorbed into a universe of names, the shiny black Wall
> high above your head and all those panels and all those lines are uttering their
> names at you. . . . And you are in an open grave with all those names. . . .
>
> All around you are people like you, every age and color, their stunned
> faces surely mirrors of yours. They weep as you weep because, no matter what
> they expected, the stark meaning of this place has swallowed them whole as it
> has devoured you, and they lean and touch the Wall dazed by this unimagin-
> able accounting of loss, just as you do. They touch a fingertip because they
> have to feel the carving on just one of the gold-lettered names just as you
> do. They look at the American flags, the state flags, the gay pride flags, the
> flowers, the folded notes and letters, the photos, the crosses . . . all the tributes
> that lean against the panels all along both long, long sides of this Wall of
> remembrance. (239–40)

NOTES

1. Sandra Scoppettone's *Everything You Have Is Mine* (New York: Ballantine,
1993).

2. She or he might in a public reading, but in this scenario, the teller at least has
some control over her/his audience.

WORKS CITED

Cawelti, John. "The Study of Literary Formulas." *Detective Fiction: A Collection of
  Critical Essays.* Ed. Robin W. Winks. Englewood Cliffs. N.J.: Prentice-Hall, 1980.
  121–43.
de Lauretis, Teresa. *The Practice of Love: Lesbian Sexuality and Perverse Desire.*
  Bloomington: Indiana University Press, 1994.
Derrida, Jacques. *Of Grammatology.* 1967. Trans. Gayatri Chakavorty Spivak. Bal-
  timore: Johns Hopkins University Press, 1976.
Forrest, Katherine V. *Liberty Square.* 1996. New York: Berkeley, 1997.
Gledhill, Christine. "Pleasurable Negotiations." *Female Spectators: Looking at Film
  and Television.* Ed. Deidre E. Pribram. London: Verso, 1988. 64–89.

"Liberty Square." http://www.amazon.com (accessed February 10, 1999).

Roth, Marty. "Homosexual Expression and Homophobic Censorship: The Situation of the Text." *Camp Grounds: Style and Homosexuality.* Ed. David Bergman. Amherst: University of Massachusetts Press, 1993. 268–81.

Walton, Priscilla L. "Bubblegum Metaphysics: Feminist Paradigms and Racial Interventions in Mainstream Hardboiled Women's Detective Fiction." *Multicultural Detective Fiction: Murder from the "Other" Side.* Ed. Adrienne Johnson Gosselin. New York: Garland, 1999. 257–80.

Walton, Priscilla L., and Manina Jones. *Detective Agency: Women Rewriting the Hard-Boiled Tradition.* Berkeley: University of California Press, 1999.

9. *Bloods*

Teaching the Afroamerican Experience of the Vietnam Conflict

WILLIAM M. KING

This chapter describes a course I teach in the Department of Ethnic Studies at the University of Colorado, Boulder. The course, "Black America and the War in Vietnam," is the outgrowth of an article, " 'Our Men in Vietnam': Black Media as a Source of the Afroamerican Experience in Southeast Asia," published in a special issue of *Vietnam Generation* that I co-edited in 1989. My intention in developing this course was to provide a view of the war in Vietnam from an orientation growing out of the historical experiences and folk wisdom of Americans of African descent; to expand our offerings in the Afroamerican concentration for the bachelor's degree in the Department of Ethnic Studies at the advanced level; and to examine an aspect of the Vietnam story that had not gotten the kind of coverage I believed was warranted given the rising number of courses on the war. Wallace Terry's *Bloods: An Oral History of the Vietnam War by Black Veterans* is one of the foci around which the course revolves.

No, I myself did not serve in Vietnam. But I did spend four years, three months, and fifteen days in the United States Navy from 1958 to 1962 inclusive of three cruises to WESPAC (the Western Pacific) with a fair amount of time in the South China Sea beginning in 1959, the last with less than ninety days left to serve before I would be discharged to the active reserve. For this I thank Public Law 87-117 that stated, in part, "all military personnel currently on active duty are hereby extended on active duty for a period of up to one year" (King, DD-214, 1962), this because of the Berlin Crisis of 1961.

We were generally not told where we were, where we were going, or when we would get there. Imagine my surprise, then, upon examining a newspaper clipping my mother sent me from the *Cleveland Press* dated sometime in either late 1961 or early 1962. The clipping contained a map showing the position of my ship, the U.S.S. *Midway* (CVA-41), off the coast of South Vietnam, a place that would come to be called "Dixie Station" as the war increased in intensity following President Lyndon Johnson's signing of the Tonkin Gulf Resolution in August 1964. I worked on the flight deck and recall continuous air operations for a period of several days while we were in that area. Whether those operations were for training purposes or the realization of some other objective, however, I was not told.

While I have no combat experience, I do believe my military service affords me some insight into some of the topics detailed in *Bloods*. My time in the military transpired when mandated desegregation was not quite a decade old — a time when dominant attitudes and behavior were beginning to undergo a transition, a kind of stepping down from a more robust commitment to prejudice and discrimination. Partly this change reflected a growing realization that new needs demanded greater utilization of available manpower, and thus that the criteria of manpower availability had to be changed to include Afroamericans in military service. What I want to convey to my students is a sense of the period from the perspective of one who experienced portions of it, and to remind them of the truism that, while people are ordinary, experience is not. I believe it is possible to convey a sense of this period in American history by teaching the oral testimonies from *Bloods,* with careful attention to the contexts out of which the described experiences arise. My objective here is to enrich the interpretive imaginations of my students, supplementing whatever they bring with them that might foster an easier acceptance and understanding of differences.

Although black people have been involved with the United States military since pre-colonial times, beginning with the early years of the Civil War and lasting until the Korean "police action," Afroamericans, when allowed to fight, were wounded, captured, bled, and died for the most part in segregated units. Indeed, the conflict in Vietnam was the first in which it was possible to say that the military forces of the United States were truly "integrated." That does not mean, however, that misunderstandings growing out of a history of racial attitudes and racist actions did not continue to influence human relations in the field or the rear area. Consider, for example, the occupational specialties of those Blacks who went to war. Here one finds a disproportionate distribution of Blacks in the enlisted ranks and the office corps, a reflection of the social structure of the civilian labor force. In the military as in civilian life, Blacks occupied mostly the lower ranks and did mostly the "unskilled" work.

In *Bloods*, however, Terry selected for interviews only those soldiers who played an active, military role in Vietnam. All of them "had won a badge of courage in combat, whether on a patrol boat or in a POW camp, on a night ambush or in the skies above North Vietnam, as medics and platoon leaders, as fighter pilots and grunts" (Terry xvii). That is to say, employing their own parlance, they were warriors, even if some of them were also "grunts."

The origins of the book date from a cover story published in *Time* magazine in 1967 entitled "The Negro in Vietnam," by Robert Jones. Terry, assigned to the Washington bureau, was sent to Vietnam to collect several of the interviews that appeared in the article. Of the "scores of Negro servicemen interviewed by *Time* in Vietnam, all but a few volunteered the information that they were there to serve their country, however badly it may have treated them" (Terry 16). Later that year, Terry returned to the magazine's Saigon bureau as a war correspondent for a two-year tour that ended with the first troop reductions ordered by President Nixon. While there, he published an article in *Time* titled "Black Power in Vietnam" that detailed selected aspects of black and white life in Southeast Asia, and changes in the attitudes and behavior of black soldiers he had witnessed since his arrival two years earlier.

During this period, black combat casualties, which were 23 percent of all American deaths in 1965, fell to 14 percent by 1969 (Terry xviii). This was still above the 11 percent of the U.S. population that the Census Bureau said was Black, however, and the publication of this number fostered all manner of speculation about how "Our Boys" were being treated over there in the Nam specifically and in the military generally. These concerns were expressed both by civilians back home and soldiers in the field. Yet what most caught Terry's attention was the arrival of a very different kind of black soldier as the war escalated and the troop counts mounted. These new troops, mostly draftees—given that the "war had used up the professionals who found in military service fuller and fairer employment opportunities than blacks could find in civilian society, and who found in uniform a supreme test of their black manhood" (Terry xvii)—were in a number of instances

> just steps removed from marching in the Civil Rights Movement or rioting in the rebellions that swept the urban ghettos from Harlem to Watts [and were] filled with a new sense of black pride and purpose. They spoke loudest against the discrimination they encountered on the battlefield in decorations, promotion and duty assignments. They chose not to overlook the racial insults, cross-burnings and the Confederate flags of their white comrades. They called for unity among black brothers on the battlefield to protest these indignities and provide mutual support. And they called themselves 'Bloods.' The war, which had bitterly divided America like no other issue since the Civil War, had become a double battleground, pitting American soldier against

American soldier. The spirit of foxhole brotherhood found in 1967 had evap-
orated. (Terry xvi)

Clearly, to get the most out of this book's representation of the revolutionary turmoil of the 1960s in America, one needs more than a passing
acquaintance with Afroamerican life, history, and culture, and the role black
people have played in all of American society's institutions, especially the
military. In the absence of such historical and cultural knowledge in the
classroom at large, one can only dance next to the precipice of inference; one
can only suggest the presence of the "not said" or the invisible respecting the
indignities and the oppression of black experience; or one can only allude to
this context briefly along the way. What my students need to understand is
that, both in the military and the society at large, the historical contours of
black experience in America define a marginalized people brought from Africa to labor for the benefit of others. What this means is that, in contrast to
the oral histories of other Vietnam Vets, the content and character of the
stories related in *Bloods* must be understood within the overall historical
experience of Afroamerican people.

A good place to start, beyond a general history of slavery in America, is
with W.E.B. DuBois's prescient address to the Pan African Congress in London in 1900, for it conveys a truth still with us as we move through the early
years of the twenty-first century:

> The problem of the twentieth century is the problem of the colour line, the
> question as to how far differences of race, which show themselves chiefly in
> the colour of the skin and the texture of the hair, are going to be made,
> hereafter, the basis of denying to over half the world the right of sharing to
> their utmost ability the opportunities and privileges of modern civilization.
> (qtd. in D. Lewis 639)

How best to convey the meaning of being Black in this way? How best to
communicate the reality Julianne Malveaux laments when she tells us that
for black people nothing can be defined outside the context of the oppressor—neither life nor love nor any other aspect (34)? My students are mostly
White; their knowledge of the black experience in the United States is often
minimal at best and almost wholly absent at worst. *Bloods* can help make
real for them the felt experience and living memory of historical black subjects whose voices demonstrably originate from a place beyond the pages of
the book itself. Suddenly, hearing the voices of the Bloods, one understands
that DuBois's observation is anything but abstract, "historical," or obsolete:

> After the Egyptian and Indian, the Greek and Roman, the Teuton and Mon-
> golian, the Negro is a sort of seventh son, born with a veil, and gifted with
> second-sight in this American world,—a world which yields him no true self-

consciousness, but only lets him see himself through the revelation of the other world. It is a peculiar sensation, this double-consciousness, this sense of always looking at one's self through the eyes of others, of measuring one's soul by the tape of a world that looks on in amused contempt and pity. One ever feels his two-ness, — an American, a Negro: two souls, two thoughts, two unreconciled strivings; two warring ideals in one dark body, whose dogged strength alone keeps it from being torn asunder. (DuBois 8–9)

A related context of interpretation for *Bloods* is the contemporaneous conjunction of racism and war best characterized by both Muhammad Ali and the late Stokely Carmichael in their oft-quoted remark, "Ain't no Vietnamese ever called me nigger!" This remark reminds us that the history of black people in America is both a labor history and a history of attempted depersonalization and objectification. For Carmichael and Ali, black people live in a society constructed through the arrogance and myopia of imagined white racial supremacy, a society in which superficial differences in skin color have been transformed into a color caste system that, while replicating itself in all the subordinated groups, has been especially troublesome for black people, and has materially influenced their opportunities for advancement. There is no social institution, process, or belief system in American society and culture that has not been affected by an attitude of implied racial inferiority.

The voices in *Bloods* inhabit a time when black people were beginning with greater alacrity and tenacity to break free of the forces of American racism and the shibboleths of an oppressive past. The 1960s were a time when Blacks were beginning to challenge ever more effectively the myths that had been made up about them by the various sovereign and disciplinary powers. Myth-sustaining rituals like inadequate schooling, discriminatory employment practices, and the misadministration of justice had relegated Blacks to a kind of second-class servitude, a reality that was being radically questioned and exposed.

The Vietnam War exacerbated the fractures in the American system and, given the obvious racism and imperialism of the American involvement, illuminated them. Despite Westmoreland's comment of 1967, "I have an intuitive feeling that the Negro Servicemen have a better understanding than whites of what the war is about" (qtd. in Terry 16), in fact all too many of the young men, Black or White, who went to Southeast Asia, poorly understood what they were fighting for, owing to an inadequate political education. There was a superficiality to their awareness of things different from what they believed or knew. Nor did the military help at all when it instituted manpower policies like McNamara's "Project 100,000" (DOD, 1969) in 1966, a consequence of the Moynihan Report (DOL, 1965). This report argued that the deterioration of the family was the cause of the social pathology witnessed in the black community. Insofar as the assumed matrifocal character of this community made it difficult for young men to learn the male role, this condition might be corrected by bringing them under the tutelage of army sergeants. The result of this policy was literally a sweeping up of people off the streets, over 40 percent of whom were Black, so as not to unduly disturb the chosen folk who remained in college or in critical occupations.

Bloods, then, in its description of another history of the war in Vietnam, can help us to learn much about how some young black soldiers who fought in the Nam attempted to cope with the long and ongoing ordeal of race relations in American culture. During the Vietnam "conflict" (for it was not a war in the official declarative sense) Black and White shared the same fox-holes, cheek by jowl, and became dependent on each other for survival. There was no time for racism in the bush. In the rear it was a different story, however. Blacks had their part of town where whitey wasn't allowed. White boy had theirs too. By April 30, 1968, total U.S. military personnel in Vietnam numbered 543,300 (Olson and Roberts 303). Our army in Vietnam required nine service and support troops for each grunt in the bush. With a surfeit of bodies in the rear, a critical mass was effected that recreated America in Vietnam. Racism in the rear area was alive, well and virulent.

As the war dragged on and the draft calls began to multiply, protest activity intensified, not unlike a similar situation in about 1780, the fourth year of the war of 1776. As in that earlier time, some white folks found a way to get black folks to do their tours of duty for them. In the 1960s, this was called student deferment. Student deferments had been introduced into the selective service legislation during World War II as a means of encouraging study in selected areas of science, engineering, and kindred fields. The knowledge gained, not the body that produced it, was then employed to prosecute the war effort. Folk who could afford it struggled to get into college and stay there as long as they could. Those who could not went to war. A disproportionate number of the grunts in the Nam were of the "lesser breeds."

The Vietnam War coincided with the successes and failures of the Civil Rights Movement, including the Voting Rights Act of 1965, LBJ's Great Society, Model Cities, and the rise of the Black Power movement: suddenly there were Malcolm X and Cassius Clay, The Louisville Lip, who said: "Hell no, I won't go!" He had to be made an example of because he was symbolic of a rising tide of black anti-war activity whose import sent shudders throughout the land of the free and the home of the brave. His case was followed closely overseas because the consciousness of the brothers had begun to change.

When there was conflict in the urban core, there was conflict in the rear area. Blacks arriving in the Nam after Tet were very different than the Bloods who were there before. The early ones, disproportionately constituting elite units like the Rangers and Special Forces, volunteered because, even with the war, the Army was a place where you could get ahead. The latter, especially those in-country after "Project 100,000," were conscripts — the poor, the illiterate, the detritus of a throwaway society. Some were from the war zones of Detroit and Newark. All they wanted was to do their time and get back to the world. The military made the same mistake with these folks that it had made with the "enemy" — it chose not to learn anything about them until it was almost too late.

Black vets got it coming and going. Those who had incomplete schooling and no skills when they went in, more often than not came out the same way. How much use is there for a rifleman or pig gunner back in the World? No skills meant no job. No job meant that criminal activity would become a viable alternative, at least in the short run. Besides, there was the common belief that all Vietnam vets were junkies anyway; crime and drugs were kissing cousins. Too, many black vets, owing to a chronic "failure to adjust to military life," left the army with Bad Conduct or Undesirable Discharges; some few even had dishonorable discharges and a tour in LBJ (Long Binh Jail) or the Da Nang Brig to add to their records.

By the time the war was over, some 3.5 million military personnel (men and women) had done tours of duty in Vietnam, Laos, and Cambodia. An equivalent number of American civilians were also directly engaged in war-related activities ranging from diplomacy to racketeering. For every one of them, the war was different. For the brothers and sisters, it was very different indeed.

Bloods, published in 1984, contains twenty interviews with black men "who portray their war and postwar experiences" (Terry xvii) in separate chapters that allow some insight into the experience of black people in — but not always of — America, in both military and civilian life. Among them are enlisted personnel, and commissioned and noncommissioned officers, drawn from all the services including those "for whom the war had a devastating impact, and those for whom the war basically was an opportunity to advance in a career dedicated to protecting American interests." The bulk of the interviews (ranging in length from eight to twenty-six pages) were collected during the early 1980s. Twelve of the twenty interviewees had seen some degree of service pre-Tet or during Tet, while the remainder saw their tours of duty in the period thereafter. Two veterans, Norman Alexander McDaniel and Fred V. Cherry, were POWs who had been incarcerated from early in the escalation of the war until their release following the conclusion of the Paris Peace Talks on January 23, 1973, when the rules for prisoner exchanges had been worked out. The lengths of the tours of duty they describe differed also. Three of the interviewees (Huff, Norman, Anderson) had more than one tour

of duty marked by sharp differences in policies and practices respecting assignments, awards, promotion, and the administration of military justice.

Upon reading this text, my students immediately grasp the potency of
oral narrative to convey the subjective texture of a lived life. The simple yet
profound process of identifying with these Bloods, of putting themselves in
their places, is powerfully, pedagogically effective. In the classroom I begin
with a discussion of the testimony of Army Specialist 4 Arthur E. "Gene"
Woodley, eighteen years old when he arrived in Vietnam in November 1968
and, by his own accounting, an animal before he was nineteen. He served in
the war zone until December 1969, the most violent year of the war. Woodley
was from a hard neighborhood in Baltimore, had his "rep" to protect, and
sought out elite training as an airborne ranger and Special Forces trooper. He
speaks movingly about his "mercy killing" of a fellow soldier who had been
skinned, staked to the ground, and left to die because he was of no significant
value to the enemy.

> It took me somewhere close to 20 minutes to get my mind together. Not
> because I was squeamish about killing someone, because I had at that time
> numerous body counts. Killing someone wasn't the issue. It was killing an-
> other American citizen, another GI. (Terry 249)

As he pondered what to do, whether to let the man die — death was only a
couple of hours away anyhow — or take his life, he listened to the cries, the
pleading, looked again and again at what had been done by the enemy soldiers, and smelled the putrid odor of rotting, bug-and-maggot-infested flesh:

> I put myself in his situation. In his place. I had to be as strong as he was,
> because he was askin' me to kill him, to wipe out his life. He had to be a hell of
> a man to do that. I don't think I would be a hell of a man enough to be able to
> do that. I said to myself, I couldn't show him my weakness, because he was
> showing me his strength. (Terry 250)

Placing his M-16 next to the man's temple, he asked again, for the last time,
"You sure you want me to do this?" The answer: "Man, kill me. Thank you."
And with that Woodley pulled the trigger and "cancelled his suffering" (Terry
250). And after they buried him, buried him deep, Woodley cried. Later, he
tells Terry, his agony evident in the tone of his recapitulation, "I think I made
it back here and am able to talk because he died for me. And I'm living' for
him" (Terry 265).

A little later in his story, Woodley details his return to "the world" (home)
on the very same day he left the Nam. Still wearing his worn, dirty, smelly
combat fatigues, and without having had a chance to clean up, he has just
enough time to catch the big freedom bird to a place where social death was
frequently more painful than physical death in the war zone. He speaks of

how he frightened his mother because he was still an animal and sometimes acted like one. He describes how he bought weapons and joined up with the Black Panther Party for Self Defense because they appeared to be doing something real, including sponsoring free breakfast programs. And sadly, he details how he could not have a permanent relationship with a woman because anyone he hooked up with could not deal with his flashbacks once they began; nor could he share the causes of them with anyone whose experiential background rendered them incapable of understanding what he had been through. Yet the most telling part of the interview, in terms of looking at the black experience in America, is his recounting of the grocery store incident.

Back in his neighborhood in Baltimore, he goes into a small shop to make a purchase. Inside Woodley learns the owner is a Vietnamese man who remembers him from his days in An Khe. The owner even identifies Woodley as Montagnard Man, a title Woodley had in-country because of the way he dressed and behaved. He is not angry with the shopkeeper, he tells Terry. Rather, he is angry at America and how the leadership of the country treats those who, deprived of the ways and means to realize their potential, are characterized by their oppressors as useless "niggers":

> When the Vietn'ese first came here, they were talkin' 'bout the new niggers. But they don't treat them like niggers. They treat them like people. If they had gave me some money to start my life over again, I'd been in a hell of a better situation than I am right now. We went to war to serve the country in what we thought was its best interest. Then America puts them above us. It's a crime. It's a crime against us. (Terry 263)

Indeed, what makes his situation even more galling is his belief that he was lied to by the government. This belief is one that has been held by black troops returning home from overseas since the Spanish-American War of 1898. Their fondest hope was that, because of their service, conditions at home would be different for them. Unfortunately, this was not the case:

> They had us naïve, young, dumb-ass niggers believin' that this war was for democracy and independence. It was fought for money. All those big corporations made billions on the war, and then America left. (Terry 264)

No, he could not speak about the experiences of other people of color. But as far as he was concerned, life for black people in America in the 1980s was a war for survival — survival without the tools that might make it possible. Indeed,

> black vet'rans are being overlooked more than everybody. We can't find jobs, because nobody trusts us. Because we are killers. We crazy. We went away intelligent young men to do the job of American citizens. And once we did, we came back victims. (Terry 264)

Another story that powerfully illustrates the range of experiences endured by black soldiers is that of Private First Class, Reginald "Malik" Edwards of Phoenix, Louisiana, who saw duty at Da Nang from June 1965 to
March 1966. The principal event in his story is his receipt of "Bad Paper,"
a less than honorable discharge. This happened to many black soldiers in
Southeast Asia who spent part of their tour in "LBJ" — Long Binh Jail — for
Article 15 violations of the Uniform Code of Military Justice. Edwards's
dismissal from the Corps came as a consequence of his participation in a
racial incident at Quantico Marine Base in 1970 (see below), the context of
which is crucial for my students to understand. Edwards had been a potential
career soldier. He had even made sergeant, a not insignificant rank in the
Marines, but had gotten busted back to PFC (Private First Class) for his
alleged racial "attack on an unidentified Marine" (Terry 13). Following the
adjudication, he received "[f]ive months in jail [and] five months without
pay. And a suspended BCD (Bad Conduct Discharge)" (Terry 13). He goes on
to describe his treatment in the Brig:

> In jail they didn't want us to read our books, draw any pictures, or do any-
> thing intellectually stimulating or what they thought is black. They would
> come in my cell and harass me. So one day I was just tired of them, and I hit
> the duty warden. I ended up with a BCD in 1970. After six years, eight
> months and eight days, I was kicked out of the Corps. I don't feel it was fair. If
> I had been white, I would never have went to jail for fighting. That would
> have been impossible. (Terry 13)

Edwards, the first in his family to graduate from high school, tells us that
because he had no money to go to college, and because he was too small to be
hired by anyone doing serious work, he saw the military as his best chance to
earn a living. He had chosen the Marines because they "was bad. The Marine
Corps built men. Plus just before I went in, they had all these John Wayne
movies on every night. Plus the Marines went to the Orient" (Terry 16). Of
course people made fun of what he had done. But he passed the test and his
mother signed him in because he was only seventeen at the time.

As he recapitulates his experiences during training, he speaks about what
he learned as he became both a Marine and then a black Marine in combat.
His recitations make clear that in some ways Edwards was well on his way to
becoming a poster Marine. Yet his background, the culture out of which he
came, supplied only a limited kind of orientation and understanding with
which he came to cope with the social and racial stratification of the war
institution.

In those days, as he experienced them, Blacks did not hang with Whites.
Black people just did not have white friends — the oppressive character of
interracial relations, especially in the South, made this situation a given.

Indeed, Edwards tells Terry, "White people was the aliens to me" (Terry 6). So he hung out with the Mexicans because there were only two other Blacks beside himself in his platoon. Given the reality of segregation, he continued, you expected white people in particular to treat you bad. But somehow, somewhere, maybe from all those World War II films he watched about a glorious corps fighting in the Pacific, he got the idea that the Marines would be different. Everyone dressed the same, the command structure applied to everyone — Black or White, didn't it? Those things ought to have submerged some of the differences between folks. But no, he did not find that to be the case. For a platoon commander, Edwards had an Indian-hating Indian who referred to other Indians as "blanket ass" (Terry 7). And then there was the Arkansas native who liked to call Blacks "chocolate bunny and Brillo head. That kind of shit" (Terry 7). Thus was created an opportunity for cultural conflict and misunderstanding that had ominous portent for the future.

Once, while in boot camp, and while traversing the obstacle course, Edwards had difficulty negotiating a ditch.

> Every time I would hit my shin. So a white lieutenant called me a nigger. And of course, I jumped the ditch farther than I'd ever jumped before. Now I can't run. My leg is really messed up. I'm hoppin'. So it's pretty clear I can't do this. So I tell the drill instructor, Man, I can't fucking go on. He said, "You said what?" I said it again. He said, "Get out." I said, Fuck you. This to a drill instructor in 1963. I mean you just don't say that. I did seven days for disrespect. When I got out of the brig, they put me in recon. The toughest unit. (Terry 7)

Things changed, and yet in some ways they remained the same, Edwards tells us, when he went back to the States after his tour in Vietnam. Although he had been put initially in supply on his return — probably the lowest of the low jobs in the Marines — his artistic talents eventually led him to a position as an illustrator in the training-aids library. This was good duty, so he re-enlisted and was promoted. When he was transferred to Quantico, they gave him the black squad. As it turned out, the squad was peopled by a larger-than-average number of militant, post-Tet brothers whose racial consciousness was very different from their Marine consciousness. These later recruits were not prepared to accept the old ways of being and doing in Uncle Sam's army.

They began to "hip" him, he tells Terry, to what was going on and to what racism, as distinct from prejudice, was all about (prejudice is an attitude towards persons different from oneself; racism, on the other hand, includes not only prejudice but also acts of discrimination intended to retard the progress of those who are different from the perpetrator of racist acts). Too, his work as an illustrator gave him time to think about concepts like "exploitation" and "oppression." For the first time, Edwards was around people who read and thought and shared information with one another about black life and heritage. At a time when white boys were reading novels and listening to hillbilly or rock music, he was reading black history. In short order, Edwards underwent the conversion from Negro to *Black* and then announced his metamorphosis: "I didn't call them blanco, they didn't have to call me Negro. That's what started to get me in trouble. I became a target. Somebody to watch" (Terry 13). Thus, when some Whites began to use "profanity in front of some sisters," tempers flared and a fight broke out, leading to a mini riot not unlike those that had occurred at other duty stations ashore and afloat (see F. Lewis 35–41). And now he was out with nothing to do, facing hard times because of his "Bad Paper." He joined the Washington, D.C., chapter of the Black Panthers, rose in the group's ranks because of his military skills, and became an artist for the newspaper. At the time of his interview, he was drawing unemployment, working at a local community center teaching youngsters how to draw, and spending time with the nuclear-freeze movement.

Each of the oral narratives in *Bloods* gives an insider's view of being Black and of being a black soldier in Vietnam. Taken singly or collectively, the stories provide the raw human material for fleshing out the interpretive contexts of the black experience. Each oral narrative, in its own way, allows us a different insight into the human side of history that all too often has a way of becoming the victor's propaganda about the vanquished. Through the subjective narrative material of *Bloods,* students can stretch their imaginations, and their identities, by pondering the meaning of other people's experiences.

A final word about the course I teach might be of some value here. There are three major sections to the course description: "Home Front," "In-Country," and "Post War." To create talking points for class discussion, each of these divisions is further subdivided into several topics matched to selected readings. For example, under the rubric "Home Front," we find "American idealism and the rest of the world," "Black Anti-war Protest," and consideration of stateside and overseas duty stations other than Vietnam. Under "In-Country," the focus is on concrete experiences in the bush or in the rear areas, issues of racial solidarity and racism, and "Black Prisoners of War." Finally, the "Post War" section examines the return home and the influence of the war experience on the veterans' employment situations; their experiences with the justice system; and, the situation of being Black and disabled. This section of the course also discusses portrayals of black Vietnam War veterans in film and literature. I also attempt to teach the course from a grunt's point of view because that was the status of most of the brothers who went there.

A principal reason for teaching this course came from my interest in both military history and the experiences of black people in the military since colonial times (see Pendleton, Greene, Foner, Mullen, and Astor). This background explains my selections of reading materials. James S. Olson's and Randy Roberts's *Where the Domino Fell: America and Vietnam, 1945–1990* is required reading as it gives students an overview of the contours of the wars in Vietnam. The text is supplemented by additional items, both fictional and factual, that detail primarily the concrete experiences of Blacks at home and in Southeast Asia. And because my students' world is a visual world, several videos, capable of transmitting different kinds of data simultaneously, are also part of the curriculum. Among these videos are the Martin Luther King assassination episodes of *China Beach* and *Tour of Duty,* two television series about the Vietnam War shown during the 1980s; *84 Charlie Mopic;* a PBS film version of the book *Bloods; The Anderson Platoon;* and several others that provide visual and auditory information aimed at touching students' feelings in a way that words alone cannot.

Finally, the course format is more like a forum than a lecture. Students are encouraged to talk about what they have read, seen, heard, and felt, and to gain a voice so that they may speak of whatever meanings they have made out of their experiences. The course format can be problematic, though, for there is a learned passivity endemic to the schooling approach to human resource development, as Harry L. Gracey makes clear in his essay, "Learning the Student Role: Kindergarten as Academic Bootcamp." Too often in the academy, we are taught to distrust our own experiences and to place greater reliance on outside authorities. This may make humans easier to domesticate, but it does little for enhancing self-knowledge and self-reliance, two signally important attributes of a meaningful life. When you know who you are, you know what you can do. One objective of this class, then, is to create an environment that encourages students to value but also to examine their own constructs and the consequences of their creations — ideology *does* shape consciousness. And so, I push and prod and poke. Sometimes I even demand as I attempt to free students from the mental shackles that have been so tightly wrapped about their minds. With a peculiar kind of inertia, we soak up terabytes of information as we watch and listen to dramatic portrayals of events experienced by others. Still, we don't often know what to do with that information or how to find meaning in what has been presented to us. This is especially the case when the portrayed experience is foreign to that of the interpreter. But by juxtaposing film and oral testimony, it is sometimes possible to create and then navigate new pathways that can lead to vicarious understanding, if not enculturated knowing.

With my students, I inquire into the meanings they have made of their experiences thus far and share with them the meanings I have made of mine. No, the process does not work every time. But when it does, man can they go.

WORKS CITED

Astor, Gerald. *The Right to Fight: A History of African Americans in the Military.* Novato, Calif.: Presidio Press, 1998.

Department of Defense, Assistant Secretary of Defense for Manpower and Reserve Affairs. *Project One Hundred Thousand: Characteristics and Performance of "New Standards" Men.* Washington, D.C.: Government Printing Office, 1969.

Department of Labor, Office Policy Planning and Research. *The Negro Family: The Case for National Action.* Washington, D.C.: Government Printing Office, 1965.

DuBois, W.E.B. *The Souls of Black Folk.* Chicago: A.C. McClurg, 1903.

Foner, Jack D. *Blacks and the Military in American History.* New York: Praeger, 1974.

Gracey, Harry L. "Learning the Student Role: Kindergarten as Academic Bootcamp." *Readings in Introductory Sociology.* 2nd ed. Ed. Dennis H. Wrong and Harry L. Gracey. New York: Macmillan, 1972. 243–53.

Greene, Robert Ewell. *Black Defenders of America, 1775–1973.* Chicago: Johnson Publishing Company, 1974.

Jones, Robert. "The Negro in Vietnam." *Time* 89 (May 26, 1967): 15–19.

King, William M. "DD-214" Discharge Summary, 4 June 1962.

———. " 'Our Men in Vietnam': Black Media as a Source of the Afroamerican Experience in Vietnam." *Vietnam Generation* I (1989): 94–117. Special issue, "A White Man's War: Race Issues and Vietnam." Ed. William M. King.

Lewis, David Levering, ed. *W.E.B. DuBois: A Reader.* New York: Henry Holt and Company, 1995.

Lewis, Flora. "The Rumble at Camp Lejeune." *Atlantic* 225 (1970): 35–41.

Malveaux, Julianne. "Blacklove Is . . . a Bitter/Sweetness." *Essence* 4 (1973): 34–35+.

Mullen, Robert W. *Blacks and Vietnam.* Washington, D.C.: University Press of America, 1981.

Olson, James S., and Randy Roberts. *Where the Domino Fell: America and Vietnam, 1945–1990.* New York: St Martin's Press, 1991.

Pendleton, Leila Amos. *A Narrative of the Negro: Missing Pages in American History Revealing the Services of Negroes in the Early Wars in the United States of America, 1641–1815.* Washington, D.C.: R.L. Pendleton, 1912.

Public Broadcasting Service. "Frontline — 'Bloods of 'Nam.' " 1987.

Terry, Wallace. "Black Power in Vietnam." *Time* 94 (September 19, 1969): 22–23.

———. *Bloods: An Oral History of the Vietnam War by Black Veterans.* New York: Random House, 1984.

10. The Things They Saw

Trauma and Vision in *A Piece of My Heart: The Stories of Twenty-Six American Women Who Served in Vietnam*

MICHAEL ZEITLIN

I don't know how to describe it. . . . nothing could prepare you for the horrible things you saw.

—Christine McGinley Schneider (95th Evacuation Hospital, Da Nang, June 1970–June 1971)

People are starting to pick up on the fact that women were in the war and were in combat even though they didn't carry guns.

—Rose Sandecki (12th Evacuation Hospital, Cu Chi, October 1968–March 1969; 95th Evacuation Hospital, Da Nang, March 1969–October 1969)

Tim O'Brien's classic novel of the Vietnam War, *Going After Cacciato* (1978), describes an event suffered or witnessed by the American grunts in significant numbers: sudden death or mutilation caused by landmines and booby-traps.[1] When Billy Boy Watkins steps on a landmine, his foot is blown off. He sits down on the dusty ground, reaches for the boot that contains his severed foot, and tries to put his boot back on. He dies soon after. As the novel stresses, insistently, this is the "ultimate war story" (185), the "best story" (182), the one that the soldiers who witness the event seem condemned to tell and retell over and over again. The story implies an intimate connection between the victim whose trauma is untellable and the witness who, in seeing something horrible happen to another, is traumatized by what he has seen and survived. Paul Berlin, the novel's focal consciousness, witnesses the event on his very first day in the field, yet nearly two hundred pages of this autobiographical novel must pass before he can achieve a relatively clear description of what happened when Billy tripped the mine:

> and how it made a tiny little sound, unimportant, *poof,* that was all, just *poof,* and how Billy Boy stood there with his mouth open and grinning, sort of embarrassed and dumb-looking, how he just stood and stood there, looking down at where his foot had been, and then how he finally sat down, still grinning, not saying a word, his boot lying there with his foot still in it, just *poof,* nothing big or dramatic, and how hot and fine and clear the day had been. . . . But Billy was holding the boot now. Unlacing it, trying to force it back on, except it was already on, and he kept trying to tie the boot and foot on, working with the laces, but it wouldn't go, and how everyone kept saying, "The war's over, man, be cool." And Billy couldn't get the boot on, because it was already on: He kept trying but it wouldn't go. Then he got scared. "Fuckin boot won't go on," he said. And he got scared. His face went pale and the veins in his arms and neck popped out, and he was yanking at the boot to get it on, and then he was crying. "Bullshit," the medic said, Doc Peret, but Billy Boy kept bawling, tightening up, saying he was going to die, but the medic said, "Bullshit, that's a million-dollar wound you got there," but Billy went crazy, pulling at the boot with his foot still in it, crying, saying he was going to die. And even when Doc Peret stuck him with morphine, even then Billy kept crying and working at the boot. (194)[2]

Until this extended description appears, after painstaking and costly psychic preparation, the narrative can only point to the event without describing it, telling us only that "Billy Boy had died of fright, scared to death on the field of battle" (1). The formulation, "dying of fright," or "scared to death," condenses a number of tones — sarcasm, understatement, irony, euphemism — while capturing the manic poetry of childhood encounters with imaginary terror. The purpose of the formulation in this narrative of harrowing realism and richly elaborated compensatory fantasy, is to signal, while warding off, an intolerable memory. The obsessive reiteration of this formula throughout the narrative warps the temporal flow, returning us compulsively to a dynamic moment constituted by the "decentralizing energy of its displacement" (Felman 54). There is always something missing, something untellable, at the heart of the experience of war, something connected to the impossible testimonies of the dead.[3]

The "died of fright" formulation also suggests that Billy Boy's failure to confront the horror that made him crazy before destroying him was a *personal* one. If only Billy Boy, who was so green, all of eighteen years old, could have summoned his courage and not been so *scared*. . . . The failure here, that is, would be understood as a failure of character, of the ego. Billy Boy flunked the test of facing down the Medusa; the endless retelling of "the ultimate war story" suggests that the goggle-eyed witnesses of the event are fascinated by the alienating recognition that they too would have failed under similar circumstances.

The condition of being scared literally to death can only belong to "the other" who remains locked away within the interiority — the fatality — of his own experience. Yet the witness must also feel an uncanny sense of identification, a premonition that the other's inconceivable experience may at any moment become his or her own. Only one's unconscious narcissism, lying at the heart of a superstitious belief in one's own invulnerability, keeps that inevitable moment at bay.[4] The victim *stands in* for oneself as a shadow or uncanny double. As Tobias Wolff puts it in his memoir of the "Lost War,"

> Why one man died and another lived was, in the end, a mystery, and we who lived paid court to that mystery in every way we could think of. . . . In a world where the most consequential things happen by chance, or from unfathomable causes, you don't look to reason for help. You consort with mysteries. You encourage yourself with charms, omens, rites of propitiation. Without your knowledge or permission the bottom-line caveman belief in blood sacrifice, one life buying another, begins to steal into your bones. How could it not? All around you people are killed: soldiers on both sides, farmers, teachers, mothers, fathers, schoolgirls, nurses, your friends — but not you. They have been killed instead of you. This observation is unavoidable. So, in time, is the corollary, implicit in the word *instead*: in place of. They have been killed in place of you — in your place. (5, 96)

Jacques Lacan's term for this alienating mirror of the other who stands in your place, yet whose likeness to yourself you refuse to acknowledge, is *méconnaissance,* "a failure to recognize," a "misconstruction," a "concept . . . central to Lacan's thinking, since, for him, knowledge (*connaissance*) is inextricably bound up with *méconnaissance*" (Sheridan xi).[5] In Freudian terms, *méconnaissance* belongs in that constellation of concepts including *negation, denial, disowning,* and *disavowal,* modes of defense consisting in the subject's refusal to recognize the reality of an outrageous or traumatic perception. The epitome of traumatic perception is that of mutilated flesh. In Lacan's seminar on the dream of Irma's injection, in which Freud, looking into the mouth of his patient, sees the turbinate bones covered with a whitish membrane, Lacan interprets the meaning of the harrowing sight:

> This mouth has all the equivalences in terms of significations, all the condensations you want. Everything blends in and becomes associated in this image. . . . There's a horrendous discovery here, that of the flesh one never sees, the

> foundation of things, the other side of the head, of the face, the secretory glands *par excellence,* the flesh from which everything exudes, at the very heart of the mystery . . . Spectre of anxiety . . . the final revelation of *you are this* — *You are this, which is so far from you, this which is the ultimate formlessness.* (154)

Hence unconscious disavowal, negation: I am *not* this; I *will not be* this dead flesh; I am not mortal.

The oral testimonies of the American combat veterans provide the materials that, in enriching our understanding of wartime experience, enable us to render the psychoanalytic theory of trauma and *méconnaissance* as anything but abstract. The voices of the American soldiers are well represented in this volume; here I will engage the discourse of a group of veterans who may be considered the war's ideal witnesses, the American military nurses. These women were called upon to bear witness to vast suffering while serving as sources of perfect empathy for the soldiers in their care. In the words of Linda J. McClenahan, USARV Headquarters Communications Center, Long Binh, November 1969–November 1970, "The few women that were there had to fill in as mother, sister, sweetheart, confidante; you know, we filled every gap we could" (Walker 23). Georgeanne Duffy Andreason (Special Services, Vinh Long, December 1967–December 1968) continues:

> We found ourselves spending many hours in the lounge just listening to the men "ventilate." . . . they would just relate their "war stories": the number of "hits" their aircraft had taken that day, their triumphs, and, many times, the tragic stories of the casualties they had suffered.
>
> Many of the men seemed to become more frightened as their tours became shorter. (Walker 30)

Called upon to be ideal listeners and nurturing figures, caring as they did for the shattered bodies and souls of the wounded, the nurses were also compelled to see more than they ever wanted to see, and, by virtue of the demands of their professional service, to train their gaze upon scenes of unimaginable horror:

> So I go to the emergency room and they orient you to where all the equipment is, and it's getting confusing because there is so much to remember. But they don't expect you to do too much, just observe. I hear a chopper land, it becomes very windy, and they bring in a couple of stretchers. One guy I remember has no legs; they are blown off from the thigh down. I'm standing there looking at this, and I'm totally freaked out. I see a lot of blood, I see mud, his green fatigues all soaked, and I'm seeing a lot of action. [. . .] I couldn't even look to see what was going on in the second stretcher because what I was seeing was so horrifying to me that I was, like, in a hysteria. (Lily Jean Lee Adams, 12th Evacuation Hospital, Cu Chi, October 1969–October 1970). (Walker 319)

As witnesses to the suffering of American soldiers and, in many cases, of Vietnamese civilians, and bearers themselves of terrible and often traumatic memories, these women enable us to grasp a measure of the war's staggering human cost. Reading their testimonies also enables us to ground the psychoanalytic theory of trauma within the living human subjects of contemporary history.

THE PSYCHOANALYTIC THEORY OF TRAUMA

The case of O'Brien's Billy Boy Watkins dramatizes the trauma of both the involuntary witness and the passive victim, the latter suffering, typically among the American soldiers in Vietnam, traumatic amputation or mutilation in a sudden, catastrophic event beyond the mind's reckoning. In attempting to map the forces that converge on the soft and breakable human subject, psychoanalysis stresses the "economic" factor at the outset. The metaphor implies a kind of hydraulic force funneling itself violently into a complex, insulated system suddenly ruptured by the outside world. This sudden "influx of excitations . . . is excessive by the standard of the subject's tolerance and capacity to master such excitations and work them out psychically" (Laplanche and Pontalis 456). Given the psycho-somatic premise of psychoanalysis, the "influx" also inundates the epistemological domain, flooding the ego in waves of overwhelming knowledge that mobilize the dams of resistance and repression while impelling the apertures of perception to constrict themselves.

Writing in the aftermath of World War I, Freud in *Beyond the Pleasure Principle* (1920) observed of "traumatic war neurosis," or what was then commonly known as "shell shock," that "the chief weight in their causation seems to rest upon the factor of surprise, of fright . . . " (12). For Freud, the term *fright, Schreck* in German, is to be distinguished from *fear* (*Furcht*) and *anxiety* (*Angst*):

> "Anxiety" describes a particular state of expecting the danger or preparing for it, even though it may be an unknown one. "Fear" requires a definite object of which to be afraid. "Fright," however, is the name we give to the state a person gets into when he has run into danger without being prepared for it; it emphasizes the factor of surprise. I do not believe anxiety can produce a traumatic neurosis. There is something about anxiety that protects its subject against fright and so against fright-neuroses. (*Beyond* 12–13)

The *Schreck* moment produces a rupture in time itself, coming to represent the moment impossible in any sense to "get beyond." With Freud, for example, we might say that Paul Berlin of O'Brien's *Cacciato* is "fixated" upon the frightful instant: "[Paul Berlin] *couldn't stop remembering* how it was when

Billy Boy Watkins died of fright on the field of battle" (O'Brien 194, emphasis added). The shock of traumatic memory, moreover, is perpetually re-
experienced "as something real and contemporary. . . . not as an event of the
past, but as a present-day force" (Freud, "Remembering" 152, 151).[6]

Even if one *could* forget, however, forgetting is not a viable long-term
option for the survivors of war. To forget is merely to yield to the grip of
unconscious remembrance. "Forgetting impressions, scenes or experiences
nearly always reduces itself to shutting them off" (Freud, "Remembering"
148); "shutting them off," in turn, is not to immobilize let alone destroy these
memories but merely to divert their irrepressible force away from the conscious realm. Turned back at the threshold of consciousness, the force of
these memories is channeled along psychosomatic pathways leading to the
turbulent collecting-pool of the symptom. Flashback, nightmare, addictive
behavior, or the living hell of an endless mourning and melancholia: all are
produced, driven, or sustained by the force of unconscious remembrance.[7]
Traumatic memory, by definition, remains dynamically "present and operative even without betraying its existence in any way to consciousness" (Freud,
Interpretation of Dreams 612). It takes up residence in the "internal foreign territory" (Freud, "Dissection" 57) of the unconscious, whose boundary
splits the subject while enforcing a condition of permanent self-alienation:

> I had severe depression, recurring nightmares, start-reactions, and was fearful
> of things that represented Vietnam[. . . .] There has been a lot of lost time in
> those years, loneliness, frustration, medical problems relating to stress with-
> out understanding why or even how, wanting to succeed, wanting love and
> recognition, yet running, putting up barriers — my own emotional claymore
> mine perimeters. [Penni Evans, American Red Cross, SRAO, Cam Ranh Bay,
> March 1970–August 1970; Long Binh, August 1970–October 1970; Cu Chi,
> October 1970–December 1970; Quang Tri, December 1970–March 1971]
> (Walker 282)

> I was having periods of real depression at the time — very happily married, a
> good job, wonderful husband, a beautiful baby — and I would consider sui-
> cide. I didn't understand why I was so depressed. I had nightmares, but I
> didn't attribute them to the war. It took me many, many years to even inter-
> pret those nightmares. All of a sudden one day I realized that a lot of them
> were centered around gooks; I couldn't see a slant-eye without getting upset.
> And a lot of it was centered on being misinterpreted, being misunderstood,
> but I didn't realize it at the time. As soon as I woke up, I tried real hard to
> forget them. [Anne Simon Auger, 91st Evacuation Hospital, Chu Lai, July
> 1969–July 1970] (Walker 82)

> I can't believe the amount of booze we consumed. [Cheryl M. "Nicki" Nicol,
> 91st Evacuation Hospital, Tuy Hoa, February 1967–September 1967; 523d
> attached to 8th Field Hospital, Nha Trang, September 1967–February 1968]
> (Walker 291)

Again and again the war veterans speak of their tragic predicament. To remember the circumstances of traumatic experience is to reactivate its pain, terror, and grief; hence the "dread of rousing something that, so they feel, is better left sleeping — what they are afraid of at bottom is the emergence of this compulsion with its hint of possession by some 'daemonic' power" (Freud, *Beyond* 36). At first a fierce determination not to speak of the painful past, along with energetic attempts to forget it, seems the only effective means of keeping that daemonic power at bay. "I've never really talked about the painful part of Vietnam to anyone. Mostly because I don't want to think about it myself," reports Pat Johnson (85th Evacuation Hospital, Qui Nhon, June 1966–September 1966; 18th Surgical Hospital, Pleiku, September 1966–November 1967; 71st Evacuation Hospital, Pleiku, November 1967–March 1968) (Walker 55).[8] It is never less than a matter of years of such pain, isolation, and exhausting silence before the veterans can begin to talk in a meaningful and cathartic way about what they have been through, and thus to return to their memories with some degree of composure and control. Indeed, as Cheryl Nicol submits, "I think the saddest part is not being able to talk about it sooner" (Walker 293). Jane Hodge (95th Evacuation Hospital, Da Nang, July 1969–July 1970) continues, and concludes: "Since then it's just been a gradual progression of dealing with what I can and accepting that there are some things that will never be dealt with" (Walker 231).

Freud pursues a therapeutic solution to the problematic of traumatic memory by developing a distinction between *remembering* and *repeating*: "[The traumatized soldier] is obliged to *repeat* the repressed material [i.e., the memory of his trauma] as a contemporary experience instead of, as the physician would prefer to see, *remembering* it as something belonging to the past" (*Beyond* 18). The goal of psychoanalysis, accordingly, "is to force as much as possible into the channel of memory and to allow as little as possible to emerge as [unconscious mental or somatic] repetition" (*Beyond* 19). In his important study of Post-Traumatic Stress Disorder (PTSD) in American veterans of the Vietnam War, Jonathan Shay summarizes the gist of the matter thus: "The task is to remember — rather than relive and reenact — and to grieve" (192).[9]

Inevitably, as the subject strives consciously to remember the circumstances of his or her combat trauma, he or she must "re-experience some portion of his forgotten life," but the goal is to retain in this process "some degree of aloofness, which will enable him, in spite of everything, to recognize that what appears to be reality is in fact only a reflection of a forgotten past" (Freud, *Beyond* 19). Thus psychoanalysis distinguishes between the traumatic past as something that compulsively returns to dominate the subject's contemporary existence (a "flashback" is as much a return to the past as the past's irruption into the present), and that to which the subject returns with at least some measure of deliberation (thus is fragmentary flashback transformed into narrative memory). In the former case, the subject exercises little or no authority over the primary currents of his mental life; in the later case, she attempts to strengthen control over her memory by going back to the scene of trauma and "working through" its effects in a slow, deliberate, repetitive process, within a social context of mutual trust and support (see Shay passim).[10] Yoked to the therapeutic purposes of the ego, as opposed to the "daemonic" purposes of the unconscious, "[e]ach fresh repetition seems to strengthen the mastery [the subject is] in search of" (Freud, *Beyond* 307).

The psychological process of returning to the scene of trauma in order "to master [its] excitations and work them out psychically" (Laplanche and Pontalis 456) is marked by the temporal work of "deferred action," by which the subject works her way back to a time before the trauma occurred in order to activate, retroactively as it were, what was absent — indeed impossible — as she stood unknowingly before the traumatic threshold, namely an effective psycho-somatic defense against an invasive and shattering force, a force impossible to assimilate:

> It is not lived experience in general that undergoes a deferred revision but, specifically, whatever it has been impossible in the first instance *to incorporate fully into a meaningful context*. The traumatic event is the epitome of such unassimilated experience. (Laplanche and Pontalis 112; emphasis added)

The repetitive psychological work of deferred action serves the will to mastery, that is, to a retroactive psychological mastery of a traumatic influx of excitation for which the subject was originally unprepared.

Once the subject has been "flooded with large amounts of [traumatic] stimulus . . . another problem arises . . . the problem of mastering the amounts of stimulus which have broken in and of binding them, in the psychical sense, so that they can then be disposed of" (Freud, *Beyond* 29–30). To "bind" the "inflowing masses of [traumatic] excitation" (Freud, *Beyond* 30) means to channel its force through a system of psychic dams, locks, and gates so that this force can be retarded, absorbed, and contained. In the best case, the force that is seized and "bound" is then redeployed in ways serviceable and creative (the writing and publishing of a novel about traumatic war experience may be taken as a good example of the transformation of "free flowing" traumatic energy into "bound," "stable," "quiescent," and thus culturally valuable energy). This process takes time and "work," requiring that the subject go back, again and again, to the moments that occurred before the trauma in order to re-pass through its (literally) shattering violence, gathering up more of the pieces left scattered behind.[11]

Metaphorically and psychologically, this "binding" work is indeed about *reparation*, about restoring the wholeness of shattered bodies and souls:[12]

> We would see the units during the morning hours, and by the time we got back and were put in the hospital to help by doing some programming, the same guys would be in the hospital. That just blows your mind. I mean, you've seen them two or three hours ago healthy and whole, and then you meet them with everything blown apart. It's hard to take! [Jeanne "Sam" Bokina Christie, American Red Cross, SRAO, Nha Trang, February 1967–June 1967; Da Nang, June 1967–September 1967; Phan Rang, September 1967–February 1968] (Walker 67)

> I don't remember his last name — his first name was John. He was twenty-one. He'd gotten married just before he came to Vietnam. And he was shot in his face. He absolutely lost his entire face from ear to ear. He had no nose. He was blind. It didn't matter, I guess, because he was absolutely a vegetable. He was alive and breathing; tubes and machines were keeping him alive. . . . I just . . . I couldn't handle it[. . . .] There was one time in Vietnam when I came so close to writing to my mother and asking her to check around and see if she could find one whole eighteen-year-old. I didn't believe we could have any left. After John left I just couldn't handle it any more. We had too many bodies lying in those beds minus arms and legs, genitals, and faces, *and things like that can't be put back together again.* [Anne Simon Auger, 91st Evacuation Hospital, Chu Lai, July 1969–July 1970] (Walker 67, 78; emphasis added)

> We were all new at it, and I think right then I knew one of the things I was going to have a hard time with were the amputations. It just seemed like every time we turned around after that we were taking a leg off, sometimes an arm, mostly legs. That day we had a woman come in, and we had to amputate one arm and one leg. She was about five months pregnant, and she'd caught a piece of shrapnel right through her uterus and it killed the baby. I had to carry those all out . . and it was . . . I don't know, I guess from then on that was something that really bothered me. We put everything in plastic bags and hauled it out, put it in a drum, threw gas on them, and burned them. [Cheryl M. "Nicki" Nicol] (Walker 286–87)

The psychological and symbolic process of re-assembly, restoration, burial, or disposal is especially difficult and painstaking due to the powerful psychological forces working strenuously against it.[13] The closer the subject gets to the scene of shattering violence, in order to gather up the pieces, the closer she gets to liberating its repressed ugliness and so to reliving its intolerable horror and shock effects. Yet this reliving of traumatic memory is the necessary toll to be paid in the achievement of a psychological reckoning with it.[14]

Maureen Walsh, U.S. Naval Support Activity Hospital, Da Nang, August 1968–September 1969, captures the essential structure of a traumatic experienced eventually mastered by a determination to remember, and to *narrate,* the horror:

> Another night that we had some incoming, we were walking along the walk-way and I saw one of the mortars hit smack-dead on one of our units; it exploded. There was not a lot of screaming and yelling, but mostly what really hit me was the stench, the burning flesh. The Marines never screamed, which is incredible, their training is incredible. I remember going into the ward. The lights were all out, so I couldn't see a thing, but we knew there was a lot of activity. I'm not so sure I would've been prepared to see immediately what was happening. I had a flashlight with me . . . opened the flashlight and there was just chunks of flesh and blood all over the wall. Wounded men had been wounded again in the unit. Four of our corpsmen were killed that night. (Walker 211)

It is this scene — the green nurse (as she now recasts herself in memory) advancing tentatively though bravely behind her narrow yellow flashlight beam into the blackness of an unspeakable horror — that defines, I suggest, the basic epistemological mode of the traumatized subject intent on achieving a reckoning with the past. The memory of the encounter with the horror proceeds from a base of prior knowing under the pressure of forgetfulness. Hence the sense of presentiment and premonition ("The lights were all out, so I couldn't see a thing, but we knew there was a lot of activity. I'm not so sure I would've been prepared to see immediately what was happening"). The nurse now remembers how she was already sensible then of something traumatic although unwilling to believe it. She probes into the darkness, now, again, knowing she cannot avoid or erase the truth which she already knows she must re-encounter. She wishes not to bury it out of sight once it is finally seen again, but to brace herself again, retroactively, against the endlessly returning flood of traumatic revelation. The temporal rhythm of deferred action heaves back and forth over the scene of mutilated bodies, blood, and flesh:

> The shrapnel went through his eye and through his head, went through the medicine cabinet, exited through the unit on the other side, and lodged in the wall. God, that was awful, that was awful to see that. [Maureen Walsh] (Walker 211)

> You would go into the hospital and walk through the wards of torn up, mutilated bodies with . . . wounds that are so big they can't be covered properly, naked bodies, legs blown off . . . and where do you look? What do you say? [Penni Evans, American Red Cross, SRAO, Cam Ranh Bay, March 1970–August 1970; Long Binh, August 1970–October 1970; Cu Chi, October 1970–December 1970; Quang Tri, December 1970–March 1971] (Walker 276)

The memories of the nurses are often obsessed by what Lacan has called the lines of "fragilization" that so often "define the anatomy of phantasy" (Lacan, "Mirror" 5): "These are the images of castration, mutilation, dismemberment, dislocation, evisceration, devouring, bursting open of the body, in short, the imagos that I have grouped together under the apparently structural term of imagos of the fragmented body" (Lacan, "Aggressivity" 11). Traumatic memory, indistinguishable in this sense from the epistemology of the dream (as Freud describes it in *The Interpretation of Dreams*), becomes a harrowing, "cinematic" vision into the essential structure of the real:

> The thing I think is probably a scene that's in my mind more than anything: I was coming out of the workroom, and the last two rooms in our operating room had tile on the floor, and it sloped a little bit. There were patients outside each room, and I came out of the workroom — and God, I wanted to take a picture so bad, and my camera was in the dressing room — but between the water coming out of the scrub sinks that was splashed down on the floor and the mud from outside and the blood from the people lying there — it was all just running down the hall. It really was. It was mostly water, but it was like something out of a nightmare. And that's a scene that I have flashed on probably thousands of times since then. It's just right there. If I were an artist I could draw an exact picture. Probably even put the color of the hair of the guy that was nearest to me on it. And for me, that just kind of told the whole story. . . . I don't know. [Cheryl Nicol] (Walker 297)

> We have this picture. . . . It's like, my dreams and my nightmares for so many years were about distorted bodies, you know, and you couldn't even get them in a casket because the casket couldn't fit the positions the bodies were in. They were all outstretched and stuck up in the air with one foot behind and one foot way up in front of them. . . . And you had to have a huge casket to be able to fit the whole body in without cutting something off. You know, people don't die with their hands folded on their chests and their legs out in front of them and are just lying there dead like we see them in caskets in funeral homes; that's not how they die. [Chris Noel, Armed Forces Radio, 1966–1970] (Walker 307)

Such visions might be expected to mobilize the defensive agency of aversion, repression, and denial. Yet if this dialectic of knowledge and *méconnaissance* is central to the experience — the suffering, witnessing, and remembering — of those who served in combat in Vietnam, one encounters in the testimonies of the nurses a genuinely heroic effort *not* to avert their gazes from scenes of unimaginable dreadfulness. Collectively their testimonies therefore achieve an invaluable undoing of the distortions of knowledge produced when a culture refuses to look in a sustained manner at the real wounds of war.[15]

NOTHING COULD PREPARE YOU
FOR THE HORRIBLE THINGS YOU SAW

As noted above, Freud suggests that a crucial factor in causing what he termed traumatic war neurosis is the *Schreck* effect, the fright following upon

the complete absence of any kind of adequate preparation for the encountered horror. Again and again the nurses return to the threshold moment of
"total lack of preparation" (not to be confused with their medical training
per se) and unbelief:

> I couldn't believe the numbers of people coming in, the numbers of beds and
> the kinds of injuries that I saw in front of me—I really wasn't prepared for
> that. This was in October of '68, it was what they called "post-Tet"—after the
> Tet offensive—but it was extremely busy. [Rose Sandecki] (Walker 9)

> And I don't see how the Army could have done any different. I hated them for
> years for not training me better for Vietnam, but I don't think it could possibly
> be done. I don't think you can train anybody or teach anybody to experience
> something that horrible without having them simply live it. . . . [Anne Simon
> Auger] (Walker 76)[16]

Here what is "traumatic" has everything to do with a sense of betrayal, of
having been misled by the authorities and placed in an intolerable situation
by them, a theme, one suspects, as old as war itself.[17] Lily Jean Lee Adams,
12th Evacuation Hospital, Cu Chi, October 1969–October 1970, recounts
how she was lied to by her recruiting officer, who promised her that she
would not be sent to Vietnam unless she volunteered to go. When she was
ordered to Vietnam nonetheless, she discovered she was not alone in having
been misled:

> I got very angry because I was thinking, "It's not only me; there are others that
> are going too." I went down the row, "Did your recruiter tell you that you
> didn't have to go to Vietnam unless you volunteered?" "Yes." Every single one
> of them. [Lily Jean Lee Adams] (Walker 317)

One encounters in such testimonies a growing awareness of the magnitude of
the social and political betrayal, one centered as much on what the nurses
themselves were made to suffer as on what this betrayal cost in the mutilated
bodies of young American boys. The situation is effectively rendered in fragments that, allowed to take their own effect, seem to require no further
explication:

> I was holding the one hand that he had left . . . [Maureen Walsh] (Walker 212)

> That was horrible, seeing those men come in wounded. They were just like
> brothers to us . . . [Maureen Walsh] (Walker 212)

> And to see them come in—they were just like having your own family, own
> brothers, get killed. Those are some of the memories in the intensive care unit.
> [Maureen Walsh] (Walker 212)

> I hated visiting days, especially when there were people coming for the first
> time. [Jane Hodge] (Walker 223)

And I've seen more guys turned into just real psychiatric cases because their family would walk in — "Oh, I'm so glad to see you" — and their faces would just be a mask of horror at what they were seeing. The poor guys would lie there and they knew. Even though their families, after a while, could accept what they looked like and what was happening to them, it never made a big difference because the first thing they had seen was total rejection. It was real hard to work with them after that because no matter what you said to them, it didn't matter. I found that to be true after I got to Nam. They would think if we, as nurses or as females, could look at them, take care of them, and handle what had happened to them, that their wives or their girlfriends or their mothers would be able to, too. And sometimes it probably turned out that way, but I saw so many times that it didn't. . . . It just broke your heart to know what I was sending them home to. . . . [Jane Hodge] (Walker 223)

The nurses are without illusions about the monstrous character of the bureaucratic war apparatus with its mechanized lust for "body count" (Westmoreland's strategy of attrition), human expenditure, consumption, and waste. The nurses come to understand that they were there *to process* the human bodies through the machine, to send the soldiers back into combat, to other hospitals, or to Graves Registration:

The Medical Corps's motto was, and still is, I guess, "Preserve the fighting strength." The idea of working in a military hospital is to patch up the soldier so he can go back to the battle again. [Rose Sandecki] (Walker 9)

The day I left it was just weird; I remember going into the emergency room to say good-bye to everyone, and a Chinook helicopter was landing with mass casualties. Nothing had changed; it was exactly the same as the day I had arrived. It was like, "How much longer is this going to go on?" [Christine McGinley Schneider] (Walker 43)

for me, Vietnam was just a continuous flow of bodies, one after the other from the day you got there until the day you left. [Lynn Calmes Kohl] (Walker 199)

They would come through there and then would be gone in just a short period of time, and you began to feel like you were in almost like a processing house, just passing things through. [Jane Hodge] (Walker 227)

The very first flight into Vietnam I was in awe of what we were doing. I was walking around with my mouth open, going "Wow!" A limousine came to take some dignitaries who were on the flight and then a school bus for the officers. The draftees were herded into this big, open cattle truck and were driven away, just like cattle going away to slaughter. There was no glory, no John Wayne stuff; this was war. . . . This is what people are so willing to do today, and it angers me, but if every mother could see her son going off like that they wouldn't accept it. It was a disgusting sight. [Micki Voisard] (Walker 236)

Observes Maureen Walsh: "we were in conflict between anger and grief constantly. There was just no resolution to any of that" (Walker 209).

For Jonathan Shay in his study of PTSD among American Vietnam Veterans, "betrayal of 'what's right' by a commander is almost always involved in 'the onset of the berserk state'" (xiii). "Going berserk," or "losing it," in turn, is prelude to the complete "undoing of character," to which the nurses were also vulnerable. Many nurses recount an experience in which their rage, impotence, and feeling of betrayal took them past the point of no return. In the following examples, that rage was directed against the North Vietnamese enemy:

> This POW was personally responsible for the deaths of six [. . .] GIs. When he was wheeled onto my ward, something snapped. I was overwhelmed with uncontrollable feelings of hate and rage. I couldn't go near this guy because I knew, without any doubt, that if I touched him I would kill him. I was shaking from trying to keep my hands off his neck. This scared me to death, and for twelve years after I was scared of experiencing it again. I discovered I was capable of killing and of violently hating another human being. I had been raised to be a loving and giving person. As a nurse, I had vowed to help *all* who need it. As a human being I should love my brother, whoever he was. I was forced to confront a side of myself I never dreamed existed before. [Anne Simon Auger] (Walker 80)

> And that's the last thing I remember for about two days. They told me later that I just reached over and got my hands around the VC's neck, and I wasn't about to let go. So they knocked me out. When I came out of it there were two things that were very hard for me to accept. Number one, that I had the capacity to kill a human being — and God, I wanted to so bad. The other was that as a nurse, you know . . . And that just wiped me out. [Cheryl M. "Nicki" Nicol] (Walker 291)

For Freud after World War I, "war neurosis" was essentially a result of the "conflict . . . between the soldier's old peaceful ego and his new warlike one . . . " ("Introduction" 209). Developing this point, he wrote: "[T]he immediate cause of all war neuroses was an unconscious inclination in the soldier to withdraw from the demands, dangerous or outrageous to his feelings, made upon him by active service. Fear of losing his own life, opposition to the command to kill other people, rebellion against the ruthless suppression of his own personality by his superiors — these were the most important affective sources on which the inclination to escape from war was nourished" ("Memorandum" 212–13). When escape from war was not an option for the combat soldier, the more and less total devastation of the "peace ego" commonly resulted. The fear of being changed forever by the ugly violence of war — of being held permanently under the imperializing sway of the "war ego," of having one's character permanently "undone" in Shay's sense — lies in the deepest part of the nurses' experience of war trauma.

Finally, the nurses were also in a position to witness the effects of the air war upon the Vietnamese civilians. Their worst memories involve the killing and wounding of children, whether from enemy or friendly fire. The nurses express their rage at a war that had no effective means of separating civilians from soldiers:[18]

> An orphanage was rocketed, and I think we put about two hundred kids through the receiving and pre-op areas. These were children from infancy to adolescence. I mean, literally had their eyes blown away, their shoulders — you could see all their bone structure just blown away — limbs. One kid came in with an arm between its legs — intestines out on their abdomen, brains out on their forehead, blood everywhere. I can remember saying to my mother in the tape I sent her, "Mom, I had kids coming out of my ears: they were on chairs, they were on desks, they were on the floor, they were in the hall, they were stacked up, they were everywhere." That was just incredible, that was just incredible. [Charlotte Capozoli Miller] (Walker 266)

> I was twenty years old when I went to Vietnam and celebrated my twenty-first birthday there. I had come back from a background of twelve years of Catholic schools and had a somewhat sheltered life — midwestern parents with midwestern values — and I don't know what I was expecting by volunteering to go, but what I encountered was unimaginable. I think I was kind of okay seeing wounded soldiers coming in, because that was the soldier's fortune, so to speak, although I guess I wasn't expecting the wounds to be quite so graphic. But I wasn't as prepared for that of the innocents, especially the children. I had a lot of trouble dealing with that[. . . .] These kids — of course, they were all victims of war, obviously — a lot of them were missing limbs; all of them had sores all over their bodies; many had infections. When you got playing with them, they actually were fairly happy. They would smile and laugh, but like a lot of the soldiers, they had very old, sad eyes. [Linda J. McClenahan] (Walker 21)

> They were older at the age of four than I was at eighteen. And I'll never forget that look on their faces, that old-man look on those young kids' faces, because they'd live through so much. That still haunts me today. [Anne Simon Auger] (Walker 79)

> The saddest thing I saw had nothing to do with a GI — and in a way I feel guilty about that — but it was a mother who took a rocket in her face, and she had a cross section of her face missing. She was pregnant at the time, and she also had an eighteen-month-old. She didn't complain or anything. But one night she was just kind of complaining and complaining, and I checked her dressings and everything. Finally I looked under the covers, and she had had a miscarriage, like about a five-month-old fetus. I said, "Johnny" (my corpsman), "Johnny, come here." We called the doctor, and he said, "Well, what in

the hell am I going to do about it?" He was probably tired from working. He said, "Just put it in a basin or something." I just felt like I was on sacred ground there, and I felt so bad for that woman, and little tears rolled down her face. That wasn't the saddest thing. She missed her little eighteen-month-old so they arranged for her to come and see her mother. But the woman was disfigured — had a bandage all over her — and when the baby saw her mother, it just screamed in fright and had to be taken away. I thought, "That has to be suffering beyond all." [Donna B. Cull Peck] (Walker 158)

The critical problem for any reader of such testimony is to find the appropriate kind of response to it. Intuitively, in the interest of asserting some minimal control, one reacts with moral condemnation, but now that the war is over, who or what can serve as an appropriate polemical target for one's rage? These accounts are horrible beyond reckoning, and yet one reads them in order to deepen one's sense of historical realities and what Lacan deceptively called the Real: that which resists the power of narrative and symbolization "absolutely." This sense of the Real must disrupt, even if only temporarily, a certain *méconnaissance* sustained by the ongoing war romance that continues to be projected by the culture industry in a steady stream of films. To be sure, the Vietnam oral narrative itself cannot help but circulate around our culture in its own commodified form; yet clearly it cannot be placed among the culture industry's privileged products, what Shay has termed those "popular melodramas of moral courage [which] provide satisfaction through the comforting fantasy that our own character would hold steady under the most extreme pressure of dreadful events" (Shay 31). The courage inherent in the testimonies of *A Piece of My Heart* is the radical subversion of any comforting war romance or fantasy.

NOTES

1. "Only 3 to 4 percent of American causalities in World War II and Korea were from booby-traps, while 11 percent of the deaths and 17 percent of the injuries in Vietnam were from these lowest-echelon attacks of surprise and deception" (Shay 34). "American tactics called for use of infantrymen as decoys. Instead of seizing ground and holding it as in previous wars, American troops sought to flush the enemy from concealed positions in order to destroy them with superior firepower. . . . The enemy's single most frightening response was use of the booby trap and the ambush" (Smith xi, x).
2. That trauma is "unrepresentable" is perhaps an unavoidable cliché. In a review of Paul Celan's poetry about the Holocaust, however, J. M. Coetzee suggests that implicit in Celan's writing is the premise that "language can measure up to any subject whatever: however unspeakable the Holocaust may be, there is a poetry that can speak it" (5). One of the main themes of this volume concerns the extent to which the special language of the combat veteran, his or her spontaneous "oral poetics" (see, for example, McGuirk in this volume), helps to speak the unspeakable.
3. "After a year I felt so plugged in to all the stories and the images and the fear

that even the dead started telling me stories, you'd hear them out of a remote but accessible space where there were no ideas, no emotions, no facts, no proper language, only clean information. However many times it happened, whether I'd known them or not, no matter what I'd felt about them or the way they'd died, their story was always there and it was always the same: it went, 'Put yourself in my place' " (Herr 31). To which James William Gibson responds: "Death determines much of what can be known and what will never be known. . . . How do the living put themselves in the place of the dead? It is a good question and no answer will be offered here. . . . The analytical appropriation of the warrior's knowledge has its limits. In this corpus men and women live and die; the stories of their lives and their deaths have their truths beyond incorporation in any theoretical arguments" (Gibson 475–76).

4. "It is indeed impossible to imagine our own death; and whenever we attempt to do so we can perceive that we are in fact still present as spectators. Hence the psychoanalytic school could venture on the assertion that at bottom no one believes in his own death, or, to put the same thing another way, that in the unconscious every one of us is convinced of his own immortality" (Freud, "Thoughts for the Times" 289). Freud goes on to suggest that this unconscious narcissism is perhaps the key to acts of heroism on the battlefield.

5. For an extended discussion of *méconnaissance* as the fundamental agency of the ego, see Lacan's "Aggressivity in Psychoanalysis" and "The Mirror Stage."

6. In one form or another this sense of the present-ness of the past is reiterated by every veteran whose testimony I have encountered. Lynn Kohl, 71st Evacuation Hospital, Pleiku, June 1969–June 1970, gives a representative formulation: "[the war is] still not quite finished as far as I'm concerned" (Walker 199).

7. "Hysterics suffer mainly from reminiscences" (Breuer and Freud 58). See also Philip Rieff: "[P]sychoanalysis encourages its subjects to live with a reduced burden of memory, closer to the surface of life, where tensions cannot take root and feed off the accumulated energies of the past. Though Freud is commonly thought to have measured neurosis against the ideal of an unimpaired sexual efficiency, it would be more accurate to say that he measured it against an ideal contemporaneity" (44).

8. "I returned home from Vietnam in March 1969. . . . But I was still an inarticulate teenager, confused and exhausted by my year in combat. There was no way that I could express what I had seen and knew to be true. So for ten years I said nothing. . . . Ten years later, in 1979, as if coming out of a shock-induced trance, I stopped running from my experiences there. I began interviewing and soul-searching with fellow veterans for an oral history of the war" (Santoli, *To Bear Any Burden* xix, xii). "Like most Vietnam veterans, I went to the war alone and I came home alone. And like most others, in the years afterward I rarely talked about what I saw and experienced in the combat zone—I sealed the war in a compartment, a place of safekeeping for which only I had the key" (Wilson xvi).

9. It is surprising to note that Shay, whose work is fundamentally Freudian in its conception of trauma, memory, and catharsis, cites Freud nowhere in his book.

10. Writes James R. Wilson, editor of *Landing Zones: Southern Veterans Remember Vietnam:* "As I conducted the interviews for this book, interviews that not infrequently called forth spirits from the vasty deep for both my subjects and myself, I began to understand that Vietnam has at last become a shared experience for all whose lives were touched by its fire" (xvi).

11. The psychoanalytic theory of trauma and repetition thus illuminates the es-

sential narrative principles governing O'Brien's *Going After Cacciato* and *The Things They Carried*.

12. Reparation in this sense is to be understood as involving an unconscious process of phantasy-work. The principal theorist of reparation in this regard remains Melanie Klein. See, for example, Laplanche and Pontalis: "Reparation: Mechanism described by Melanie Klein whereby the subject seeks to repair the effects his destructive phantasies have had on his love-object. This mechanism is associated with depressive anxiety and guilt" (388–89).

13. Keith Walker observes: "I get the distinct impression that none will be satisfied until they bring everybody 'back home'" (Walker 6). Yet sometimes this proves impossible. Carey Spearman, Medic/X-Ray Technician, 91st Evacuation Hospital, An Hoa, II Corps, recalls blasted, mutilated bodies, not persons, at all: "I used to go down to the Wall in D.C., but I knew nobody on the Wall. I know wounds, you know? I know faces. But I didn't know any names on the Wall at all. I couldn't go mourn for anybody" (Steinman 162).

14. An emblem of this struggle between the moral will to remember and the unconscious drive to forget — a kind of standoff between the pain of knowing and the painful guilt of forgetting — seems captured by the following observation of Keith Walker as he sat down to interview Anne Simon Auger: "When she began talking, she put one hand over her eyes, and it stayed there during the entire ninety minutes the tape recorder ran" (Walker 75).

15. The hypocrisy is captured in the following exchange between Karen "Kay" Johnson Burnette and Donna B. Cull Peck, 24th Evacuation Hospital, Long Binh, October 1968–October 1969:

Kay: I want to talk about when Pat Nixon came. My version may not be the same as Donna's but this is what I remember. President Nixon came, and he flew someplace safe to visit. I voted for him too, but that was right after I got there and I never made that mistake again. Anyhow, Pat Nixon came. We prepared for a week for her visit. We had our ward scrubbed; we had our patients fixed up as best you can — what can you do with the patients? We did everything. We were so proud; we were straight that day — we were perfect. The Red Cross were the only ones that got to talk to her. We were like lepers; they put up ropes and we had to stand behind the ropes. Here's what they showed her: the medical ward, the one Donna used to be on . . .

Donna: No dressings could be shown.

Kay: If I remember right they faked some dressings on those guys.

Donna: No, they were not allowed to show her a dressing because it might turn her stomach.

Kay: So she saw guys — and I'm sorry — but some of them had VD; this is what they showed her: VD, malaria . . .

Donna: That could smile and wave.

Kay: That's what she saw when she came, and all that did was just add to your frustration. We couldn't even say hello to her. And we have dear friends in the Red Cross, but that day they were not our dear . . . They showed her around; they socialized with her. I know it would've meant so much to our patients if she had come in and been compassionate and spoken to them. I don't know whether it was her choice; it probably wasn't.

Donna: It wasn't.

Kay: I'm sure she's a nice person, but that was an incident that I'll just never forget. (Walker 160–61)

16. This sense of being inadequately prepared upon arrival "in-country" is mirrored by the "shock of re-entry" experienced when the nurses returned to the States once their tours were completed: "I think the Army made a drastic mistake in that they didn't do any deprogramming" [Pat Johnson] (Walker 56). Observes Cheryl Nicol, "When the fellows came home from World War II and Korea, they came home by boat. They had that decompression time; they could talk to their buddies. It's a time to get out some of the things that you've been through. Good detox time. I had been working in the middle of Tet and twenty-four hours later was sitting at McChord AFB, and I was just wound up like a ten-day clock" (Walker 298).

17. The master theme of Jonathan Shay's *Achilles in Vietnam: Combat Trauma and the Undoing of Character* is the presence of betrayal at the heart of what is "morally traumatic" about war. "Bad leadership is a cause of combat trauma" (Shay 196). Under the category of bad leadership would be included the subordination of the soldiers' lives to the SOPs (standard operating procedures) and the routine phenomenon of "friendly fire": "According to Colonel David Hackworth, 15 to 20 percent of American deaths in Vietnam were due to 'Friendly fire'" (Shay 125). The "bad leadership" of generals, politicians, and war managers is also implicated in the production of moral trauma. In 1917 British World War I veteran and poet Siegfried Sassoon, winner of the Military Cross for bravery under fire, resigned from the army and spoke out against the war in terms precisely analogous to the Vietnam situation: "I have seen and endured the sufferings of the troops, and I can no longer be a party to prolong these sufferings for ends which I believe to be evil and unjust. I am not protesting against the conduct of the war, *but against the political errors and insincerities for which the fighting men are being sacrificed. On behalf of those who are suffering now I make this protest against the deception which is being practised on them;* also I believe that I may help to destroy the callous complacence with which the majority of those at home regard the continuance of agonies which they do not share, and which they have not sufficient imagination to realise" (qtd. in Gilbert 352, emphasis added).

18. See Tobias Wolff's "The Lesson," in which he recalls the destruction of the beautiful provincial town of My Tho during the Tet Offensive: "As a military project Tet failed; as a lesson it succeeded. The VC came into My Tho and all the other towns knowing what would happen. They knew that once they were among the people we would abandon our pretense of distinguishing between them. We would kill them all to get at one. In this way they taught the people that we did not love them and would not protect them; that for all our talk of partnership and brotherhood we disliked and mistrusted them, and that we would kill every last one of them to save our own skins. To believe otherwise was self-deception. They taught that lesson to the people, and also to us. At least they taught it to me" (140). See also O'Brien's "How to Tell a True War Story," in which even the water buffalo are included among the enemy: "Later, higher in the mountains, we came across a baby VC water buffalo" (78).

WORKS CITED

Breuer, Joseph, and Sigmund Freud. *Studies on Hysteria. The Standard Edition of the Complete Psychological Works of Sigmund Freud,* vol. II. Trans. and ed. James Strachey. London: Hogarth and the Institute of Psycho-Analysis, 1966.

Coetzee, J. M., "In the Midst of Losses." *The New York Review of Books* 48, no. 11 (July 5, 2001): 4–8.

Felman, Shoshana. *Writing and Madness: Literature/ Philosophy/Psychoanalysis.* Trans. Martha Noel Evans. Ithaca: Cornell University Press, 1985.

Freud, Sigmund. *Beyond the Pleasure Principle. Standard Edition* 18: 1–64.

———. "The Dissection of the Psychical Personality." *Standard Edition* 22: 57–80.

———. *The Interpretation of Dreams. Standard Edition* 4 and 5.

———. "Introduction to Psycho-Analysis and the War Neuroses." *Standard Edition* 17: 205–10.

———. "Memorandum on the Electrical Treatment of War Neurotics." *Standard Edition* 17: 211–15.

———. "Remembering, Repeating and Working-Through." *Standard Edition* 12: 145–56.

———. *The Standard Edition of the Complete Psychological Works of Sigmund Freud.* Trans. and ed. James Strachey. London: Hogarth and the Institute of Psycho-Analysis, 1966.

———. "Thoughts for the Times on War and Death." *Standard Edition* 14. 273–300.

Gibson, James William. *The Perfect War: Technowar in Vietnam.* Boston: Atlantic Monthly Press, 1986.

Gilbert, Martin. *The First World War: A Complete History.* New York: Holt, 1994.

Herr, Michael. *Dispatches.* 1977. New York: Vintage International, 1991.

Lacan, Jacques. "Aggressivity in Psychoanalysis." *Écrits: A Selection.* 8–29.

———. *Écrits: A Selection.* Trans. Alan Sheridan. New York: Norton, 1977.

———. "The Mirror Stage as Formative of the Function of the I as Revealed in Psychoanalytic Experience." *Écrits: A Selection.* 1–7.

———. *The Seminar of Jacques Lacan.* Book II: *The Ego in Freud's Theory and in the Technique of Psychoanalysis 1954–1955.* Ed. Jacques-Alain Miller. Trans. Sylvana Tomaselli with notes by John Forrester. New York: Norton, 1991.

Laplanche, J., and J.-B. Pontalis. *The Language of Psycho-Analysis.* Trans. Donald Nicholson-Smith. New York: Norton, 1973.

O'Brien, Tim. *Going after Cacciato.* 1978. New York: Dell, 1992.

———. *The Things They Carried.* 1990. New York: Broadway Books, 1998.

Rieff, Philip. *Freud: The Mind of the Moralist.* 3rd ed. Chicago: University of Chicago Press, 1979.

Santoli, Al. *Everything We Had: An Oral History of the Vietnam War by Thirty-Three American Soldiers Who Fought It.* New York: Random House, 1981.

———. *To Bear Any Burden: The Vietnam War and Its Aftermath in the Words of Americans and Southeast Asians.* New York: E.P. Dutton, Inc., 1985.

Shay, Jonathan. *Achilles in Vietnam: Combat Trauma and the Undoing of Character.* New York: Atheneum, 1994.

Sheridan, Alan. Translator's Note. *Écrits: A Selection.* By Lacan. vii–xii.

Smith, Clark. Foreword. *Brothers: Black Soldiers in the Nam.* By Stanley Goff and Robert Sanders, with Clark Smith. 1982. New York: Berkley Books, 1985.

Steinman, Ron. *The Soldiers' Story: Vietnam in Their Own Words.* New York: TV Books, 1999.

Walker, Keith. *A Piece of My Heart: The Stories of Twenty-Six American Women Who Served in Vietnam*. 1985. Novato, Calif.: Presidio Press, 1997.

Wilson, James R. *Landing Zones: Southern Veterans Remember Vietnam*. Durham, N.C., and London: Duke University Press, 1990.

Wolff, Tobias. *In Pharaoh's Army: Memories of the Lost War*. 1994. New York: Vintage, 1995.

CONTRIBUTORS

Paul Budra is Associate Professor of English at Simon Fraser University. He is the author of A Mirror for Magistrates *and the* de casibus *Tradition* and co-editor of *Part Two: Reflections on the Sequel*. He has published articles and book chapters on Shakespeare, Marlowe, Renaissance non-dramatic litera-ture, and twentieth-century popular culture.

Thomas Carmichael is Associate Professor of English and Associate Dean (Research) in the Faculty of Arts at the University of Western Ontario. He is co-editor of *Constructive Criticism: The Human Sciences in the Age of The-ory* and *Postmodern Times: A Critical Guide to the Contemporary*. He is also the author of several articles and book chapters on contemporary American fiction, postmodern culture, and theory.

Jen Dunnaway is currently completing a Ph.D. in English at Cornell Univer-sity, where she has taught classes on both Vietnam War literature and tech-nology in American culture. Her dissertation will incorporate literary and cultural representations of the war into a broader discussion of national mythology and iconography.

Craig Howes is the Director of the Center for Biographical Research and a Professor of English at the University of Hawai'i at Mânoa. He is the author of *Voices of the Vietnam POWs*, the editor of the journal *Biography: An Interdisciplinary Quarterly,* and the series scholar and a producer for the television series *Biography Hawai'i*.

William M. King is Professor of Afroamerican Studies and Associate Chair of the Department of Ethnic Studies, the University of Colorado at Boulder. He is the author of two books, *Going to Meet A Man: Denver's Last Legal*

Public Execution, 27 July 1886, How To Write Research Papers: A Guide for the Insecure, and numerous articles, essays, and other materials. He is currently at work on *Black Denver: A History.*

Kevin McGuirk is an Associate Professor in the department of English Language and Literature at the University of Waterloo. He has published essays on contemporary poetry and poetics in *Postmodern Culture, Cultural Critique, Open Letter,* and other journals.

Van Nguyen-Marshall is an Assistant Professor of Asian history at Trent University in Ontario, Canada. Her research interest is in modern Vietnamese history with a focus on poverty and charity in the French colonial period. She is presently working on Vietnamese mutual-aid societies of the early twentieth century.

Priscilla L. Walton is Professor of English at Carleton University. She is the author of *The Disruption of the Feminine in Henry James, Patriarchal Desire & Victorian Discourse: A Lacanian Reading of Anthony Trollope's Palliser Novels,* and co-author, with Manina Jones, of *Detective Agency: Women Re-Writing the Hard-Boiled Tradition.* She is the co-editor of *Pop Can: Popular Culture in Canada,* and has published numerous articles in such journals as *Narrative,* the *Henry James Review, Literature/Interpretation/Theory, Ariel;* she is also co-editor of *The Canadian Review of American Studies,* and a member of the Advisory Board for *PMLA.*

Michael Zeitlin is Associate Professor in the English Department at the University of British Columbia where he teaches courses in American literature. His recent work has focused on Faulkner, Modernism, Postmodernism, Psychoanalysis, and other twentieth-century subjects. He is co-editor of *The Faulkner Journal.*

INDEX